Houseboat Days in China

by

J.O.P. Bland

With a New Foreword

First published in 1909

Reprinted by
Earnshaw Books
Hong Kong 2008

Houseboat Days in China

By J.O.P. Bland

With a New Foreword

ISBN-13: 978-988-1762-12-2

Houseboat Days in China was first published in 1909.

Series Editor: Andrew Chubb

This book has been reset in 10pt Book Antiqua. Spellings and punctuations are left as in the original edition.

EB006

Published by Earnshaw Books Ltd. (Hong Kong)

Foreword

By Andrew Chubb

THIS book's title is liable to mislead. On my first flick through the original book, the prospect of a large yellow tome on houseboats and hunting written by a long-forgotten tri-initialed dilettante filled me with foreboding.

But in spite of the affected, bigoted persona he assumes in the first few pages, the author was one of the most sympathetic and knowledgeable Western authorities on China and its people of his time. It's not surprising then that this book, first published in 1909, is much more than the "record of Idleness" the author promises: the eloquent renderings of gorgeous 'Celestial' landscapes are at hand, naturally, but his encounters with the lives and ways of the Chinese, combined with a 'common-sense' British view, result in a deep and colorful insight into the east-meets-west riddle on the eve of a critical fork in China's history. The bigotry, it turns out, is what is affected.

But first, let us make proper acquaintance with our host aboard the *Saucy Jane*, the sportsman-philosopher and scourge of snipe, Mr John Bland (you can see why he used his initials).

John Otway Percy Bland arrived in Shanghai in 1883, the year he turned 20, and joined the Chinese Imperial Maritime Customs under Sir Robert Hart. For his services to the Chinese Government over the next 13 years, he was made a Mandarin of the fourth class, and received the Imperial Order of the Double Dragon (an honor created for foreigners). He remained with Customs until 1896, including two years spent as Hart's secretary, before taking up the post of secretary in the Shanghai Municipal

Council, a powerful position in the most powerful political body in the city. Here he remained for ten years before moving to Beijing, where he negotiated four massive loans of British capital to the Chinese Government.

Equipped with formidable Chinese language skills and official connections, he concurrently acted as correspondent for the London *Times* from 1897 until he left China in 1910, a period encompassing the Empress Dowager's *coup d'etat*, the Boxer Rebellion and the 1904 Russia-Japan war, along with the deaths of the Emperor and Empress Dowager. In total, he authored twelve books, the first two under the pseudonym 'Tung Chia' (whom he mischievously quotes in *Houseboat Days*). With Edmund Backhouse he co-authored a volume on the Empress Dowager, fooled, like so many others, by Backhouse's discredited imperial diary. Yet in 1932 the *New York Times* still described him as "undoubtedly the best informed Westerner on China in the world today". *Houseboat Days in China*, Bland's third book, was well received on both sides of the Atlantic. "[T]he seeker of truth, as far as Chinese characteristics are concerned, will find more of value in Mr. Bland's description of his innumerable experiences 'up country,' than he is likely to find in half a dozen ordinary books on Chinamen and their ways," gushed the *New York Times Book Review*.

Even more than most, this is a book rooted in a special place and time. For many years, houseboating was an almost required pastime in Shanghailander society. But the Yangtsze Delta that Bland and his fellows plied at the turn of the century was nearing the end of its halcyon days as a territory for houseboating shooters. The age of road-building in China had not yet arrived, and the mish-mash of intersecting creeks, rivers, lakes and canals was still the principal means of transport. And the horrendous slaughters of the Taiping Rebellion (1850-64) not only decimated the Delta's population, they led to a mass exodus from what has traditionally been one of the most densely populated regions on earth. The result of this tragedy, as Bland describes in haunting detail, was eerie deserted cities and a fleeting respite for Nature that was rapidly drawing to a close as migrants moved in where the earth was "dense with dead men's bones".

Unfortunately for the houseboat posse, although game was still plentiful, we hear of the recent emergence of Chinese trappers who had "devastated our happy hunting grounds for the benefit of floating hotel passengers". While there is no doubting Bland's passion for hunting, he is refreshingly frank about his own hypocrisy in alternately admiring, then killing, magnificent ducks, pheasants, geese — even whole settings:

> "Amongst the reeds the white mist rises slowly, like incense, from the river-banks, and the bright yellow of the rape glistens through unbroken veils of gossamer. One has to admit the innate savagery of man, to explain his desire to slay food, with noise of gunpowder, under such conditions. Thus one meditates, full of intelligent sympathy with the vegetarian movement, until the first bird rises; then certain unphilosophic muscles bring the gun automatically to your shoulder, and you proceed to shoot . . ."

This schizophrenic struggle between the predatory hunter-colonialist and the doubtful, bashfully progressive contemplator are a fascinating backdrop throughout the book.

From today's perspective, the obvious manner in which Bland cultivates his whimsical and superior air seems like nothing so much as provocative posturing. But at a time when the legitimacy of the world's greatest empire hung by the thread of assured moral superiority, Bland appears to have decided to firmly establish some orthodox credentials in Chapter I, before foisting his less palatable conclusions on his readership. He certainly seems to have had fun doing it. "The houseboat, like all Gaul," he writes, "is divided into three parts — the white man's, the yellow man's, and the dogs'." But though "many good people quarter their Chinese servants worse than their dogs", better treatment is indeed justified — on the basis that a better service would be rendered. He continues:

> "Smoking the sunset pipe, your body tingling with the health of a long day in the open, and your mind at peace with gods and men, you may watch the soft sinking of twilight to dusk, and dusk to night, deriving a very human sense of added ease from the contemplation of the coolies' labours."

It would be difficult to dream up a sharper parody of the zeitgeist. On the question of the stray rifle shot burying itself in some unfortunate peasant, it's almost surprising to see any concern at all — but indeed: "Like everything else in China the cost of peppering a native has increased absurdly of recent years, and for those who do not speak the language it has become almost prohibitive . . . now a dollar a pellet is cheap enough as prices go." But this, as he puts it, "fly in the ointment of our up-country joys," is not attributable to ill-will or bad temper on behalf of the Chinese, but to the pernicious influence of the West on the Middle Kingdom — an issue that recurs through the remainder of the book.

No doubt, many of Bland's Shanghailander contemporaries could have served up the promised book of trivial boating anecdotes. But behind this book is a philosopher who lives to ponder the "vast harmonies underlying the ear-splitting discords around us". In fact (and in spite of his purported "distaste for studying the native and his ways") Bland expresses an almost deferential awareness of the ancient ways and philosophies the 'Chinaman', who is "far nearer to [the philosophic attitude] than we, for all our many inventions". In Chapter VII, we meet 'The Lord of the Soil' — the countryman — who speaks "in hoary idioms whose origins stretch back to the days before Nineveh and Babylon", and

we sit on a sunlit hillside and wonder at the countless quiet centuries the green fields below have been tilled "by men like him
over yonder . . . in the sheltering peace of the East's simple philosophy". Bland is admiring, if not jealous, of what he sees as the
Chinese's essential rationality, in contrast to the Anglo-Saxon's
constant battle to suppress his emotions. Yet equally strong is his
contempt for 'Young China', that small stratum with a measure
of Western education. For Bland, their talk of democracy was utterly impractical, a concept so incompatible with their own country's hard-wired traditions that it could only result in disaster — a
view that for all the upheaval of the last century, for all the old
ways that have been smashed, still finds widespread support to-
day, not least among China's own people.

None of this should suggest, however, that Bland was a fan
of the status quo in China at the time. The iniquities of the Mandarin class — about which he had specialized knowledge — are
described in gratifying detail through Chapter XI and elsewhere.
Nor is he rose-tinted in his view of the populace's docility: "Hopeless patience," he writes, "has ceased to be a virtue and become a
national habit of mind."

And neither should my focus on the author thus far suggest
the book is anything less than overflowing with characters. Perhaps due to its birth as a retrospective, an obituary to the beloved
Houseboat Days, the roll call stretches to at least 20 (25 including
dogs rendered familiar). First among these is a lovestruck British army Major, who is the author's default companion aboard
the *Saucy Jane*. The *Saucy Jane's* default companion, in turn, is
the *Heart's Desire*, owned by an ageing King's Counsel who often travels with the young, gregarious Wilden, who might just
be the literary embodiment of the book's illustrator, Willard D.
Straight, a correspondent, diplomat, banker, publisher, and one
of the brightest sparks in the Far East.

Only slightly less honorable in his own circles, the houseboat *lowdah* — the skipper, whose complex, scheming ways are

described in all their brilliance and treachery. Belonging to a low-dah guild — a specialized "corporation of rogues and scoundrels" sealed from outsiders — the lowdah's position is virtually impregnable. "He knows, therefore he thrives," writes Bland. "He knows the European's limitations and the necessities of his fellow-natives, and from both he derives profit sufficient to make him a personage in the tea-house." Meanwhile Ah Kong, the faithful 'dog-coolie' aboard the *Saucy Jane*, likes to dress in the finery of the author's discarded apparel and adopt a lordly air around the "velly stupid countlymen" — but only when safely away from Chinese Shanghai.

Wimple, the Mormon missionary of Soochow (Suzhou), comes in for special attention due to the author's interest in the (abject failure of the) missionary effort in China. Bland sees good intentions but no chance of good results from meddling with the Chinese moral system. Writes Bland: "Here was Wimple, representative of a race of conscience-ridden hustlers, preaching his distorted version of an Asiatic religion to Asiatics."

Addressing the tactics of Western governments and Empire in general, Bland's earlier posturing as an agent of civilisation in a benighted heathen land may have gladdened his speech. "What we are pleased to call economic pressure," he says, "means greedy men with quick-firing guns." He quotes the 16th century French essayist and statesman Michel de Montaigne in denunciation of the so-called civilising mission — "Oh mechanicall victories, oh base conquest." Indeed, throughout the book he frequently refers to this man who declared more than 400 years ago, "Everyone calls barbarity what is not his custom." A far cry from the "exigencies of racial division aboard" outlined in Chapter I.

Bland's utilitarianism, however, coupled with his observations of China, also led him to become an outspoken advocate of birth control and a favourite of eugenics figurehead Margaret Sanger. A particularly agonized passage from *Houseboat Days* even found its way into Nanking University's exhaustive 1934

China population study, where it is cited as "a complete picture of the Chinese population problem".

Despite his prominence before and between the World Wars, J.O.P. Bland has today been largely forgotten. In his final book, published in 1932 when he was 69, in a chapter titled *Is there a Red Peril in China?*, he argued that the Communist leaders' political convictions were no more genuine than the conversion of Chiang Kai-shek to Russian communism in 1926. He argued that communism could never be imposed on China's social structure, and on today's evidence he was right. But he was badly mistaken in writing off the ideological zeal and capabilities of the leaders who, ironically enough, would finally institute Bland's suggestions for the salvation of China: birth control and compulsory cremation.

J.O.P. Bland died in 1945, but with this book he preserved lost, precious China worlds of sailing and salt smuggling, of geese, graves, dead cities and ancient ways — worlds that have indeed disappeared in the face of the "money-mills and counting-houses" that he so desired to escape.

Andrew Chubb
Series Editor
Shanghai, September 2008

HOUSEBOAT DAYS IN CHINA

THE LOWDAH

HOUSEBOAT DAYS IN CHINA

BY
J. O. P. BLAND

ILLUSTRATED BY W. D. STRAIGHT

TO ALL GOOD, COMPANIONABLE MEN,
WHO PREFER THE SKY TO ANY CEILING,
AND THE SONG OF THE WEST WIND TO ALL THE WISE TALK
OF PEDANTS, PHILOSOPHERS AND STALL-FED CITIZENS,
GLADLY DO I COMMEND THIS BOOK
IF ONLY BECAUSE IT IS NOT (AND NEVER CAN BE)
A STANDARD WORK ON CHINA.

PEKING, *December*, 1908.

CONTENTS

CHAPTER I

THE BOAT AND ITS PIDGIN 1

CHAPTER II

THE LOWDAH AND HIS CREW 12

CHAPTER III

THE MÉNAGE AFLOAT 20

CHAPTER IV

OF DOGS 27

CHAPTER V

THE NEARER HUNTING-GROUNDS 35

CHAPTER VI

THE QUARRY 42

CHAPTER VII

THE LORD OF THE SOIL 54

CHAPTER VIII

THE ETHICS OF HOUSEBOAT TRAVEL 69

CHAPTER IX

OF THE ETERNAL FEMININE 80

CHAPTER X

OF DUCKS, RAIN, AND OTHER MATTERS 90

CHAPTER XI

MISSIONARIES, MANDARINS, AND MORALS 101

CHAPTER XII

ON THE HYPNOTIC INFLUENCE OF THE P'UTZU 110

CHAPTER XIII
PREPARATIONS FOR A GRAND SORTIE 121

CHAPTER XIV
TO THE CHIENTANG RIVER 130

CHAPTER XV
DISCIPLINE ON BOARD THE ARK 148

CHAPTER XVI
OF RIVERSIDE MEMORIES 162

CHAPTER XVII
OF SMUGGLING AND SOME ASPECTS OF THE ART OF GOVERNMENT . . . 174

CHAPTER XVIII
OF SPRING SNIPE AND THE COMING OF THE RAILWAY 188

CHAPTER XIX
OF GEESE AND A DEAD CITY 201

CHAPTER XX
OF BOOKS AND POETRY AND BABUS 209

CHAPTER XXI
ON COMING HOME 221

LIST OF ILLUSTRATIONS

PLATES

THE LOWDAH . . . . *Frontispiece*

A BOATMAN OF THE CHIENTANG RIVER . . . . *To face p.* 144

MAP

MAP OF COUNTRY NEAR SHANGHAI . . . . *At End*

THE ·BOAT·AND·ITS·PIDGIN·

CHAPTER I

"We are what suns and winds and waters make us." — LANDOR.

"Perpetual devotion to what a man calls his business is only to be sustained by perpetual neglect of many other things. And it is not by any means certain that a man's business is the most important thing he has to do." — STEVENSON.

OR those to whom the Yangtsze is but a name, the existence of the European's houseboat thereon requires explanation; for, like many another feature of life on the fringe of Eastern Asia, it is an exotic growth, slowly evolved as the white man has adapted himself to a new and medieval environment. To most people the word will no doubt call up visions either of those unwieldy floating parlours which line the comfortable banks of Thames in summer, or that more navigable but cheerless craft discovered by Mr. Bangs on the cold tide of Styx. But to us in China the houseboat is become as much and as intimate a factor of existence as Taotais, the chit-system, or any other of the parochial matters which differentiate our lives from those of Upper Tooting. And so, though I may be tedious, I shall explain matters for the benefit of the uninitiated.

Imprimis, however, a word to the enlightened reader, the old resident (bless his querulous ways!), who, rightly enough, asks to be informed of your book's *raison d'être*. A record of Idleness, my dear Sir, trivial things set down in garrulous mood and chiefly for the delectation (if so it may be) of fellow-Idlers. Herein you shall find little geography and even less science, except it be such as all may take, by favour of the gods, from "pleasure trips into the lands of Thought and among the Hills of Vanity." A little chronicle, Madam, in memory of glad sunlit days, of cheery companions, and the joy of living. No great matter at best, and yet, to those who, smoking tolerant pipes, perceive through the haze something of relative values, our boat and its affairs may, from a philosophic standpoint, be as worthy of attention as any of the world-shaking matters that reverberate from the House by the River at Westminster.

The houseboat of the lower Yangtsze regions owes her existence to several causes, of which the first is the *wanderlust* inbred in the Anglo-Saxon, and, second, the absence of all roads, except waterways, in China. She is the embodiment in canvas and timber of European ideas adapted to Celestial ways and byways, ideas of accommodation, watercraft, and common humanity. This for the general; but beyond this, of necessity, lies the expression of individual identity common to all ships, so that, crossing the gang-plank of the *Water-Baby* or the *Mighty Atom*, you shall say at a glance what manner of men their owners be.

In the beginning of things the houseboat of Shanghai, such craft as the gentlemanly opium smugglers used in the days when the Eight Princes held their tinsel Court at Nanking, were nothing more than the native *wusieh k'uai*, equipped with camp beds to keep down vermin, and curtains to keep out the winds of heaven. And in remote spots one may yet fare right well in these native boats; of which more anon. But your Chinese ship,

big or little, is an unwieldy craft, built on the principle common
to the life of this people that there is always room for one more,
and indifferent as to how or where he shall bestow himself. It is
eminently adapted for a race which travels as a matter of choice
in the patriarchal manner, which cooks its food in the helmsman's bunk and eats it on the cabin floor; but British ideas of
"ship-shape" as well as the exigencies of racial division aboard
called for gradual amendment of the type. Therefore, our boat
was brought to a form combining the qualities of house comfort and ship speed; Chinese rigging gave place to English sails;
lee-boards were added, and finally brasswork, awnings, and a
coat of paint made the thing complete. Its evolution, which may
be traced in old photographs, has taken forty years, and the last
word has not yet been spoken.

Philosophers are agreed that the common fate of all noble
and great devices of man, unless restrained by abiding virtue
or an energetic police, is to fall away from the first ideal state,
and this by reason of the cankerworm of luxury. It is an old-
world struggle this, of Stoic and Epicurean, to be found for the
seeking at every turn of the grim human comedy. In the matter
of houseboats one may see clearly its evidences and portents.
Let us say nothing of such elephantine freaks as Simeon may
build, whereon to give his Gargantuan feasts, *al fresco*, on summer nights; tavern-ships with pianolas and plush fittings, happily unseen beyond harbour limits or, at their worst, disturbing
the stillness of the nearer hills. Nor need I refer to those boudoir
boats, lace-curtained and mirrored, whose owners must needs
find a way to spend their money, and whose chief use lies in up-
river picnics, entertainments wherein gramophones, parasols,
much food and some gallantry combine to relieve the dullness of
Whangpoo scenery. In another place, if I find myself in a proper
and delicate humour, I shall refer to the question of the fair sex
in its relation to houseboats; as for these vessels of the Sybarites,
let us leave them at their moorings. For they are excrescences, of
their nature ephemeral, unworthy of serious regard. Let us not

speak of these, but only of houseboats *pour le bon motif,* and even here honesty compels the admission that there exists evidence of the insidious cankerworm aforesaid.

It is a curious fact that as the flesh-pots of the white man in China have waned in their fatness, as the conditions of his life have gradually come to conform more closely to the standards of the lands which sent him forth, as the profitable hazards of the game have grown less, so has the candle of his comfort's needs waxed ever greater. The fact scarcely calls for demonstration; its evidence meets us on the threshold of every villa residence, protrudes itself in all our dining-rooms, in our clubs, and on our backs; and the houseboat, compared with the craft of twenty years ago, affords proof of the advances we have made in comfortable materialism. The thing was at first of its nature simple, a fitting answer to the call of the wild; but now, when transcontinental railways are making us one of London's remoter suburbs, and the voice of Israel (*via* New York and Moscow) is in our ears, our boats are becoming finicky things, tricked out with marble baths and gold paint. 'Tis an easy descent, its impulse the same which leads many a good woman to turn her house into a restaurant, but its results are unpleasant. To give you an instance: I have lately been told of a boat built to contain four persons in luxury, a thing in itself so contrary to the philosophy of up-country wanderings that one can only explain it as due to continental influence or the yellow peril at our gates. This monstrous invention has folding beds of full size, a bathroom with hot and cold water laid on, dining-room for six, and a patent card-table; moreover, she is provided with a petrol motor-engine which drives her through the water at six miles an hour, with hideous noise and stink. True, this is an extreme case, and Grandison, her owner, is the sort of man who goes to the theatre with his compradore; but the germ of an unholy competition is abroad, and there is need for us, the brotherhood of Idlers, to walk home carefully in the paths of simplicity. The cigarettes of Egypt are well enough in their place, but on the hillsides give me the honest briar.

It is not given to the works of man to combine all the virtues, and the reader will observe that our houseboat, being useful, is not a thing of absolute beauty. Those who desire an exact description of her build and equipment will not find it here, for, in the first place, your technical details are but dry stuff, and, in the second, this is a matter on which, as with feminine loveliness, we do not all agree. Let me therefore but roughly outline the *Saucy Jane*, so that those who have never crossed her gang-plank may know something of her interior economy and uses. The houseboat, like all Gaul, is divided into three parts — the white man's, the yellow man's, and the dogs'; and since the object of its being is that all these should dwell together, for days or weeks, in such good content as may be, the proportion of space which each enjoys is a matter on which much depends. I speak of the boat for two, whose, average length is forty-five feet, with an eight-feet beam amidships. In such a one a cabin twelve feet by eight should suffice for any decent pair of Christians and sportsmen; all good fellowship and much peace of mind can travel easily in a smaller space. For your free-moving man, who in his waking hours must have room to swing a cat, or indeed in any event, it is an excellent thing to have bunks which fold and fit nicely into the walls, for not only do you thus avoid during the day that dormitory aspect which has been known to offend sensitive minds, but these bunks being provided with locks, you can enjoy the pleasant certainty that no unsavoury native will sleep on them during your absence.

Forward of the mast the ship is decked some three feet higher than the level of the cabin floor; in this place is the kennel, as ample as possible, while leaving room in the house for a chain locker and those mysterious depths where, under our protection, the lowdah carries his smuggled salt and other perquisites. Bluff bows of the Chinese type are best, affording grateful space above and below; as our journeyings are usually on pacific inland waters, we can cheerfully take the risk of an occasional bumping in a head sea. Much of the joy of houseboat days depends on good deck-room forward, which should give place at least for two cane chairs. There, smoking the sunset pipe, your body tingling with the health of a long day in the open, and your mind at peace with gods and men, you may watch the soft sinking of twilight to dusk, and dusk to night, deriving a very human sense of added ease from the contemplation of the coolies' labours; or, as the dawn comes up over the edge of your flat, sail-dotted world, you may here fill your lungs with the morning breeze, blowing sweet-scented from the rape fields, and thank God that you are alive. All of us, if we stop to think it out, would sooner share

what Whitman calls "the cooling influences of external nature" with a congenial friend or book on the quarter-deck of our wandering boat than sit in the busiest money-mill on earth; the pity of it is that we go on, nevertheless, most of our days, groping in our subterranean ways, while, far overhead, larks are singing and the sun is shining on God's wonderful world;

The Dingy.

and so the swift years pass, until from our narrow path we emerge to find Charon waiting for us by the cold stream. Every day that we rescue from the gloomy routine of our counting-houses and gas-lit streets to spend under the open sky is a day of grace; this is a truth which even Chicago may recognise, as its spasmodic cult of the 'simple life' bears witness. All of which digression comes from the memory of hours fortunately spent beyond the frontiers of fancy on our houseboat's foredeck.

Aft of the cabin belongs to the yellow man; seeing the space he occupies, a stranger would be surprised at the number of our Aryan brothers and the manner in which they dispose themselves and their impedimenta. Ten Celestial souls, at least, journey (without sentiment) in our company — the boy, the cook, and the crew, — and each has his allotted place for work and sleep. In a well-ordered boat the space between cabin and kitchen is generous; partly because one is thus spared many of the unsavoury harbingers of dinner which arise from the frying-pan, and partly because the boy and cook have no other sleeping-room than that which the "pantry" affords. I know that there exists a theory, widely held, that a native can sleep anywhere, and that to concern oneself for his comfort is foolishness; many good people quarter their Chinese servants worse than their dogs. No doubt that the Oriental survives bad treatment and that he accepts it, like other sublunary happenings, with stolid patience; at the same time, there is an old saying about the merciful man which comes to mind when one sees the "boy" sleeping *en pelotte* in a cupboard five feet by three, while the cook lies uneasily curled between his stove and the water-kong. Humanity apart, these people would better appreciate our excursions and sorties, and render us, therefore, a better, because a more willing, service if their necessities were a matter of more concern to us.

Of other matters on which depends our boat's wellbeing, that of light and ventilation in the cabin is immediate. To get both in plenty, without the thousand natural ills that come of draughts; to avoid gloom and glare by day; to prevent on wintry nights those swift alternations of stuffiness and cold, wherefrom spring rheums and vapours, — these are problems to which the complete answer still eludes us. Yet there are certain principles of universal acceptance. Our windows should be wide, and one of them on a level with the bunkhead, so that, without moving from the pillows, the silent message of the kindly stars may reach us as we turn to sleep; that, waking, we may see the wonder of rosy-fingered dawn come, soft heralded by twittering of birds. As to fresh air, tastes vary; I have seldom known two men, and never a woman, to hold a reasonable and temperate view of the subject, and I have journeyed pleasantly enough with a German who would have none of it. The question is greatly simplified, however, by firmly abolishing that abominable source of woe, the American coal-stove. 'Tis an invention good enough, no doubt, in its own place, where men make it the rally-point of society, expectorating towards it as to the centre of gravity, but in the houseboat it is a fearsome thing, disturbing the even tenour of life. Unlike the Church of Laodicea, your small stove is always red hot or stone cold; windows and doors in its vicinity must be for ever opened and shut, clothes doffed and donned, to meet its varying humours. Replace it by a movable kerosene stove of the non-odorous kind, and you may sit snugly through the coldest evening with the temperature you desire, and as much fresh air as the stronger vessel may want.

I speak not here of the servants' quarters, nor of that unsavoury place wherein the crew sleep, eat, and spend lives which to us seem curiously purposeless and unpleasant; to these tribes on our frontier I shall refer in another place.

For the cabin's equipment, every man in his humour. Certain things there must be, such as good lamps, so fixed that one may read cosily abed; bunks that invite to sleep; a bookshelf and some odd nooks and corners for stowage of boots, bottles, and other unsightly things. In boats, as in houses, there is a happy halfway resting-place between Rome and Capua, of which the sign is comfort with simplicity. With a few good pictures we soon become intimate, and fitness may be observed even in the colour of drugget. I have a friend who carries the Spartan mood to extreme limits, whither I follow him with difficulty; his cabin has the severity of a casual ward, and, like Mrs. Battle, he plays the whole game with rigour. At his frugal dietary I cavil not (though a glass of port on a winter's night is grateful), but I draw the line at his bunks. For he will not hear of spring mattresses, quotes the Immortal Bard on the blessed state of him who snores upon the flint, and thinks a bed of shavings with alpine bosses and declivities "good enough for any tired man." I mention this case merely to show how the best of customs, if overdone, may corrupt our little world, and to observe that spring mattresses in a houseboat

A Ferry.

are desirable, if only because you can take them out and wash them; and where one travels with Asiatics, cheek by jowl, this is a matter not unworthy of consideration.

Our good ship is thus set forth in all her parts; to your realist a thing of timber and tarpaulin, full of jabbering Orientals, but to the eye of faith an Argosy wherein we may sail gladly into worlds unexplored and return not empty-handed. For each one of us, though the poetic fires may be damped and the young man's fancy turned to lumps of lead, life has yet voices that call ever to the Enchanted Isles, hands that guide us to the gate called Beautiful. It is when the day's work is done and our quantum of meals eaten that life begins; then we have time to realise the wonder of our being here at all, and to distinguish something of the vast harmonies which underlie the ear-splitting discords around us. In the glory of the sunset, in the piping of Pan beneath the trees, in the beauty of a woman's face, each of us hears at times these undying voices universal, but for many a man the whole joyous world of imagination may be conjured up by homelier things, by a trout-rod, a bag of golf-sticks, ay, even by the wind shrieking in suburban chimneys. For myself, I never see a houseboat lying at her moorings but straightway I sail away in fancy to the happy hunting-grounds.

Sailing, — the word reminds me that of recent years there has grown up amongst houseboat Idlers a tendency to discard the sail in favour of steam towing. Everywhere, since the days of the Shimonoseki Treaty, native and Japanese companies compete on the main waterways to tow your boat, one of a serpentine train, carrying you a hundred miles while you sleep. For Nimrod the advantage is plain, and to carp at the inevitable advance of our material devices were churlish; one may sigh for the time when no puffing engines disturbed these peaceful waters, besmearing their lilies and eglantine with soot, but after all, you may sigh with as good cause over every navigable river in England. Of this, then, we need say nothing; at the temperate use of launches let us not cavil; but that it should ever lead any man to abolish the sail, wherein lies the essence of houseboat joys, is a melancholy result. Yet I know men who have removed the mast boldly, henceforth towing their poor dismembered hulks dismally from one shooting-ground to another. Motor-launches, too, have appeared within our borders, machines which act as tenders, snorting up and down the shallower creeks and relieving the houseboat of all purpose in existence except that of a floating inn. True it is that all the base uses of the lowdah and his crew are directed, naturally enough, towards inducing the foreign devil to rely entirely on steam, and that to overcome these passive resisters requires determination of a high order. True, also, that the largest bags may possibly be made by those who use these latest inventions; nevertheless, an old-fashioned person may be allowed to hope that the thing will not be overdone, and that the houseboat may continue to move with life upon the face of our inland waters; for the killing of game, after all, is only one of the objects of our up-country days, and there are higher joys than to make a bag which shall be recorded in the papers.

Of all our good store of houseboat memories, none, I think, linger more fragrantly than the *moments perdus* of sport, those half-hours spent listening to the ripple of waves breaking from under our bows, and the whisper of the wind in the rigging. After a morning on the marshes, to sail among the lagoons or out into the lake, with the sunlight dancing ahead and Black Care a hundred miles behind; down the long reaches dreamily to watch the banks go by, to the creaking of buffalo wheels and the thousand familiar (yet unknown) sights and sounds of Chinese life afloat and ashore; or, seeking a quiet anchorage, to steal down a silent creek at dusk, a white shadow among the grey and brown, where no sound mars the spell of coming night — hours like these we would not willingly forgo for any invention of rapid transit.

There is, methinks, something in the Anglo-Saxon, landlubber and ledger clerk though he be, some fluid in his system diluted from that of his Norsemen and Dane forebears, which unconsciously quickens to the throb of any craft that sails upon the face of the waters; as the canvas bellies to the wind, and the foam goes rippling astern, he feels a glorious tickling of his spinal cord, a message, echoing faintly down the long corridors of Time from those stout mariners of old, that the joys and fears of their long forgotten lives are still a very part of his being.

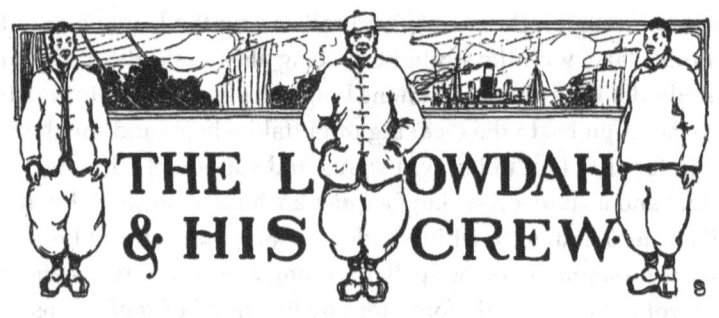

THE LOWDAH & HIS CREW

CHAPTER II

The skilled Milesian man who, with half-open mouth and dreamy eyes,
Stood steering Argo to that land of lies.

JASON.

KNOW a man who has conceived and executed the brilliant idea of putting his houseboat crew into uniform — a rainbow thing of scarlet and blue, with heraldic devices in green across breast and back. His reasons for this are, first, to distinguish his retainers from the aborigines; secondly, to impress the cities of the plain with the importance of the strangers in their midst; and, thirdly, to conceal from himself that exceeding squalor which marks the houseboat coolie for its own. Arraying these poor waifs in garments suggestive of a pantomime chorus, he is able to contemplate them, he says, without continual heart-searchings on the subject of Destiny and its rugged inequalities. Vastly creditable, I think, both this spiritual distress and the manner of its alleviation.

For the crew of a European's houseboat consists generally of the pariahs of our floating population. That it should be so is

unnecessary; the fact, like many others of the kind, is due to our
distaste for studying the native and his ways – or, to put the matter plainly, to our ignorant laziness. Good and notable exceptions
there are – boats that use and keep workmen; on long trips, even
your easy-going man may inspect his wastrels before starting,
but of the ordinary week-end trip it is safe to say that half the average crew should be in hospital and the other half in gaol. And
this is partly because the lowdah has come to expect that you
will travel by steam, and partly because long impunity in fooling and fleecing the foreign devil has made him greatly daring.
Which brings us to consideration of the lowdah.

In the ancient vernacular his name means "old and great" – no
doubt, like another word with us, it was originally "a term of en-
dearment among sailors," an archaic equivalent of 'old cock,' and
its actual meaning is helmsman or shipmaster. On a houseboat he
is the only permanent official; in theory, a faithful watcher who
keeps the *Saucy Jane* spick and span; guards her inner parts from
river thieves, rats and vermin, and her hull from dry rot and the
poles of passing junks; sees to her safe mooring, and engages the
crew when wanted. In practice he is one of a close corporation of
rogues and scoundrels, who for five days in the week riots and
gambles (probably in the cabin of the *Saucy Jane*) with his fellow
ruffians on what he has 'squeezed' from your last trip. The native
mafoo[1] is something of a villain, but compared to the houseboat
lowdah he is a guileless person of good morals.

And when you come to think of it, the thing is natural enough,
for here, as in all the Seven Seas, the leisured classes are prone
to evil, and the innate virtue of a Chinaman is not proof against
luxurious idleness; and the lowdah is idle, exempt even from the
master's eye, for 300 days of the year. In such case he must perforce fall from grace; but the mystery of the thing is that, having
fallen and being the reprobate he is, he should retain his pride
of place and continue to swell it on the after-deck of any decent
boat. No doubt the secret – like that of all native villainy – lies in

[1] Horse-boy.

organisation; these fellows keep the ring against outsiders, and to get a new lowdah, under these conditions, is simply to draw another card from a very filthy pack. Dismiss your man to-morrow: what happens? Brown will take him, because Brown's has left him suddenly — and you get Brown's. There is one truculent ruffian of my acquaintance who has been lowdah on nearly every boat on the river; he never keeps a place more than a month after the shooting season begins, and is generally thrown overboard up country; but he finds, like Tristram Shandy, that in the propagation of geese Nature is all-bountiful, and I see no reason why he should not continue successfully in his profession unto the end. A remedy for this state of affairs may possibly lie in engaging young and artless lowdahs from another district under police protection; but the experiment requires more energy and leisure than most of us can afford.

Seven coolies go to make the ordinary boat's crew which the lowdah professes to engage. You pay each man forty cents a day (say 8d.). Off this wage the lowdah 'squeezes' three or four cents as the price of his favour; next he makes profitable terms for running the ship's mess, and levies a claim on "cumshaws." Eventually he engages a couple of able-bodied men in case of accidents, ships his wife's cousin (suffering from incipient beri-beri) and his own nephew (ætat. 13), the remainder of the crew being usually opium-smoking ricksha men whose vehicles have been impounded by the police. Is it any wonder that, if you insist on travelling twenty miles under "yuloh,"[1] the elements, mysteriously working, and the stars in the courses combine to forbid it; that time, tide, head winds, the size of your boat, and the state of the creeks prevent any such undertaking?

Knowledge, as sages have frequently observed, is power. In no country upon earth is this axiom made manifest as in China, where the 'knowing' man lives in fatness, preying upon those whom Imperial Edicts describe as the "stupid ones." The lowdah's place in creation and his survival therein aptly illustrate

[1] The long stern sweep.

this simple truth. He knows, therefore he thrives. He knows the European's limitations and the necessities of his fellow-natives, and from both he derives profit sufficient to make him a personage in the tea-house. There is, moreover, as with friend Reineke, a certain artistic merit in the rogue's methods which compels our sneaking admiration; he has brought his villainies to such a pitch of studied perfection, based his systems on such foundations of laborious knowledge, that at times you are inclined to let him enjoy the fruits of his ingenuity. It is the same feeling that prompts you, when the peregrine swoops deftly on your wounded quail, to let him get away with his quarry.

In the gentle art of presenting bills the lowdah is a past master; give him his head, and the upkeep of your boat will equal that of a suburban villa. There are, of course, the usual and recognised squeezes of his profession; the annual overhauls — on which he lives riotously for months — the incidentals of each trip, coal, oil, candles, soap, and the unnumbered mops and poles whose mysterious life is but a

"A personage in the tea-house."

little day. Every lowdah knows to a nicety, by experience and by that delicately-gauged repute in which each European stands in native opinion, the breaking-point of your endurance; also he knows that you will pay something, however monstrous the claim, for peace' sake and to be rid of importunity. And so the

wind is tempered to the shorn lamb and many a bleating victim of my acquaintance not only submits to the shearing, but
becomes curiously attached to the shearer. This, too, is not un-
natural, for your typical 'savez' lowdah, the man who knows
and does his business up country, often displays, rogue though
he be, a very wholesome and engaging interest in your sport;
take him away from his accustomed purlieus and the sons of
Belial his friends, and you find him decent enough, serviceable
and keen in the matter of your bag. These pleasing traits in his
character are, however, reserved exclusively for his so-called
master; the world sees them not. Let a stranger borrow the boat,
and with it he borrows a very pestilent rogue.

An intelligent[1] observer of Chinese life — unduly neglected by
the present generation — pointed out years ago this side of the
lowdah's character in an entertaining passage which I may fitly
quote: —

It is to the outsider, the casual tripper, that our friend reveals the
choicest beauties of his nature. Which of us has not sat down over the
cabin-stove and cursed the unwritten law which forbids the chastisement of another man's menial? The lowdah, still sleepy from yesterday's
debauch, revels in this impunity, which preserves him from the *argu-
mentum ad hominem*; right well he knows too, that, storm as you may, it is
unusual to look the borrowed horse in the mouth, and that on Monday
you will pay without demur, for the lender's sake.

You start gaily enough, wondering only how the wretched crew of
decrepid men and small boys is going to yuloh the boat to your happy
hunting-grounds; but a friendly launch takes you as far as Sungkong,
and with this aid it should be easy for them to get you to Kazay before
the morning. Therefore, having seen them start work at ten o'clock, you
turn in after describing with much detail the spot where you wish to
shoot. "My savee," says the lowdah, and you go to bed. At 3 A.M. you
awake to find the boat snugly anchored under a mud-bank. Then the
fun begins — at least, it is fun for the lowdah. When you have roused

[1] Tung Chia

him from his lair (it takes time, and you are half-frozen), he says, "Head wind, head tide, no can yuloh." There is no wind, and no tide to speak of, but that is a mere detail. When you ask where you are, he says, "Velly near Kazay," by which statement the memory of Ananias is put to shame. Then, with the threats and promises, you persuade him to go on, and for half an hour—until you are asleep again—two small boys propel the boat at the rate of one 'li' an hour. Eventually, the next morning you find yourself moored in the salubrious vicinity of Fungking, a spot endeared

An ancient Bridge.

to the lowdah by the presence of a lady friend, but otherwise only re-markable for a total absence of game; there, while you tramp the highly cultivated mud-fields, he spends a happy day in congenial society. At dusk he returns, explaining that certain supplies of coal and oil were required for the return trip, and these defects he has provided, the bill being presented in proof of good faith. Then you start homewards; and should your latent wrath be inclined to manifest itself in unpleasant-ness, you will, if you are wise, refrain therefrom, for our friend is quite capable of running the boat violently into a convenient bridge while you are at dinner; he knows you will have to make good the damage, and there are pickings in such accidents for himself.

Next morning, at the hour when you should be in a ricksha on the Bund, you find yourself facing the first of the flood at the top of the seven-mile reach. At this stage you tell the lowdah what you think of him in the plainest and worst language. He receives it in silence, his mouth being full of rice at the time; but when you have done, he confides to the comfortably-resting crew what he thinks of you, and his remarks are the cause of considerable native merriment. There appears to be nothing for it but to walk home, until by a lucky chance a launch looms in sight. The lowdah knew all about that launch before you started — he has a cousin on board and three out of the five dollars which you pay for the tow are his reward for a carefully-devised stratagem.

Much water has flowed under our bridges since then; many hopeful men have returned, sadder and wiser, from fierce struggling on inland waters with the lowdah tribe, but the latter remains unchanged, fixed in its destinies and smiling at the pitiful struggling of its victims. In this smiling immobility, as in his lust for coin, there is something in the lowdah suggestive of that grim helmsman who waits for us by the banks of Styx. When all's said and done, one rather likes the fellow for his very stolidity, and 'tis undeniable that most of his misdeeds are due to our own foolishness. If only he were a trifle more human in his relations with those pitiful scarecrows, the crew, we might well forgive him his other enormities.

And here, until we meet them again anon, we may take leave of these our humble fellow-travellers; but before we go, Sir and Madam, let us cast a glance at the place where these atoms of superfluous humanity live aboard our boat. Imagine this after-deck on a day when the rain comes driving sideways before a northerly wind, picture the condition of this black hole wherein seven men bestow themselves, *tant bien que mal*, to sleep. Perhaps on a cold night, as we sit comfortably over our second glass of port, recollection of these things may incline us to tolerance for some of the shortcomings of our Mongolian brother; and if so, not a soul will be any the worse for it.

THE · MENAGE · AFLOAT ·

CHAPTER III

"Take us the foxes, the little foxes, that spoil the vines."

— Song of Solomon.

GOOD housewife of my acquaintance — one of those worthy people who make themselves very uncomfortable in the pursuit of comfort — tells me that she could never bring herself to visit the cook's den on a houseboat. Herein, I think, she is wise; nor would I recommend to those who hold extreme views on sanitation and hygiene too close a scrutiny of the boys' quarters. At the best of times, and giving him all facilities, there is a wide gulf between the Chinaman's standard of cleanliness and ours. He endorses that scientific definition of dirt which calls it matter in the wrong place, and his philosophy teaches him that, sooner or later, the wanderer will find its way home without the help of man. Each one of us, he knows, must eat his peck o' dirt in a lifetime, and if length of days or inscrutable destiny increase the peck to a bushel, what of it! If kings must needs go a progress through the guts of a beggar, if imperial Cæsar's dust should stop a bung-hole, the cook knows, without word of the immortal Dane, that this also is but one of Nature's fantastic ways, and that the beggar is none the worse for the vagaries of these poor atoms. Let us admit, strictly between ourselves, that many of us have a sneaking fellow-feeling for the Oriental attitude in this matter. Doctors, of course, cannot indulge it, nor sanitary inspectors, nor good women brought up in the household wisdom of Penelope, but to the plain man these strident voices of Public Health authorities in our kitchens and boudoirs are something too emphatic. They would have us go in fear all our days, bringing the imminent shadow of Death before us in guise of grisly microbe at every street corner, at the tiffin table, ay, even on Clorinda's ruby lips. We hear them, shuddering, and then, harking back to our unguarded but joyous youth; — remembering our salad bachelor days when filters were not, and the cook was a law unto himself, — we take heart of grace and go our unregenerate ways in cheerfulness. Nevertheless, and as a compromise between conflicting theories, it is not a bad thing to descend suddenly at intervals upon the boy and cook in their lairs, ejecting things unseemly and of purely native origin; hygiene apart, it is not fitting that our omelette should be cooked with, but after, the lowdah's sea-slugs.

Our immediate followers up country on ordinary occasions are three — boy, cook, and dog-coolie, and on long trips, where steady work is before us, it is wise to include in the ship's company two sturdy beaters, men of tried prowess in covert.

The boy and the cook have between them, for their respective duties, impedimenta and the disposal of their own persons a cubic area something less than that of a Saratoga trunk. Cast your eye, my Lady, on this kitchen equipment, observe its limitations, the nice adjustment of necessity to space, and you will wonder with me how one small stove can carry all its brew. Dine with us, Madam, and as each course, *réussi* and fittingly served, emerges from these mysterious regions, pause not to ask how the plates were washed, nor where the baked meats lay before they came to table. If to-day's fillet and to-morrow's trussed fowl came aboard neatly packed in the cook's wardrobe, why, ignorance is bliss and the saucepan covereth a multitude of sins. And so for Ganymede, whose labours, between the kitchen devil and the deep sea of clamorous white men, are compassed about so narrowly with crockery and pendent glass that he looks for all the world like some contortionist juggler at his tricks—pray you, indulgence. Which of us has not wondered beneath the armour of their stolidity what these followers of ours think of our excursions and sorties? To the severely practical mind for which we usually give them credit, the whole business must be a monstrous enigma, one of those mysteries inseparable from foreign devildom, which Confucius bids them neither consider

nor discuss. For they must recognise the astounding fact that the cost in sycee of the game we bring home, after long toilful days, is ten times more than we could buy it for in the market; even with the best of luck there can be no profit in shooting with cartridges that cost eight cents apiece, and they know us for men who can afford the luxury of leisure. All the ways of this "White Peril" are indeed inscrutable; those who recklessly waste money, enduring hard labour up country, are of the same mad world which pursues divers balls with bats and clubs; rides violently, without errand, across the face of the earth, and postures to the sound of horns with other men's wives. Such beings are classed in the native mind with prodigies, monsters, and the immortal gods, and accepted accordingly, without, question or complaint.

Despite their *res angusta* afloat, I believe our followers are rather partial to upcountry life in their own way; Ah Kong the dog-coolie welcomes it, I know, in spite of his aversion to long walks, his wife being a notorious vixen and his home a place of wrath. The boy who answers cheerfully to the name of Gehazi. and Wang-hi the cook, enjoy their peaceful days on board, especially when our programme includes cold tiffin in a basket. 'Enjoys' is perhaps too strong; their attitude is one of philosophic calm, due to the fact that for a while they can eat, sleep, and gamble undisturbed. In none of them have I ever perceived any signs of interest in the country itself or its inhabitants; whether we go to the lakes or to the hills appears to be a matter of absolute indifference, and the only spots for which they ever display preference are those where they can buy salt or other commodities, which, smuggled to Shanghai, will show a profit. Gehazi will sit in his pantry reading an absurd chronicle of the Han Dynasty, while the boat takes him, all unconscious, through unknown places where men live by strange crafts; to him they are such stuff as dreams are made of, and he can provide better dreams of his own. This, at least, is the impression the native's *nonchalant* stolidity conveys, but who shall say what are the thoughts that lurk behind these wall-faces?

Now and again they will surprise you, these Chinese, with glimpses of unsuspected thoughts and motives in their mental depths unfathomed by us who live amongst them. Strange breaths of spring stir at times the dusty recesses of their emotionless souls; voices call to them from the past through opium haze and cult of cash, and for a moment their commonplace lives are touched with a ray of the light which, ages ago, sent Chinese artists and poets to teach Corea and Japan. In some squalid courtyard you will find ragged fellows listening in long silence to a caged thrush's song; sometimes, on the sorriest beggar-boat on the creek, or in the tea-house of a dingy by-street, you shall see a sprig of flowering plum-blossom; on the walls of country rest-houses I have found not only verses from the classics, but the original work of passers-by — student or pilgrim — singing of autumn winds in the bamboo grove and the flight of wild geese between the hills. I am by no means sure that Gehazi himself does not invoke the lyric muse with compositions of this kind in spring, for I have seen verses at the end of the book in which he keeps a record of what he is pleased to say I owe him.

Ah Kong, master of the hounds, and his fellow-beaters arrayed for the chase, suffer "Shame-face" in the eyes of the crew; and not without reason, for they are indeed figures of fun. Their own kit being useless in covert, I provide them with boots (originally made for Indian policemen), wide trousers of sail-cloth cut in the fashion of clowns', and old hats. Ah Kong, being an enthusiast, sports a grey Monte Carlo and a pair of ancient kid gloves; good fellows these, of Spartan philosophy and wondrous patience, who will beat their way through scrub and sword-grass for days, and take a friendly interest in your bag. One ragged suit of clothes to their backs, no certainty as to next week's rice, yet they face the world and its back-bending affairs cheerily with hearts undismayed. I like to hear them when, after their long tramp, they have hung the game, seen to the dogs, and foregathered round the lowdah's rice-pot with the crew; the day, with all its chances and events, will keep them talking for hours. In their tales the beater often cuts a more heroic figure than his master, if only because it is denied to him to relieve himself by cursing audibly the adverse Fates. They sum us up, these heathen, all our little weaknesses and some of our virtues, in racy opinions, as just, and quite as kind, as those recorded by our friends of the club smoking-room.

I have written of the up-country ménage as I know it, but there are, I believe, people who go into remote parts of these provinces with hirelings — boy and cook engaged for the trip. In most cases, no doubt, this is the outcome of the married state, and criticism halts at the recognition of necessity; but the results are, nevertheless, not to be commended even to a benedict. I, who am no epicure, have suffered many and grievous things at the hands of the short-job cook; and your 'hotel-boy' on board is a sorry rogue at best. Often you do not know your friend's habits or necessities in these matters; you start for a week's outing, learning the truth too late, and these varlets take from you much peace of mind and bodily content. To the leisurely enjoyment of houseboat life you must bring a soul unharassed by the sordid things of domesticity.

And this brings to mind an adventure of my friend M'Nab, a parlous case of the hireling not without its humorous retrospect. He had taken a varlet for a week, one of the 'oiled and curled Assyrian bull' type, reeking of gambling dens and petty larceny. On the second day out, in the wild country beyond Haiyee, the fellow showed signs of eccentricity—laid tiffin on the bunks and made curious gurgling noises in his throat. Next day, grasping one of the crew, he jumped overboard, was rescued, dried, and locked up in the pantry, where he lay, cursing horribly and scratching on the partition. Towards morning he contrived an escape, and thereafter gave M'Nab and his friend, an unsuspecting British sailor, one of the most exciting hours in life. The trip was abandoned, and they took him home chained in the dog-kennel. It was subsequently stated that he adopted insanity to avoidance of settling certain urgent debts—a ruse not infrequent in his class. The explanation is not as important as the fact that M'Nab, by agreement with his wife, now takes his No. 2 boy up country and that travelling on his hospitable boat is much pleasanter in consequence.

In the matter of cuisine, your houseboat should strike a cheery midway note, avoiding Scylla of the superfluous and Charybdis the unlovely. Grandon, who takes his chef with him, and feasts hugely, after unwonted exercise, on truffled entrées and port, is more attractive in food and philosophy than the man who professes to rough it on a badly-cooked chop and a bit of cheese; but both are unseemly. A stock-pot, ever simmering, is one of the secrets of houseboat economy; into it should go all the odds and ends of the bag — except perhaps civet cats and foxes — and from it should come a savoury mess such as Esau loved. For dinner, after all, is no inconsiderable moment in the healthy human animal's day, a thing not to be despised even of philosophers. It was one of the cheeriest of these who said, "A good meal and a bottle of wine is an answer to most standard works upon the question of life. When a man's heart warms to his viands, he forgets a great deal of sophistry and soars into a cosy zone of contemplation. Death may be knocking at the door, like the Commander's statue; we have something else in hand, thank God, and let him knock."

Therefore, friends, let us have viands that our hearts can warm to.

·CHAPTER·FOUR·
·OF·DOGS·

"It is sweet to establish that, at least in appearance, there is on the planet where, like disowned kings, we live in solitary state, a being that loves us." — MAETERLINCK.

SHOOTING without a dog is like a song without words — there is joy in it, no doubt, but the fulness of satisfaction is lacking. I know a mighty hunter, one after the manner of Bahrám (o'er whose head wild asses stamp in vain), who stoutly proclaims the belief that in this part of the world dogs are no help, but a hindrance. A retriever for water work he might endure, though even here a hardy coolie, mother-naked in the wind, would be more to his liking; but pointers, setters, and spaniels he holds in contempt. Certainly he makes good bags, his plan being to stride, with a beater on either side, through cotton and beans at ten-league ferocity of speed, so that running birds are terrified to a rise; but it is not given to every man to be twenty-two and a sprinter. *Pour moi*, satisfied with a leisurely ten to fifteen miles a day, half the day's sport lies in watching the swift signals of good dog Tray, doing for me the work which Bahrám does for himself; and if, through his over-zeal or our own lack of field-craft, we lose a shot here and there, what of it? I, for one, would sooner watch the spaniel nose a false scent than go rushing blindly across country without him.

This from the standpoint of sport, but there lurks in most of us a certain human quality which loves dogs for their own sake and apart from the size of the bag. These "wagging humourists" of ours, as Meredith finely calls them, are often the only company we desire — friends ever ready with silent sympathy to respect our changing moods. If they have a defect — I speak not of foibles — it lies in their brief mortality; so short their little day that the thought of it comes ever to mind, laden with memories of past bereavements, to warn us of the penalty of affection. Payn knew this feeling when he wrote:

> And never more shall our knees be pressed
> By his dear old chops in their slobbery rest.

The warning is a vain one; Melampus, Duke, and Ponto in turn have gone beyond to that dogs' paradise in which Southey believed, and their memory brings at times a feeling that is very near heartache; nevertheless, the newcomer makes his dogged way into our affections and will not be denied; the bonds tighten as we fall into each other's grooves, and he learns to read us like a book, giving us "ten years of loving loyalty" in return for what he gets out of life in our society.

The human idea of blessed immortality is variable, dependent on age, the set of the wind, conscience, and other matters, but there is a feature in the Red Indian ideal of heaven which commands my sympathy: in his celestial mansions, as in the theatres of Saigon, the dog is ever welcome. One of our minor poets feels this, though he expresses it deprecatingly, with an eye on the village pulpit: —

> Is a man a hopeless heathen if he dreams of one fair day
> When, with spirit free from shadows grey and cold,
> He may wander thro' the heather in the unknown far away
> With his good old dogs before him as of old?

Horsfield's verse is open to criticism, but the sentiment does him credit, and I confess to liking him for the choice of a good steady old dog (it was a setter) in Paradise, where there can be no question of making a bag before sunset. A pretty vision, is it not — the heather, the old shikarri and his dog, pottering gently through the Elysian fields, world without end!

What cheery souls they are, these silent comrades of ours! At night, when all is snug aboard the *Saucy Jane*, when dinner is digesting under the soft influences of book and pipe, 'Bob' and 'Jess' lie there, best of company, dreaming of deer in the covert or wild fowl in the reeds; tails that will wag on the slightest pretence, eyes that have never looked unkindly on you in their lives; and in the morning, what a greeting it is they give you as you emerge on deck to take stock of wind and weather; no 'katzenjammer' here, no misgiving or question as to the purpose and value of life! A tonic, my dear Sir, in every movement of their nimble bodies; the boat that has no such passengers is like a house without children — a poor place at best.

For field work in this part of the world your homebred pedigree dog is not usually a success; the best all-round animal is a retrieving pointer born in China; equally good in many cases is a cross of pointer with setter or spaniel; and of imported dogs the German wear best. The first thing to be borne in mind by any man who wishes to be merciful to his beast is that no rough-haired dog can be used until the grass-seed has lost its sting, that is to say, until the first sharp frosts of December; to take a thoroughbred spaniel or setter through grass country earlier in the season is sheer cruelty, often killing the beast, and always inflicting grievous injury. No lover of dogs that has once seen the results of grass-seed in the ear, or even in the feet, of his beast will ever again risk the infliction of such misery — therefore 'earthlier happy' is the owner of the dog smooth-coated. I use a spaniel myself, for old times' sake, and because I love the breed; but he does not take the field, except in paddy, until December, and then with many precautions. And for these tender mercies he reviles me, poor ignorant mortal, from the depths of an impatient heart, which demands its day's pleasure regardless of consequences. Herein is revealed the humanity of the beast.

The best dog I ever knew for all-round work, field and covert, point and retrieve, was a cross between poodle and pointer, a great lanky beast with the head of a deerhound, the speed of a lurcher, and the *savez* of all his motley forefathers combined. On his wiry coat grass-seeds fell harmless — the thickest covert had no terrors for his soul; he would work for a week, untiring; all the thousand natural ills to which dogs' flesh is heir left him scathless; and he took a more intelligent interest in his business than any dog of my acquaintance. Wherein, for those who ponder these things, lies a moral and the possibility of several conclusions. Of these I will mention only one, to wit, that your halfbreed appears to be exempt by some mysterious dispensation from those subtle and swift-slaying diseases — such as worms in the heart — which often reduce the life of the ordinary imported dog in China to a matter of two or three seasons. The ideal sporting animal for this country has not yet been discovered; pending the arrival of a scientific observer and breeder we continue to experiment with exotics. Californian and German pointers pass, brief-lived shadows, through our troublous days. Therefore to future sportsmen I commend the poodle-pointer breed in all seriousness and sincerity. And, for the man of small purse, impatient of tardy experiments, let it be said that results, by no means to be despised, may be obtained with trained native dogs — wonks pure and simple; which if any man doubt, let him hire a native of Chinkiang with one or two of his beasts — 'tis a matter of seventy-five cents a day for the lot — and report progress. These miserable-looking curs, half-starved and bedraggled, often work covert and retrieve with more credit to themselves than many a lordly taipan's pointer imported from the Shires.

It has seemed to me at times that with the close of the shooting season, when the last spring snipe has been slain, and when, in the first warm days of May, the pointer is eclipsed by the punkah, some of the keenest of sportsmen are apt to forget the dog-days and their necessities. To keep any animal healthy, and to give him length of days, he should have real exercise — not the chained weariness of a coolie's stroll, but running and swimming — all through the summer months. The simplest plan is to train him to follow the carriage or ricksha, with an occasional romp in the fields, and a bathe in the river daily; thus handled, your dog will take the field in autumn with shining coat and a stout heart.

In the Wuhu country, and in certain parts of Chêkiang, there is scope and congenial work for the home-bred pointer, but in the districts around Shanghai he is apt to be disheartened, partly by reason of the scarcity of game, and partly because of the nature of the country. When a thoroughbred pointer takes to covert work, *faute de mieux*, the speciality of his education is lost; I know nothing more demoralising to these dogs than bamboo-partridge shooting, at which the steadiest beast that ever lifted paw will gradually develop spaniel tactics. In this respect the German-bred dog is superior to our own; he seems to be less influenced by environment, more phlegmatic, apparently remembering even in our reed-beds and bamboo-copses the turnips and stubble of his Vaterland. A heavily-built dog and usually slow, but a pointer in spite of all temptations.

For all-round work in these parts there is no dog better than a spaniel, but he must be of the bustling, eager breed, a dog that can run pheasants out of paddy by sheer speed and noisiness, chase hare and deer in covert, and follow bamboo partridge through thick undergrowth. Most of the breed imported from England are of too heavy a build for this work — useful as retrievers, but lacking the quality which follows game through sword-grass and heavy scrub. For the man who will rear and train a good strain of fast-working spaniels in China there is prospect of reward. These dogs contract dysentery easily and suffer seriously from grass-seed, but as a rule they live longer than pointers or setters.

But, after all, every decent dog and decent man, both intent on healthy sport, will eventually establish an *entente cordiale* and attain their common end, either scientifically or by God's good grace; given good-will, they accommodate themselves, like married folks, to circumstances and each other's weaknesses, forgiving the same for a good cause. Therefore it is, that when we call our dogs aboard and set sail for sunlit lagoons or oak-scrub hills, as it may please our fancy, each one of us is well persuaded that his kennel contains the best possible example of canine sagacity and worth, which is just as it should be — testimony alike to the ingratiating nature of dogs and the honest simplicity of man. With what different feelings, how fearfully, we regard the kennel when the mother of invention has filled it with the dog we have borrowed from a friend, or (worse still) hired from a stranger.

Most of us, necessity compelling, have taken the field with a borrowed dog, and some, because of the hopefulness of humanity, will do it again; but few will recommend the practice. Two recent cases come to my mind, each of their kind instructive. One is that of Colonel Gatewold, a gallant officer of the Indian contingent, who in 1900 spent a year in our midst, waiting for the fun that never came. Despairing of sorties and martial feats when once the talkers had resumed business at Peking, he took a month up Yangtsze, borrowing two dogs, one of which was Weston's pointer, a yellow Californian of sinister appearance called Nero. Nero was a retriever by reputation, but he had one peculiarity which Weston forgot to mention; he always ate his first two birds, and he bit any one that attempted to prevent him from doing so. The result was unfortunate; Gatewold, endeavouring to rescue a quail on the point of disappearing down Nero's throat, was bitten in the leg and lamed for a week. Nero was kept chained on deck for the rest of the trip; yet I have seen him since, under happier auspices and in the company of Weston, doing most excellent and docile work.

The other case is worse, but it does not reflect on the dog, and I mention it simply as showing the depravity of man and the evils of borrowing. My friend Boulden, whose kennel had been emptied by hydrophobia, advertised to hire a dog for the Christmas holidays. M'Cormick, whose reputation for being the meanest man in China few cared to dispute, replied, and eventually Rover, a handsome Gordon setter, was hired for a reasonable sum. M'Cormick, however, being (as he said) a prudent man, had a subsidiary agreement drawn and signed, stipulating that, in the event of Rover's loss or death, the sum of one hundred taels would be payable. The sequel might have been foreseen by any one who knew M'Cormick, which Boulden didn't. Rover, true to his name, disappeared into the depths of the Kashing plain on the first morning out, and was never seen again—at least not by Boulden; and M'Cormick's bank account swelled with his passing. It was M'Cormick who made Sandy Wilson a present of a pointer pup, and then sent him a bill for $30, the alleged cost of milk supplied to its mother before the days of weaning. I do not wonder at these things, because the air of China sometimes affects men from the neighbourhood of Glasgow in this way, but I wonder at any self-respecting dog condescending to belong to him; and yet, who knows, perhaps Rover was trying to find M'Cormick and his numerous unsuspected good qualities when he left poor Boulden dogless on the edge of the Kashing plain?

It was my fate, once upon a time, to own an Australian dog named Hector. I have never been to Australia, but my feelings are respectful for a country which declines to import Asiatic labour, and is able to get good money for exporting such articles as that dog. He was the best of a lot of five guaranteed setters, imported at £10 apiece; the only conclusion which a charitable person could form about those animals was that they had been exclusively trained to the pursuit of kangaroos. Hector had a mournful way of mooning about the country, indifferent to any birds in his vicinity, which said, as plainly as a dog can speak, that he was looking for the familiar things of his youth; and as the chances of flushing a kangaroo grew daily less, his interest in our proceedings waned visibly, and finally expired. A masterful

head withal and a noble brow, but a furtive, cat-like way of walking round covert that suggested four-footed leaping prey and a
taste for blood. He was eventually disposed of by public auction,
without reserve; I mention his case as a warning against dogs of
unknown origin in general, and Australians in particular. Now
and then, as in the case of people who get married by advertising
in the matrimonial agency papers, it may turn out all right; but
as a rule it is wiser to get your dogs from a man you know, and
whom you are likely to meet again.

"Here where earth is dense with dead men's bones." —SWINBURNE.

NOT quite a sportsman's paradise, the hunting-grounds of Kiangsu, yet happy for the brethren of the houseboat guild, for every man that loves to see the blue sky overhead and to breathe the unsullied air of lake and hill. Happy too for us, in memories of bygone days, is many a well-frequented spot; hardly a landmark but brings to mind some heart-warming echo of the past, kind faces that have passed beyond our ken, friendly voices that reach us no more. Wonderfully, from the secret treasure house of memory, is restored to us, in sudden recognition of some familiar scene, the essential fragrance of long-lost days. Often, standing at the corner of a sunlit bamboo-grove waiting for the beaters, the mind, in a flash, bridges the chasm of Time and one finds oneself back in the past; many half-forgotten happenings, trivial incidents of our half-buried lives, are brought back so vividly, that for the moment we cheat ourselves with a swift-born, furtive hope that the Scythe-bearer has spared us, that the gulf which lies between us and our youth is but a mirage and the shadow of a dream.

Twenty years ago game was plentiful from Shanghai, westward and north and south, in all the great region dotted with the ruined cities that mark the track of the Taiping's devastation. In and around those old cities it is still true to-day that

> The quail, the partridge, and the pheasant keep
> Their court, where Chinese in their thousands sleep,
> While the predestined devil from the West
> Stamps o'er their heads through many a grass-grown heap.

But their number is rapidly decreasing as the resistless tide of Chinese humanity flows back, first to cultivate and then to over-crowd the places made desolate forty-five years ago. We who in the eighties have shot deer on the wide desert plains, where every inch of ground is now under thrifty cultivation, have seen that which in any other land would be a miracle — city after city repopulated, thousands of miles of land reclaimed within the space of half a generation. Intelligent observers of that long-drawn and hideous carnival of slaughter say that three million Chinese were killed in the region which Gordon conquered, cane in hand, between Nanking and Hangchow; but the ranks have closed up, and to-day the struggle for life is almost as fierce here as in any other part of China; fierce enough to spoil our chances of making the old-time bags, for the native sportsman and trapper is abroad, earning a livelihood by the supply of game, in and out of season, to the nearest markets.

A few of the ruined cities remain much as the Taipings left them — Cholin, for instance, and Chapoo; the old grass-grown battlemented walls enclosing scenes of desolation such as only the callous East could tolerate. Here you will flush teal from ponds that were once the marbled glories of a rich man's garden, and pheasants from long grass that covers the ruins of his home; scarcely a habitable building from end to end of the city. True, the activity of Shanghai contractors, and their keen demand for broken bricks, has of late years done something to clear these places of their melancholy fragments, and many a Bubbling Well villa is founded on the remains of what was once a Chinese bourgeois

home in Kashing or Kazay; but the mark of the Taiping lies still
on the land, and will not readily be effaced. Curious supersti-
tions and prejudices of haunted places influence the new generations; though most of the old cities have gradually been repopulated, a few are so informed with memories of terror, that none
will venture to live in them,—in others, the new-comers have
approached timidly, first building up busy suburbs beyond the
silent walls and gradually advancing, thus supported, into the
grim places of the unhonoured dead. Instances have occurred
where the wandering spirits of those whose very names are for-

"The mulberry lands of the Grand Canal."

gotten have been propitiated *en bloc*, and sacrifice made to an
ancestral tablet, specially devised by the new settlers to appease
the unknown ghosts bereft of the uses of filial piety. In nearly all
the walled towns where the Imperialists and Taipings committed
their alternate atrocities, there are spots which every sportsman
has noticed, bleak and unoccupied in the midst of cultivation or
crowded streets; these usually mark a place whither have been
brought skulls and bones collected from all parts of the city. At
Kashing, for instance, a thriving town has sprung up, where ten
years ago the footfall of man was seldom heard on the ancient
flagged streets; yet you will find an open grass-grown space just
inside the wall whereon no man builds, and where you may shoot
pheasants at sunset—for it is their favourite roosting-place. I shot

birds there quite recently from the wall, that fell into the court-
yards of astonished citizens, and had to be retrieved through the
street door. There are old English guns on that wall, lying just as
Gordon's men left them for the use of the Imperialist forces.

Snipe-shooting apart, however, the happy hunting-grounds
of Kiangsu to-day are not what they were twenty years ago,
nor can they ever be so again; each year sends us farther afield
to harder work. But the land is wide; its undeniable beauties,
even under close cultivation, appeal to the man of streets and
wharves, and it is no small interest in life to watch the stealthy
advance and change of the seasons on hillside, river-bank, and
sea-wall marsh.

To each man his favourite haunts and to every season its
hunting-grounds. The number of places to which houseboats
make their way from October to May is legion; every sportsman
has his warm corners and his own ideas, about which argument
were vain. Some love the wild-goose chase, and the pursuit of
water-fowl, from Woosung along the bleak wastes of the sea-
wall country; one man I knew whose peculiar delight it is to pur-
sue bustard with a rifle on the grey mud-flats beyond Battery
Creek. For some the silent places of Haiyee and Chapoo offer
continual joys, where partridge and woodcock lurk in the undergrowth; others follow for choice the wandering winter snipe,
whose habitation varies with the distribution of surplus water
from the Yangtsze. For some the mulberry and paddy lands of
the Grand Canal, the quiet by-creeks off the great arteries that
connect Shanghai with Chêkiang and the interior of Kiangsu;
for others the hills beyond Soochow, the lagoons and the great
lake region, or the vast burial-lands around such ancient cities as
Chang-ja and Wukong. There is room and to spare for every man
in his humour.

At the outset the reader was warned that herein he would
find no precise guide to the hunting-grounds; this because, in
the first place, it is idle to dogmatise on matters of taste, and, in
the second, because what is worth having is worth working for;

nevertheless, for the benefit of the uninitiated, a few suggestions as to the seasonable jaunts, given without guarantee and in the spirit of true benevolence, may be here set down. They reveal no secrets and deal only with beaten tracks, but even in these I have seen men as sheep wandering without a shepherd.

Of the autumn snipe, that goodly bird which, after replenishing the earth with its species in Siberian solitudes, comes south again on the wings of the first north winds, and reaches the Yangtsze about the end of August, it is unnecessary to say more than that he who seeks shall find; for the bird is ubiquitous, dropping from the long line of his migrating hosts wherever marsh or watery furrow offer prospect of food. His favourite haunts — as in the spring — are decided  by rainfall and the force of the gales behind him, so that in the vicinity of Shanghai he gives us both lean and fat years; but in certain places, to wit Cholin, Sakong, and especially Hangchow, you will always find him, and good bags may be made by feverproof sportsmen, provided with sun-hats, mosquito nets, and an icebox.

During October, and much of November, in fact until the gathering of the rice crops is well forward, the pleasure of pheasant shooting is derived chiefly from the charms of the fertile landscape, for the paddy affords unlimited cover from which the birds can hardly be flushed. The best spot, within my experience, for the first autumn pheasant shooting is at and beyond Changchow and the Pen-yu Creek, where harvesting begins early; unless the season is unusually backward, good sport can always be had here in the beginning of November, and there is no better trip for a race-week holiday. For this work a bustling spaniel is the best dog, a beast that will scurry through the patches of standing rice wherein the birds find shelter. Mixed shooting in covert-country is weariness and vexation to dogs and beaters alike until late in November, when the natives have begun to cut the long grass and undergrowth for winter fuel; and until the first fierceness of the grass-seed has been nipped by frost. Awaiting these reliefs, however, there is fairly open country and passable shooting to be had in the Meichee Creek and on the high ground to the east of Hsi-tai Lake.

When, with December, comes the beginning of six weeks of cold bright days of brilliant sunshine and frosty nights, that make life worth living anywhere out of doors, wild fowl and wood-cock descend on our inland waters, and the dwindling cover makes life precarious for pheasant and partridge in all their abid-ing-places. For week-end trips Taitsan, Cholin, and Bingwu are amongst the best, the two former offering, in addition to sport, picturesque examples of once prosperous cities in decay. Farther afield on one hand lie Haiyee, Chapoo, and the sea-girt lands to the mouth of the Chientang river, the long stretch of the Ta-men Creek, and many good spots in the region of Huchou and Meichee; on the other lie the shores of the great Lake — barren of game in many places — and beyond it, towards the Yangtsze, a goodly land overflowing with fur and feather. *Pour moi*, once the heavy cover is cut and there is frost o' mornings, the best of all the nearer hunting-grounds lies in the Haiyee country, for there the partridge is prolific, the bamboo-copses are favourite resting-places of woodcock; mallard, teal, and an occasional mandarin duck lurk in the frequent ponds, and the pheasant, though rarer than of old, is not extinct. And, withal, it is a good land, pleasant underfoot and pleasant to the eye.

When all is said and done, the man who wants really good sport — sport without fear of long tramps for an empty bag — must fare far afield. We of the houseboat fraternity will exist and persist so long as there is water in the creeks and while our "bird of Time is on the wing"; but it is as much for the love of the craft, its liberties, and the sweet air of heaven, than because of any remarkable excellence in the sport on our immediate borders. We have, like every dog, our days, when it pleases us to think that prospects are improving; but if we steadily face facts at the end of each season we must acknowledge that things are not what they were, and — to put it plainly — that much of the nearer country is "shot out." There have been times when, after trudging for hours without flushing a feather, I have felt something like compunction in killing a pheasant wondering whether it was not perhaps the last of its species in all that lonely land — not a pleasant feeling for any decent dog or man. And so, for the sake of both, when by meritorious service I have earned a fortnight's furlough, I, like to make for the wilds of Chêkiang, with one or two congenial souls, to spots where the foreigner is almost unknown, where the heathen is still unsophisticated, and where a man may shoot to his heart's content without fear for next season's supply. True, to do this means exchanging the foreign houseboat and its amenities for the unadulterated native article and the manners of strange men; but with a little trouble, the exchange can be made to afford a very profitable and pleasant experience, and bring into our wanderings that variety which is the salt of life. In another place I shall tell of the native houseboat and its ways on the Chientang river.

THE·QUARRY·

CHAPTER VI

"And God created great whales and every living creature that moveth, and every winged fowl after his kind; and God saw that it was good." — *The First Book of Moses.*

N all the East few places that I know afford so great a variety of small game as the lower Yangtsze. No doubt Corea, Manchuria, and other northern regions can show better pheasant-shooting and fair chances of big game, but for all-round sport, combined with pleasant conditions, the country which runs from Wuhu on the great river to the upper reaches of the Chientang in Chêkiang offers an unequalled field to the sportsman who takes an intelligent interest in his bag and the manner of its getting; and much of it remains practically unexplored.

The South has its birds and beasts, and a man with a gun may enjoy his day in the Malay States or Tonquin, but there he has to deal with a climate which makes a burden of the grasshopper, whereas here — well, give me a December morning on my houseboat and I resign my claims to all the jungle fowl on earth.

It is in the variety of the quarry, in the chances and surprises of the day, that lies the essential charm of our sport, a charm which comes home to one with renewed force after a season of pheasant- or partridge-driving in the old country. I imagine that most of us have realised this, more or less, during a day on English stubble-fields or by the coverts, where the quality of unexpectedness is almost entirely lacking, however warm our corner; where, unconsciously at first, but definitely at last, the scene before us is focussed into comparison with certain bamboo-groves and fern-clad hills that we know on the other side of the world. Thereat, our compassion goes out to the generous host whose half-guinea birds follow each other in such gorgeous but monotonous succession. For sport has this in common with love, that you find it in perfection where the joys of expectation and imagination have their fullest scope. It is the obvious, the foregone conclusion which kills, and *toujours perdrix* (however game the bird) is a bitter cry. For which reason (permit the digression) when, by the sale of this book, or other more remunerative labour, I come again out of the land of Sinim unto mine own people, I propose to seek in the wilds of Ireland those conditions of sport which most nearly approximate to that of our houseboat days. If there be truth in the man who writes to *The Field*, I hope to find them there.

Let me not in this matter appear churlish or ungrateful. The comparison of our driven game in England with the rough shooting of the Yangtsze suggests itself inevitably, and I set it down in all honesty, but in its conclusion there lurks no doubt something of that spirit of cussedness which makes purblind humanity ever to prefer the beauties of the distant scene to those of its front garden. In the same way I have heard many a man up country, especially after a long day when birds have been scarce or wild, sing the praises, in no uncertain tone, of some snug little place in Norfolk. Be this as it may, I would not that this frankness of mine should ever prevent any hospitable man from asking me down to shoot his birds.

With us the piece of resistance, the first object of our excursions and sorties, is the pheasant, that goodly fowl (*Phasianus torquatus*), progenitor to the more delicate and gentle sporting poultry of England, whose habitat extends practically throughout China to Mongolia and Corea. When I think of how much this brave bird has done to build up in me the delightful character which my friends appreciate but dimly, how much more he has endeared himself to me than most of my near relations, I find it in my heart to spare him all further harassing and threats of violent death – in my heart only, for apart from the irradicable bloodthirstiness of man in the chase, there is something in the wild pheasant of China, in his courage, his infinite resource, and (I verily believe) in his enjoyment of all this business of bustling dogs and men, that brings to his pursuit a perennial flavour of delight. I speak here of the cock-pheasant only, a bird as beautiful as anything in Nature, and infinitely finer here in his native wilds than in the semi-domesticated state. When, sitting between the dull walls of a brick and mortar house, I think of him rising swift and straight from the gossamer-spangled bracken, with the sunlight gleaming on all his gorgeous jewelry of colour, sounding, as he goes, a clarion challenge, a note of derision unmistakable, my eye travels instinctively to the corner where dog Rex lies snoring, and I thank Heaven that both of us are still good for a long day in the open.

There are still places in the lower Yangtsze where the pheasant may be found in a comparatively unsophisticated state, but these are few and rapidly disappearing. In such spots you may flush him close to the dog's nose in warm grass at mid-day, or even from the uncut paddy. In such spots the beaters will send him out over your gun from the little copses that stand behind the farm-houses. Not of this confiding nature, however, is the bird with whom we have to deal in the nearer hunting-grounds, but a very Ulysses among fowls, wary, subtle, of many devices, a sprinter of no mean quality through cotton or beans, a rare judge of distance and the carrying capacity of a twelve-bore, a strong flier, particularly skilled in placing cover between himself and the gun, and an expert in distinguishing between the various races of dogs and men that come within his purview. Remarkable, indeed, is the rapidity with which pheasants, by a sort of local consensus, come to discriminate between the "smell-dog" and "the run-dog," the "gun-man" and the "walkee-man," and to act accordingly; that they know English voices from Chinese is most certain, and the ingenuity they display in selecting feeding- and roosting-grounds with a clear line of retreat would do credit to a Kuropatkin. If, however, you wish for an example of cunning approaching the devilish, then study the ways of the "runner," an old bird for choice, winged in the open. Dropped in a field so bare that you would swear it could not conceal a mouse, he makes like a hare for the nearest thicket, doubling all the while amongst the furrows, head, back, and tail one dull indistinguishable line of brown; at the first cross furrow he is lost to sight, and eventually hides, quarter of a mile away, in the opening of a grave or under some shelving bank. Creeks baffle him not, for he swims them like a duck. Once lost, unless you have a dog that is fast and lucky to boot, that "runner" is not for your bag. Yet, when one thinks of all the perils that environ the ground game of these districts, the hawks that hover by day, and the foxes, cats, and countless vermin that prowl by night when one remembers that the native trapper and snarer knows no close season and no mercy for a sitting hen, one realises that these resident game-birds of ours, the pheasant and partridge, must either become exceeding "slim" or follow the dodo down the path of extinction.

And the bamboo partridge of this country is a bird even harder to circumvent than the pheasant, hard to flush from cover, and hard to shoot. In size and general appearance he resembles his French cousin, the most noticeable feature of the bird being his bright red underwing that catches the eye, as a soft note catches the ear, with a vague sense of unanalysed pleasure, as he flashes through the undergrowth. Throughout the province of Chêkiang he is to be found on all the hillsides and in the wooded copses that lie scattered amongst the cultivation, in coveys ranging from six to a dozen or more; but in Kiangsu he is fastidious in choice of location, and this for no apparent reason. You will find him in the Haiyee country, and again at Esing, west of the Great Lake, but the Soochow hills know him not, nor is he to be found in the Wuhu country. We await better information in regard to this bird and his distribution and many other matters which we may get perhaps when that most knowledgeable and kindly of naturalists, Mr. Styan, gives to the world his garnered wisdom of years; in the meanwhile, from the sportsman's point of view, we may write him down as a fowl well worth following, as tricky as a corncrake and as game as a bantam.

At feeding-time you may flush the coveys in the loose undergrowth "that just divides the desert from the sown," and if your dog knows his work, the birds can be made to break outwards and head for the nearest adjoining covert. Rising in a compact bunch with a mighty whirring of wings, they divide swiftly, like minnows startled in a pool; flying hard and low, some will come at you with most disturbing directness, pass within a foot, and disappear into the thicket ten yards behind you; already the rest are vanished, *perdus,* and your beater's ideas as to their whereabout are hazy. The whole performance is uncommonly like a firework, a sort of feathery Roman candle, and it frequently ends, like the candle, in noise, smoke, *et præterea nihil.* In time one learns to stand clear of the covert, taking the birds as they rise, but here again there is cause for uncomfortable perturbment of body and mind, for they give you but little time for thinking, and all the while there is at the back of your mind the horrid knowledge that they are flying at the height of a man's head, and that there are always natives gathering fuel in the woods at this season. It is certainly nervous work, and I have known careful men give it up with cold perspiration of the brow and a weakness of the knees.

Once flushed and scattered, you may find the birds again with keen beaters and good dogs unless they have made for the hillside. There the quest is well-nigh hopeless, for they invariably head upwards in the thickest covert, taking to the trees as readily as to the ground. I know of no other partridge that has learned this device, nor is there any evident cause for such subtlety unless it be that polecats and stoats have taught them to roost in the bamboos; by day they do it only when hard-pressed. When you have marked a bird into a copse, and the dogs can find no trace of him, look carefully through the bamboo-tops and you shall see, luck permitting, your little brown friend swinging on a branch and doing his best to look like a thrush. He succeeds very passably.

With pheasant and bamboo partridge in good numbers, no better sport need we ask; in circumventing their wiles we attain to craft of field and forest, and many hitherto unheard voices of Nature and man become distinct and speak to us out of the silent places of this ancient land. Far from "the great town's heart-wearying roar" we, who wander in unconscious obedience to the hunter instinct of primitive man, amidst the quiet grave-strewn hills, may hear and understand something of the eternal truths that whisper through their memorial trees; let the bag be small or great at the end of the day, there have been moments in the deep places of the woods, and by the green-fledged river-bank, when all the shoutings and pushings of our materialism seemed but a pitiful waste of breath; when we have realised that a man may do worse than go to bed at night without having added his voice to the shrill clamour of the market place. Socrates, Plato, Omar, the Lord of Montaigne, all the wise men whose words lie bound in the undisturbed volumes on our shelves, tell us these forgotten truths in vain while the noise of the counting-house is in our ears; but here, as we make our ways homewards at dusk, as the soft cadence of an old-world temple bell comes drowsily across the water and the last rearguard of Care retreats before the "familiar glimpses of the moon," we learn to love this patient deep-breasted Mother Earth, old and grim though she be; we are glad to be alive, to breathe the pine-scented air and hear the voices of our fellow-men. In such mood, if it be only for a moment, we

learn to see life steadily, gauging its relative values, and we catch
an echo of the comfortable songs that first old Homer sang "on
some vast headland of the Cyclades."

But we were talking of game, of the birds and beasts that call
us to the wilds. It is not everywhere nor everyday that the beaters
return burdened with pheasant and partridge, and in the nearer
hunting-grounds we must look for another quarry. For this we
depend largely on migratory birds, on the chances of wind and

"Amidst the quiet grave-strewn hills."

those other mysterious laws that
determine the flight and resting-
places of woodcock, snipe, quail,
and water-fowl. Quail, it is true,
are to a certain extent residents
of these parts, though their great
breeding-grounds lie in Manchuria
and the Siberian plain. It is thought
that their main line of migration
branches westward and south
from Manchuria, passing us by;
but occasionally, like the children
of Israel, we get our providential
sendings of quail, when the little
brown fighting bird is to be found in every patch of cotton and
grassy field, providing good shooting and excellent training for
your dogs. There are men, I know, who profess to despise quail-
shooting, but most of us have had cause to be grateful enough
for his presence and cheery chirp on days when other shots were
few and far between.

The woodcock, except on red-letter days, is always something
of a joyful surprise when he rises silently from a damp bottom,
or comes wheeling round the edge of the covert; yet there are
certain spots in every district which, after November, seem to
have a sort of prescriptive right to a long bill or two. How the
supply is so regularly maintained, by whose direction, and from
what unseen headquarters of the tribe they come, is one of the

many mysteries of bird-life. One learns to know these haunts, and to head for them instinctively; rarely are they drawn blank unless, indeed, some other gun has been there before us, and the deceased incumbent's successor has not arrived. To find this silent tenant of the coverts in good numbers the best chances are after a fall of snow. I do not attempt to account for the fact any more than for the sudden unanimous vanishings of winter snipe in certain changes of weather, but fact it is. Is it not recorded in the log of the *Mighty Atom* how at Haiyee, one afternoon of the year of the great snow, we accounted for twenty-seven?

And when all else fails there are always wildfowl or snipe to be found, either in the sea-wall country that runs along the coast from Woosung to Hangchow or in the creek-infested region which adjoins Soochow and the Grand Canal. If the water-level is propitious, the great lagoons that lie between the 53-arch bridge and the hills afford as fine a snipe district as heart of man can desire. Here, as in all the creek country, the day's chances generally include mallard and teal; widgeon and pintail duck are common on the lakes, and good flighting may be had by any man who will study the craft and brave the rigours of a winter's evening behind a grave. The Bean goose comes with November in mighty squadrons, high flying before the north monsoon. As winter sharpens, they seek the inland feeding-grounds; on the Chientang river and in the Bingwu country you find them, vedettes posted, a grey and silent army on the bare-swept fields. In a high wind they fly low at sunset, in twos and threes, following a line between the river and the fields which varies not, which was their forefathers' before them, since the first goose found and laid down the law. Finally, the great bustard haunts the sea-wall, a rare bird and shy as the ostrich — a quarry for the elect.

So much for the feathered tribes on our frontiers and their ways. Of the beasts, less may be said. The hare is with us, and the river deer, but both are comparatively uninteresting, beasts of little resource, bourgeois habits, and no individuality. The hare, it is true, has learned to swim and live underground (chiefly in

graves), but in the process his body has shrunk to rabbit-like pro-
portions, and his existence appears to consist almost exclusively
in dodging hen harriers and Chinese dogs. A poor thing, yet for
some inscrutable reason an object of perennial interest to Chinese
husbandmen. Our river deer is a timid, hornless creature that
seeks the thickest hillside covert by day and the farmers' crops at
night. Twenty years ago, when around Kahsing and all the Taipings' silent cities lay the uncultivated wilds, these pretty beasts
were plentiful; but now they are rare enough. As venison 'tis a
poor thing, of little flavour; nevertheless, a haunch makes a gift
presentable to thrifty housewives. For our own use we will keep
the liver only, commending it as very delectable for a houseboat
breakfast; and for the rest, there is no better food for your dogs
on a long trip (where beef cannot be bought) than deer-meat,
soup, and biscuit.

Of larger game, such as the wild pig and leopard of the further hills, I say nothing here; they are beyond the range of our
houseboat wanderings. Sometimes, both on the Yangtsze and the
Chientang, pigs of more than ordinary enterprise and *wanderlust*
may be seen at daylight close to the cultivation, but to find them
in their own place you must camp out among the higher hills;
there too, if native testimony be creditable, are the leopards and
many strange and fierce beasts, referred to collectively by villag-
ers as *yeh wu* — wild things. I have seldom met a native who has
not seen and heard the *yeh wu*, but the descriptions given conflict
so wildly both as to the habits of these ferocious beasts and their
anatomy that I cannot identify them. From all accounts, however,
I conclude that hills in the vicinity of Chinese farms are inhabited
by an omnivorous and unclassified quadruped well worth the
attention of adventurous naturalists and sportsmen. Leopards
may, of course, be responsible for some of the bloodthirsty leg-
ends these quiet people tell, and perhaps the fox, badger, coon-
dog, and civet-cats might claim the credit for others; but I have
heard tales from guileless men that compel me to believe in the
existence and nightly prowlings of a beast which combines in

one fearsome body the qualities and panoplies of the Snark, the Poom, and the Icthyosaurus.

The Major, who has offered rewards for anything bigger than a civet-cat, disagrees with me on this subject; yet how else can even he account for an animal that admittedly destroys not only standing crops but also goats and hens; that cannot be shot at close quarters with a ten-foot gingal; that opens locked gates with ease and devours everything in sight? How else account for the disappearance of his own leggings, left by night on the deck of the *Saucy Jane*, and the loss of edibles without number from the after-deck on many occasions? Either this was a Poom's work or I know nothing of field-craft.

So much for our quarry. Let me observe, however, that I have dealt with the subject from the Anglo-Saxon's point of view only. I know that there is another, and that for our Continental friends, as well as for the well-meaning sportsmen of Dai Nippon, there are other objects in the chase. Some of these we may guess at, by furtive inspection of the trophies hanging at the rear, of their homeward bound boats; others we may glean from the indiscretions of lowdahs and boys. *Cælum, non animam, mutant*, and for a certain class of Frenchman, the shooting of thrushes and larks is a national pursuit, sanctioned by custom and tradition, and greatly approved by thrifty wives. I know one boat which usually brings back with its sporting owner a collection of small birds that calls to mind the ornithological wealth of an Italian market-stall; *que voulez vous?* Pheasants are scarce, and snipe extremely hard to hit. But he has a noble-looking dog, carries a goodly flask, and enjoys his Nimrod days with the best of us; in fact, to hear him, *à la* Tartarin, recounting his exploits, one is inclined to envy an enthusiasm which thrives so cheerily on the day of small things. Another acquaintance of mine, a subject of the great White Tzar, frankly disclaims all idea of pot-hunting on his wanderings; he takes a gun because it is the proper thing to do, and, sticking to the river-bank, he shoots anything that sits or walks slowly within range. His young wife accompanies him on these excursions, and I shall not easily forget the joy and pride with which, when last I ran across them near the lakes, she showed me the corpses of six crows, a sea-gull, and some miscellaneous small birds. Well, well, to every man in his humour, and happily crows are plentiful. Frankly, I prefer those scavenger birds, untimely slain, to the pheasants and duck which always hang in triumph on M'Alpine's boat, and which, as every lowdah on the river knows, his boy buys in the market and smuggles on board for "face-pidgin."

But there is one animal which none of us willingly shoots, yet which, sooner or later, figures in every bag — *Homo sinensis* to wit, our Chinese fellow-man. When one remembers how ubiquitous and numerous is this blue clad creature, how its innate curiosity and other forms of cussedness invite disaster, the only wonder is that we bag so few. Suddenly rising between you and a flushed quail in the cotton, or bobbing up from behind a grave, as you are snapping at a partridge — how often have we seen his sheepish grin as the gun comes away just in time, that grin which broadens as the marrow trickles in our bones, and we curse him in the ecstasy of our relief? But every pitcher has its appointed day, and most of us, either for our own or for another's offences, have heard the *vox humana* rise strident from cover and seen our undesired "bag" emerge, loudly bemoaning his (or her) impending doom. If it be a man, reason and sycee salve will often adjust matters unless the wounds are serious; but if your quarry is an old woman, or if one of these shrill viragos appear screaming on the scene, your best plan is to make swiftly for the boat, and from that coign of vantage discuss matters through the lowdah. Like everything else in China the cost of peppering a native has increased absurdly of recent years, and for those who do not speak the language it has become almost prohibitive in some of the more turbulent districts. We all remember the days when a dollar and a bit of sticking-plaster would atone for half a charge of No. 6; now a dollar a pellet is cheap enough as prices go, and the nearer you are to schools of Western learning and the unspeakable Baboo, the higher the value of a native's injured feelings. In the farther wilds you will still find sturdy country folks to whom the pattering of a stray shot or two on their padded clothes is a joke; nearer home it means the welkin rent with wailings and aged beldames rolling in the dust, the parading of predestined orphans, and the price of blood discussed with half a village. This fly lurking in the amber of our up-country joys is one of the inevitable results of our civilising theories about the rights of man; happily it comes but rarely to the surface. And, after all, this is the Chinaman's country through which we stride so blithe and *débonnaire* with beaters, dogs, and guns, and if we have to pay occasionally for our bad luck or his stupidity, why, let us pay cheerfully, and thank Heaven he is still unsophisticated or good-natured enough to dispense with barbed-wire fences and the laws of trespass. There is one rule inviolable if you have trouble with natives inland; settle the matter somehow, but settle it before you move on. To give largesse is easy, but it creates a bad precedent and an itching for more; to "talk reason" costs time and temper, but pays best in the end. But to fold up your tent like the Arab and to leave the thing unsettled means bad blood in that neighbourhood against all foreigners for many a day. In other words, to quote the Major, if you have done it "pay up and look sweet."

All of which brings us naturally to consideration of that much-described enigma, the Lord of the Soil.

CHAPTER VII

"Along the cool sequester'd vale of life
They kept the noiseless tenour of their way."
GRAY.

RMA virumque, of the Man I sing; not in his relation to humanity at large, nor as a specimen for the sociologist, but simply as I have seen and known him since first I wandered, gun in hand, through his well tilled fields and marvelled at the infinite patience and industry of his race. No doubt that, like the rest of us, the Celestial offers wide scope for religious, philosophical, and psychological speculation; he is undoubtedly a complex monster (even as you and I), ever capable of surprising those who flatter themselves they know him well, by some swift variation from the accepted type, some unsuspected mood or outburst of unfathomed devilry; and all this without more obvious cause than, shall we say, pretty Fanny's April tears. Complex and mysterious he is, being human (and it is a farther cry from Peking to Canton than from London to Berlin), but he gains nothing in simplicity when we consider him from the half-dozen standpoints, and apply to his dissected anatomy the latest panaceas, of all the political, medical, biblical, and whimsical persons who are good enough to interest themselves in his present behaviour and future salvation. If one may judge by the amount of attention he has recently received, and by all the wind-puffed nonsense written about and around him, our poor friend's character should by this time be satisfactorily disposed of and put away amongst the half-digested crudities which make up our so-called public opinion. It is possible that in diplomatic circles there may still be an open (even if occasionally empty) mind on the subject, and the political problems emanating from the Celestial Body will continue to serve (that those may write who run) for the transient tickling of amateur statesmen; but for the rest, the thing has been overdone, and the Chinese race, one-third of the world's bustling ant-heap, has been neatly labelled under suitable, moral, and descriptive headings, its manners and morals tabulated, and the once-doubtful specimen occupies its definite place in the museum of humanity. The man in the street and his board-school offspring are well posted on the subject; Primrose Leaguers, Passive Resisters, and Seventh Day Baptists have all learned precisely from their particular and divergent oracles what manner of perilous yellow man looms yonder, what are the habits of his heathendom and the uses to which he may aspire in the cosmos, as seen from Shepherd's Bush. To add yet another voice to the Babel were waste of breath; why disturb the complacency of that wisdom which explains the Boxer movement as blithely as the impending doom of Confucian scholarship? These things have been revealed by scores of peripatetic observers, *solvitur ambulando*; knowledge, swiftly acquired, has been as quickly assimilated, through the medium of *Titbits*, by minds whose earlier impressions were limited to hazy visions of tea-chests, pig-tails, and bird's-nest soup.

Yes, the thing has been done—overdone—and to tell the truth, I marvel at the hardihood of those last gleaners in our

Celestial stubbles, those dogged forlorn souls who solemnly continue to describe China and the Chinese. Remembering all the tomes which burdened our shelves even before the days of travelling M.P.'s, one wonders, as the stream of books rolls on, what and where are the people who buy them? But that, after all, is not my business and since the patient blue-clad object of all this pother remains in happy ignorance of the sudden stir he is making, since it will never be his lot to read these descriptions of himself, nor to decide between the opinions of the "two-and-seventy jarring sects," why should we trouble ourselves about it? I will only reassure you, good reader, that from me you get little or nothing of useful information; this book, at least, can serve neither politician nor trade dissector: not a line in it for all their dreary purposes. Surely the world has had enough of these well-meaning but deluded folks; let us have no more books about this people except those of a light and whimsical humour, calculated to leaven the lump of stodginess.

If now I write of the Lord of the Soil it is from the sportsman's point of view and within the little region of our wanderings. Even within these limits there is room for surprises and much revising of dogmatic opinions, for the native of East Chêkiang is farther in tongue and temper from him of North Kiangsu than Glasgow is from Cork. And yet, how little do we know of him, here or there, after twenty years of rambles through his land? What is he more to us, this silent toiler of ancestral fields, than a dim shadow moving in a land of things unfamiliar, elusive, and remote? We speak with him, and he tells us, in hoary idioms, whose origins stretch back to the days before Nineveh and Babylon, of obvious surface things, of the immediate side of his material existence, of the price of food, rice, of the feeding-grounds of game, of wind and weather; but what do we know of the real man, of his inner life, his thoughts? And if we knew, would we understand? To appreciate his attitude towards gods and men, his mysterious beliefs, the origin and motives of any one of the thousand enigmatical things we see him doing, we must divest ourselves of the traditions of Aryan experience, and reconstruct our ideas on foundations older than the Homeric period. I have not time for these flights myself, even if imagination sufficed; I continue, therefore, to regard my agricultural friend as a gentle, half-simple sort of elder brother, a primordial stay-at-home, unable to sympathise with this nomad modernity of ours, disliking many of our noisy new-fangled ways, but tolerant and kindly withal, forcing no issues, desiring no church militant here on earth.

> Who can see the green earth any more
> As she was by the sources of Time?
> Who imagines her fields as they lay
> In the sunshine, unworn by the plough?
> Who thinks as they thought,
> The tribes who then roamed on her breast,
> Her vigorous primitive sons?

Imagination stands aghast at the mental and ethical equipment of this cobwebbed civilisation; yet I love to sit on the sunny side of a hill, looking down on the tender green of the rice bearing valleys, to dream of the forgotten centuries, the uncounted generations that have passed, leaving the patient toiler of this land as they found him, adding little to the knowledge and the needs that were his before our mushroom Empires were dreamt of. Here, if anywhere on earth, is ancientry of pedigree, a landed gentry whose tutelary ghosts hovered about these pine-shaded tombs in the beginnings of recorded time and determined their ancestral *feng-shui* for ever. Here, before all the storm and stress of our conflicting creeds, ere the first Roman set foot in Britain, these fields had been tilled by men like him over yonder, men who dreamed of no world beyond their Middle Kingdom, and asked nothing better of life than to be able to live it after the manner of their fore-fathers. I like to think of them peacefully weaving and dyeing their celestial cloth, learning to read their musty

books, obeying their mothers-in-law, and rearing countless saffron broods down long vistas of uncounted years what time Europe still lay wallowing in primitive savagery. Coming nearer
to our own days I like to think of all the myriad lives that have
"dwelt their appointed hour and gone their way" in the sheltering peace of the East's simple philosophy, undisturbed by all
our earth-shaking progress; red men and black and brown have
struggled and gone under since first the white entered upon his
"civilising" mission; in the word of old Montaigne, "the richest,
the fairest, and the best part of the world, topsiturvied, ruined,
and defaced for the traffick of Pearles and Pepper; oh mechanicall victories, oh base conquest"; but the yellow confronts his au-
dacities calmly as of old, resisting pressure with ideas and beliefs
that are stronger than all the panoply of science. And, judging by
recent history, and the present position of affairs, these dogged
Celestials are likely to continue yet awhile in their established
ways, to plant and reap, to breed and die, oblivious of all our
clamour at their gates. All our fleets and armies, our religions
and huckstering activities, affect this people as much, or as little,
as my afternoon stroll on their quiet hillsides; they look on us and
all our works as apparitions permitted to emerge in the fulness of
time from the shadowy overseas lands, those lands which they
know are tributary, even if troublesome, to the Son of Heaven.
And so long as we disturb not their ancient ways they are ready
to accept us placidly as unexplained phenomena, "unaccountable, uncomfortable works of God," extending to us that gentle
courtesy which is part of the surface morality of Orientals. I, for
one, am quite ready to accept their hospitality on these terms.

One of the results of that gentle courtesy and of the East's wise
conception of man's place and business in the universe is that for
them the earth is free and common to all men to go their ways in
peace. From one end of China to another, if you will but respect
the growing crops and the privacy of men's homes, there is none
who will question your right to wander at large by land or water.
No fences here nor barred gates; no man-traps, gins, or spring-

guns to protect the sacred rights of landed property. The Asiatic claims in the soil only the fruits of his labour and the burial of his dead; for the rest, is not the Earth the common mother of all? He knows no laws of trespass; he claims and gives a general right of

"On the way to market"

way, and asserts no rights of ownership in the beasts of the field or the fowls of the air within his borders. We, the heirs of centuries of feudalism, take this, like many other of their ways, for granted, often despising while we enjoy their democratic equality and simple communism; but as it is in these green-fledged valleys, so it was in the golden age when the world was young

and Pan still piped in the thicket, when there was room to spare
for every man and his adventures.

No doubt that the teachings of Gautama the Merciful have
much to do with the abundance of birds and beasts in this
closely-cultivated land, and with our opportunities of shooting
and eating them. Customs and local option vary so greatly in
China, we so frequently see yesterday's conclusions upset by to-
day's experience, that to generalise is the business of the unwary.
I claim no fixed ideas as to the consensus of public opinion
amongst natives in regard to this matter of sport; very possibly
there is none. In these central provinces the ideas of a certain
utilitarian class (happily for us it is as yet a small one) have
gradually been affected by the knowledge that pheasants and
other game command steadily-increasing prices in the Treaty
port markets; with these the gentle teachings of Buddha and the
duty of kindness to all living things have gone down before the
hard fact that a basketful of partridges or quail trapped without
violation of the first Law are worth more in cash than many days'
labour. It is not in Western lands only that economic pressure
affects a man's interpretation of his religious beliefs. Around
Shanghai especially, and up the Yangtsze in districts where the
great mail lines vie with each other in bidding for enormous
consignments of game for cold storage, a race of expert trappers
has sprung up; these have devastated our happy hunting grounds
for the benefit of floating hotel passengers, and but for the
vastly creditable energy of Commissioner Rocher and Customs
vigilance the pheasant would have come near to extermination
all along the river. Given a close season, the game supply should
suffice for our local markets, and within these limits the pheasant
trapper's existence is justified by our housewives' needs; but
there are other clouds on our horizon, much larger than a man's
hand, that fill me with nervous apprehension. I frankly dislike,
for instance, the growing tendency of Young China, taught by
Japanese soshii, to assert their vigorous independence of mind
by the adoption of our Western menus and manners. *Persicos*

odi: I hate their semi-European restaurants, places where the deportment of the *clientèle* equals in villainy the cuisine and the *couvert*, and I view with positive horror, in the streets of Soochow and Hangchow, the festoons of pheasants and wild fowl, cheek by jowl with the *bêche-de-mer* and varnished pig that tempt the native gourmet. Herein is augury of evil days to come, as in the growing efficiency of the native trapper, enlarging his craft and the field of his operations to meet these new demands. A few years ago the bamboo partridge escaped his attentions; now he has learned its habits, watches the birds taking cover at sun down, and bags half-a-covey in a hand-net, bringing them to market alive like his quails. Since he allows me to shoot on his land I can hardly take serious exception to his proceedings; they strike me, nevertheless, as a deplorable lapse from the high ideals of the East, brought about, like all such lapses, by too close contact with our iconoclastic civilisation. For if Buddha proclaimed the sanctity of life in every form, did not that most philosophical of sportsmen, Confucius, modify the law by prohibiting "the use of snares, or the making of pitfalls in catching game"?

I profess a general inability to determine in any given case whether the controlling impulses that underlie these people's lives originate in Buddhistic or Confucian traditions; most probably, as in Japan, the two teachings have fused. But our native friend is on the horns of a dilemma in either case; he can only escape the eight hot hells hereafter, and reincarnation in vermin form, by abandoning the Sages altogether. The Major, with that cheery and swift analysis of other nations' souls so characteristic of the British soldier, remarks that "the blighter does not think about it at all; if he can make a dollar, that's good enough for him or any other Chinaman. Religion? Rats! Money talks." It would be futile for me to suggest to him that this race, like our Indian brothers, would gladly give us all its available wealth for a pledge in perpetuity that we would go our ways and leave them in peace to be relieved of the burden of our presence, of our restlessness, all our intolerable and endless talk of morality and mining rights, of peace and progress and quick firing guns; if we would just drop the white man's burden, and go away and leave them to enjoy their own kind of peace. The Major would describe that as sheer flapdoodle.

We were talking, however, of Chinese sportsmen. In certain districts the native gunner is in evidence and increasing; particularly around the great cities you find him of the modern type, sporting a muzzle-loader, some rudimentary English, and a half-trained wonk. There is a tentative and bashful swagger about this fellow, a clumsy attempt to give and take something of the freemasonry of sport, that rather appeals to one in spite of the competition which his genesis forebodes. I have even known cases in which the sporting instinct has triumphed utterly over all the voices of the ancient East, producing humorous but somewhat melancholy results. I once went up river at Newchwang with a gentleman whose pigtail stretched its dark length on a tweed Norfolk jacket, who boasted a pair of Purdeys and a fine assortment of English smoking-room stories, pipe-stem legs in leather gaiters, and a remarkable knowledge of international law; but he had to travel in a boat by himself because he filled the cabin with opium a dozen times a day. But his was a rare case. As a general rule the Chinese sport is a strict utilitarian; he shoots for the pot, or rather for his pocket, is an adept at stalking, and has no silly prejudices about letting a bird fly if he can get him sitting. His powder is of native origin (generally leakage from the nearest arsenal), and his shot is a mixed lot of old iron; yet he contrives to make a very decent bag at times, for he knows all about the movement and habits of birds, their flighting- and feeding-grounds.

Occasionally one meets with an older and more interesting type of native chasseur, one whose forefathers hunted before him, who asks no new fangled devices. His weapons are archaic, his manners generally unconciliatory, and his livelihood a doubtful quantity; but he is grateful to the eye, picturesque in all his equipment, a wandering survival of former days. This type is varied and widely scattered, cropping up in unexpected places, often unable to account for itself; so that one can only guess at the causes, outside the general celestial economy, which produce it. Why, for instance, should the hunting of hares be a solemn public business, officially recognised, in Shantung, while in other provinces puss goes unmolested? Why should duck-shooting with a gun of the Plantagenet period (fired with a slow match) be the hereditary pastime of certain clans in Chihli and Anhui? Since when have they taken life, and provided food for Oriental dissenters? Who knows what occult laws regulate the Chinese dinner-table, why pig and duck and fish are more lawful food than oxen and geese and sheep? Why should the quail be a table bird for the literati of Hangchow and a fighting bird only for the men of Canton? The native hunter does not explain these things.

But the Lord of the Soil, as a rule, concerns himself little enough with sport of any kind. In bygone days, when first the foreign devil was permitted by the All-wise to disturb the peace of the Flowery Kingdom, his presence attracted the curious wonder of the villages; his dogs, his guns, his strange garments and bold women would bring men from the fields to stand in silent, awe-stricken crowds around his houseboat. Now the monster's novelty has worn itself out, his many inventions have been explained by priests and elders versed in demonology; he is accepted as part of the established, though mysterious, order of things, so that the wood cutter on the hillside scarcely raises his head as we go by, and the women no longer run from us in terror. Only in the village children human curiosity survives; for these quaint little bundles of fatalism we are still a raree-show. Our coming is an event, a welcome change from the sober joys of buffalo-rides and the terrors of the trimetrical classic, and they follow us, trailing out like a long blue string along the narrow paths that lead from one hamlet to another. Merry little imps, as a rule, who will show you the way round a creek or carry your bird, shouting the while unspeakable names at their retinue of yapping curs. They take a keen interest in sport, cheerfully getting in the line of fire if they can, anxious above all to retrieve the empty cartridge that makes so melodious a whistle. In covert their company is undesirable (though they never recognise the fact) and trying to the temper; but, *mes amis,* imagine what would be the following of Chinese sportsmen in the wilds of Galway?

"*A daughter of the soil*"

One cannot see a Chinese village and its inevitable pullulating horde of children without realising the vital problem of the East, a problem so immediate and tremendous that it dominates the mind like an evil dream. "Ils poussent comme des punaises," said the good Abbé Huc years ago of this race, in which every human instinct is subordinate to that of replenishing the grievously-burdened earth — the whole life-force of the people spending itself in a blind frenzy of reproduction. The picture is the same from one end of the country to the other: cities and villages innumerable taking their toll of the land; hamlets huddling ever closer in the valleys, where every field already supports more lives than would be possible in any other country except India; a third of humanity struggling hopelessly and unceasingly to procreate and maintain its swarm of predestined hungry ones. And for these there is no outlet; the untilled lands beyond the seas will have none of them; here they must live somehow or die. In its blind lust for posterity the race has acquired fixed mental and bodily habits of thrift and frugality unknown in the white man's fiercest struggle for life: "scorning delights, they live laborious days," and to spectators like ourselves all the vast energies of the East seem to be concentrated on this pitiful business of bringing into the world beings for whom there is little room and no food.

And this is a matter which, for obvious reasons, our missionaries leave untouched; neither the superior wisdom of our philosophies nor any of our comfortable creeds profess to deal with this the crucial problem of the East's infirmities; and so the inexorable Law works out its own pitiless solution, and they go down, these superfluous lives, by millions to fatten the tired earth which could not fatten them. The whole sorry tragedy goes on before our eyes: infanticide, rebellions, and disease, swift slaying famine or slow starvation; Nature ruthlessly applies these her remedies while our Consuls prate solemnly of administrative reform, and earnest Christians struggle pathetically with their foundling homes and hospitals to prevent the inevitable. What are all the shrill miseries of our submerged tenths compared to the inarticulate sorrows of this people in which hopeless patience has ceased to be a virtue and become a national habit of mind? The little section of humanity that reads its Wells and listens to its Bernard Shaw is mightily moved at the results of economic errors and overcrowding in our little corner of the globe, but I cannot help wondering what would become of our best humanitarians if they had to apply their panaceas — the standard of comfort, for instance, and the minimum wage — to the Chinese problem? And I wonder, too, what would happen to all our European civilisation, its labour saving machines and little Bethels, if there should ever arise a Mahommed to lead these starving millions westward in search of food and glory? Could anything short of Ocean's boundaries stop their march? I never pass a village school-house and hear these little Confucianists howling themselves into the classical condition of mental paralysis without a feeling of gratitude for the system which has petrified the race's imagination, and wonder at the purblind folly of those who long to instruct the Chinese in earth hunger and the science of modern warfare. Happily, they have no desire to learn it.

Meanwhile, pending the coming of Malthus or Mahommed and the infusion of vivifying ideals into the "wholesale man-making" of Cathay, the Lord of the Soil bends his patient back to the task that is never done, asking no questions of Destiny. Grateful to his ancestors for existence (however unpleasant) as a transient phenomenon, and hoping to acquire merit for the next turn of the wheel, he labours to leave behind him as many little phenomena as possible before his going hence shall take from his scanty fields the space of one more grass-grown mound.

If I were a missionary, that is to say, could I soberly persuade myself that any of these transitory phenomena might be led to consider seriously the arm-wavings and gibberings of such shadowy forms as they know us to be, I would preach to them the virtue and beauty of cremation. If Mrs. Archibald Little can set forth hopefully, and get Viceroys to subscribe for, the abolition of lily-feet, might not something possibly be done, if only as a temporary alleviation, by reclaiming for cultivation the vast area of land now covered with tombs, memorial groves, tumuli, and matted coffins? Painstaking statisticians estimate the proportion of the soil thus devoted to pious misuses at about a seventh of the whole; might not these people, if approached by organised eloquence, understand a reform that would give them fifteen per cent more rice? I doubt it myself, just as I doubt the ultimate wisdom of increasing the population of any crowded land; but I suggest the idea, as containing germs of practical benevolence, to any preacher who may have come to doubt the native's capacity and desire to absorb sectarian dogma and the Athanasian creed.

But I would not leave our friend, the Lord of the Soil, under any imputation of melancholy. If to us his lot, and that of his too numerous progeny, seem hard, it is probably because our feather-bed humanitarians have a tendency to promiscuous pity for all sorts and conditions of men, and from them we have learned the trick of uninvited sympathy for all those who have not known the joys of our poor-law system, our commercialism, and our sex-problems. To do him justice, the Celestial asks for none of our pity. Despite the ever present spectre of hunger — because perhaps of the very lessons it teaches him — there is in him little of the sorrowful countenance and nothing at all of the intolerable ennui wherewith the heirs of all the ages have purchased knowledge. It is a cheery soul, *bon enfant*, even where an unconscious race antipathy makes him wary; possessed, moreover, of a kindly and gentle humour racy of the soil and wise with all the ghostly wisdom of his past. This humorous quality of the man is that which brings him nearest to our sympathies; no doubt it is also that which enables him to accept life with such *bonhomie* and good grace. No collar-grinning yokel humour his, but the precious faculty of seeing the incongruous in life and in himself, of hearing the Lohan's laugh amidst all the growlings of the Thunder-god. Few Chinese peasants are so cross-grained that they will not spare the time to crack a joke at your expense or their own: in the village elders and story tellers you will often find the qualities of Scheherazade and Sancho Panza combining to produce a very pretty wit and nimbleness of repartee. And, withal, these people have certain things that we, with all our superiority, may well envy, — the faculty of contented industry, of finding joy in simple household things. Let us not too greatly pity them: I doubt if my boat-coolie, sunning himself after a meal of fish and rice, and telling his pals a story bluer than the deepest azure of the *Arabian Nights*, would change with John D. Rockefeller. If he did, John might be a happier man.

In the grey shadows of false dawn, as I stand at the boat's bows and watch the last stars faint and die, I hear the farmers making for their fields, laughing as they go, by twos and threes, and singing (in that quaint falsetto which Europe outgrew in the Middle Ages) their bucolic joys and legendary amours. Singing they go, to their back-breaking labour, to toil as monotonous as the buffalo's eternal penance at the water-wheel; yet all day long, by field and forest and hill, in sunshine and storm, we catch the echo of laughter and song. And again, as we fare homewards at dusk, as the mist rises ghostly from the river, and all the life of the village gathers and nestles in the wide-spreading shelter of its memorial trees, with what cheerful bustle and murmur of life they take the day's reward — the evening rice, the old wives' tales, the tapping of frequent pipes, voices of children in the temple courtyard, cries of the wild-fowl overhead, languor and thrill of weary resting limbs, glamour and peace of the dying day. And then, like fireflies lost in the bamboo-groves, the tiny lights go out, and sleep, "care-charmer Sleep, Son of the sable Night," takes them all under his dark wings and bears them to the dream-strewn shores of the Enchanted Isles. Brothers, sleep well!

CHAPTER VIII

"He who hath no jouisance but in enjoying; who shoots not but to hit the mark; who loves not hunting but for the prey; — it belongs not to him to intermeddle with our schoole." — MONTAIGNE.

"Fortunatus et ille, deos qui novit agrestes." – *Georgics.*

HE *Saucy Jane* lay moored to a high bank, under the mulberries, near Haiyee. It had been an ideal day, bright with the "nipping eager air" that sends the blood dancing through the dullest veins like wine. There had been a sending of woodcock in the morning, fair sport in the copses, and the bag had been pleasantly rounded off with teal, mallard, and snipe from the ponds of the deserted city.

But the Major's mind had not yielded to all the soft influences of contentment. His shooting had been a bit off, and Wilden had undoubtedly wiped his eye; also I had observed a difference of opinion between him and Ponto early in the day as to the fitting limit of a spaniel's range; but these are not matters that usually disturb his equal mind. That he was in love, I knew; but with him that blissful state, varying only in its objects, nearly approaches the chronic, and, being an Irishman, its effect is a "lively and blithe agitation" rather pleasing and advantageous to his friends. Nevertheless, there was evidently a fly somewhere in the amber of his philosophy. He had taken his tub in meditative silence; not a note of the accustomed "Toreador" had come from those usually melodious ablutions, and now he was lying on his back, thoughtfully counting the flies on the ceiling, impervious to the soft seductions of the hour, not to be charmed by comfort of tobacco nor any of the soothing household sights and sounds that mark the close of our houseboat day. Not a word had he spoken for half an hour: truly, a most unfathomable mood.

But it is the unwritten law of the houseboat that we accept and respect each other's varying humours — wherein lies the secret talisman of good fellowship. Let questions and explanations plague our work a day world; at least when we travel afield we can put them behind us. So, leaving the Major to exorcise the spirit of melancholy, I made my way on deck to smoke the pipe (ay, Calverley, the sweetest) of closing day. Ye gods, how good a thing it is to be alive and hear the whisper of the evening breeze in the reeds, to see the moonlight steal ghostly through the deep shadows of the camphor trees! How sweet and clean the air, fresh blown from the sea; how restfully one's tired limbs stretch themselves, and revel in the balm of laziness! Sitting on the ice box, the thought of dinner looming pleasantly on the mental horizon, at peace with all the world, I was in the mood to indite an ode in praise of Idleness, but for the protest of an inner voice which declared all such effort to be sinful. It was at this point that, by a sort of reflex action of the mind, I remembered that the Major had been reading poetry.

I sat and ruminated in the gathering dark. On the bank the dog-coolies were performing the kennel's evening toilet, washing feet and extracting grass-seeds, while they recounted the day's exploits to the cook's "larn pidgin," busy cleaning and hanging the game. From astern came the clicking of chop-sticks and a confused undertone of grunts and labial noises that indicated the gathering of coolies round the rice pot; above their heads a coil of blue smoke drifting on the breeze, with savour of frying fish, proclaimed the first activities of Gehazi and the cook. All was well ordered, regular, and quiet, the domestic economy of the *Saucy Jane* working, as usual, without jolt or creak of its machinery. Truly, the world was a good place.

Suddenly, from close at hand, where the *Heart's Desire* lay moored, came the voice of Wilden, strident and cheerful, shattering the soft nocturne; proclaiming first, in song, the complaisance of the cosy-corner girl, and thereafter a prosaic desire for cocktails, bridge, and the pleasure of our society. A convivial soul is Wilden, free from sentiment and introspection; gregarious, of Rabelaisian temperament; a blithe pilgrim to whom life sings, in no uncertain tones, the virtues of good cheer and boon companions. I often wonder at the freakishness of those imps of perversity that have led him to consort habitually with Thurlsby, for the K.C. is a studious and scholarly man (with lucid intervals of gaiety) who reads *The Economist*, and can, if provoked, quote Swinburne and Arnold by the hour. He, I think, takes Wilden as a corrective for the sobering tendencies of advancing age. Be that as it may, they manage to strike between them a golden mean of tolerant common-sense, and the intellectual activities of the boat have a pleasant and invigorating range between the Pink 'Un and the Elizabethan poets. I know few places where the sack is so nicely proportioned to the bread as in the cabin of the *Heart's Desire*.

Lucullus, after much experience, limited his dinner guests to six; had he owned a houseboat there would have been two less. I have never quite made up my own mind whether a *tête-à-tête* or a *partie carreé* is the better arrangement, but I do know that outside of these lies vexation of spirit. Our humours are variable; what pleases us to-day may not attract to-morrow, but my inclination on long trips is to travel with another boat: for our week-end forays the *Saucy Jane* asks no company. For these are easeful and gentle excursions with which the Major and I clear the cobwebs from our bodies and souls: companionable books, perhaps a hand of picquet, "a little talk of Thee and Me"; these suffice us. But on our further journeys, when the long daily trudge ends fittingly in convivial evenings, we are the better for the company of another boat. The best of friends may see too much of each other; there are human vapours which only "variety dissolveth and shifting dissipateth" on these occasions. We shoot in pairs, each taking one bank of the river, and there is a pleasing rivalry between the boats which adds flavour to the sport. In the evening, over our glass of port, the day's chances are discussed, old tales retold, and the morrow's route planned. "No viands are so sweetly pleasing," says the wise Lord of Montaigne, "no sauce so tasteful, as that which is drawn from conversable and mutual society, which company a man must seek with discretion and with great heed obtain before he wanders from home. With me no pleasure is fully delightsome without communication. I do not so much as apprehend one rare concept, or conceive one excellent good thought in my mind, but methinks I am much grieved to have produced the same alone, and that I have no sympathising companion to impart it unto." Most human and honest of philosophers, how well he perceived the essence and ethics of reasonable travel! Well, the gods be thanked, I have found "honest men, of manners conformable, to accompany me with a good will."

But Wilden was shouting for cocktails and bridge. A window rattled, and the Major's head emerged below me in the gloom.

"Shut up, you noisy devil," he said. "Play picquet with the K.C. if you can't read. I'm tired — besides, I've got some work to do. Bridge after dinner if you like."

Wilden whistled after the manner of men incredulous. " Love-letters should be written before breakfast," he proclaimed to the night, "songs before sunrise, old chap! Come over here, and Thurlsby will do it for you cheap."

The Major's window rattled again as a shaft of yellow light died on the ripples. Wilden whistled (something less joyfully) and disappeared.

Exempt from the law of the ninety-and-nine, *in partibus infidelium*, the Major professes to teach certain large-goggled Chinese students and others who bear the mark of Young China on their wide-spreading locks the whole art of war. Thereby he earns his living, but within the memory of man he has never been known to work after 5 P.M. Therefore curiosity began to tickle me; I went below and ordered vermouth cocktails for two. The Major was still lying on his bunk chewing a pencil, but old Rex had snuggled up beside him, and although the warrior's brow was creased with expanse of thought, his expression was that of a man in kindly, confidential mood. And I noticed a sheet of foolscap covered with something that looked suspiciously like verses.

Gehazi brought the drinks and some savoury morsels that he concocts cunningly with redfish from the Straits. The cabin was bright and cosy enough to cheer the heart of any melancholy *Jacques*. "Here's luck, Jim," I said. "What's your work? Didn't know you went in for overtime?"

The Major looked pensive. *Cherchez la femme* was writ plain on his expressive features.

"Well, you needn't give it away, old chap. I don't want those fellows to rot about it, but the fact is, I've been trying to write some verses. You know it isn't exactly in my line . . . and, you see." He took a sip at the vermouth, and his manner was artistically insouciant; it was evidently my turn to say something.

"Yes, women are keen on that sort of thing; but I didn't know . . ."

"No more did I. But there's a fellow — you know that conceited ass Staynes? And Miss Talbot seems to think an awful lot of the silly stuff he writes for her. You see, she rather went for me for coming away on this trip — missing two dances, of course, and all that. So I thought I'd like to see if I couldn't write something to take the shine out of that duffer. Something to send with a brace of birds as a peace offering."

"Ever done any before, Jim? What's the subject?"

"Well, first I thought I'd go in for the usual thing — treacly stuff about eyebrows and rosebud lips. I've done my share of that, you know." (I didn't.) "But she must be pretty well fed up on that sort of diet, so I'm making it a sonnet: something in the grand manner, I mean; something that will suggest the poetic charm of wandering in the wilderness with the idea of the perfect woman for company." Here Jim stuck, stroking Rex's head in a sheepish way. I hastened to express sympathetic approval.

"But it's not as easy as it looks," he went on. "I'm all right at a rhyme, but sonnets are the devil. Kipling isn't much use as a guide for that kind of thing."

I took Rossetti down from his shelf. "You'll find something in there," I said. "What you want to express, I suppose, is that the man with the wandering temperament is best qualified to appreciate the charms of the fairest of her sex?"

"That's it. That's the idea, exactly."

"And while a soulless person might suppose you to be walking the Philistine's way, killing birds, playing bridge, and forgetting the existence of the ever-present deity, the eye of faith is to see you worshipping her at the high altars of Nature. The wild calls you, in fact, and you go, but she is of the company, and all the voices of the high places tell her name. Listen to this: it seems to me the very thing for you: —

> Her's are the eyes which, over and beneath,
> The sky and sea bend on thee, — which can draw,
> By sea or sky or woman, to one law,
> The allotted bondman of her palm and wreath.

> This is that Lady Beauty in whose praise
> Thy voice and hand-shake still long known to thee
> By flying hair and fluttering hem, — the beat
> Following her daily of thy heart and feet,
> How passionately and irretrievably,
> In what fond flight, how many ways and days!"

"Yes," said Jim, "that's good. I'd like to do something in that line."

"I'll lend you a hand, Jim, if you like" (for I know how restless, peevish, and unsociable a spirit is the Daemon that seeks expression in verse, and I wanted him expelled before dinner); "and if Roxane. . . ."

"Her name is Betty."

"And yours isn't Christian. Well, go ahead, and good luck to you."

For half an hour, silence, while the air was filled with the soft quivering of the Muses' wings. Their subtle influences must have discovered old Rex beyond the portals of sleep, for he whined fitfully, with twitching limbs. As for me, I was away with Drake, sinking galleons and plundering cities of the South Seas, to the glory of the Virgin Queen and my own complete satisfaction, when Jim put his labours from him with the contented sigh of the artist satisfied.

"That's all right," he said, secreting the paper carefully in the pocket-book where he keeps his bridge-chits. I respected the reticence which kept his gem from profanation of the vulgar, but made a mental note to ask Miss Betty for a copy of it later on.

"When you come to think of it," observed Jim, reflectively, "it's not so easy to define the attraction of a wandering life. Even in this matter of houseboats there's an elusive something which most of us feel, but I can't put my finger on the exact spot which it touches in my sentimental anatomy."

"Mightn't you say the same of Lady Betty? Can you resolve that charming person's fascination into its component parts? If you ask me, I should say that idleness and the allurements of variety are permanent ingredients in the nature of man . . ."

"Talk sense. Of course there's the open air, and the shooting, and the physical satisfaction of walking oneself stupid; but there's something more than this, only I can't put it into words. After all, as an old Chinaman said to me on the sea-wall this morning, mightn't we find lots of other ways of enjoying life at

less trouble and expense? Why does this business get hold of one
and stick when all others have grown stale?"

"Wanderers all, I suppose, Jim. What are we doing among yellow men, anyhow? The ruling passion, and the last to go; it's part
of the Briton's heritage that within him there are voices calling
him to come out from among the chimneys and brick walls, and
hear the wind blow free. Now, if Wilden were a Frenchman, he
would not want to leave his comfortable fireside and the wife of
his bosom to go prowling about the shores of the Yellow Sea in
all kinds of weather."

"And if Thurlsby were a Dutchman, he'd be wearing a skull-
cap and playing chess at his club instead of chasing duck in the
small hours."

"That's about it. 'A man doing fit things forgets Hades,' and
our ideas of fitness shape themselves at the bidding of innumerable ghosts. But if you really want to explain to Lady Betty the
essential spirit and virtue of houseboating, the thing has been
fairly well done, some thousands of years ago, for the patient
goodly Odysseus."

The door opened and Thurlsby came in, with a rush of the
keen north wind. The lawyer's eye, in search of evidence, fas-
tened on Rossetti.

"Finished that work yet, Major? What's this — poetry?

> A book of verses and a fat bow-wow,
> A glass of wine, some pickled fish and now
> Poor Wilden singing in the wilderness,
> Oh come and put a stopper on his row!

"Don't you fellows know that dinner's ready?"

So the Major's Daemon was exorcised. In due course Miss
Betty gave me the sonnet (that dainty person treats me as an el-
derly uncle), and to my mind it affords remarkable proof of the
stimulating effect of the tender passion on the average human
intelligence; also it shows how great and well worth seeking is

the mine of unsuspected poetry to be found under familiar and
most unpromising waistcoats. Here it is; I rather like the way he
brings the wild geese into it: —

> Where the lone marshes circle Ocean's bed
> I stand and watch the pallid daylight wane,
> A phantom curlew's cry, far overhead,
> Breaks on the stillness with a note of pain.
>
> Ghostly the wind comes shuddering through the sedge,
> More pitiful than any lover's sigh,
> As if in fear, over the dark world's edge,
> The wild geese wing, in serried squadrons high.
>
> Now darkness falls, as the last hopes of day
> Forlorn against night's battlements are hurled;
> Swift shadowy sails speed silent o'er the bay,
> As if escaping from a doomed world.
>
> Yet, love, whene'er I turn to thoughts of thee
> The world is full of joyful melody.

At dinner the Major mentioned Penn, the teaman, as an
instance of the theories he was trying to prove. (The fact that
nobody wanted to disprove them only made him the more emphatic.) Penn had come in for two thousand a year and a place
in Scotland, tried it for three years and then chucked it; he had
come back quite lately to spend his summers in Japan and his
winters on the old houseboat. Some people said it was because
his wife couldn't stand the strain of the British housemaid, and
Penn wanted peace in his borders; but Penn himself said that he
had breathed too much fresh air to be able to stand the English
rural Sabbath and local politics — couldn't live in a country where
conformity to the movements of all the surrounding automata
was a necessary condition of peace and decency. We argued the

matter, from soup to coffee, without any very definite results.

Wilden said he believed in the old familiar faces and places (though he was at pains to express the sentiment bluntly), in the force of habit which can make even dull spots and people take on forms of friendliness and welcome. "How can a fellow expect to grow new roots comfortably at Penn's age, especially in Scotland, where people look on you with suspicion if they don't know all about your private affairs, your wife's family history, and your religious experiences?"

Thurlsby summed up the matter in his own way as he and I sat on the deck-rail, smoking a last pipe before turning in.

"It seems to me," he said, "that life is always more or less a matter of ruts. Live where and how you like, you cannot avoid them, and the wise man is he who chooses his ruts on a road where he can hear the birds sing and see the sunlight on the hedges. Here and there in the world you may find a man brave or lucky enough to keep his unfettered soul, his full liberty of mind; but most of us, as the years go by, have to forswear our dreams, cease our excursions into the fairyland of fancy, and stolidly enough accept the commonplaces of a world of routine. We settle down into our rut."

"I don't see how wisdom herself can prevent it. To play the Olympian, to live the hero life, isn't as simple as the copy-books make out. Even Solomon fell into an uncomfortable rut at last, and Socrates found no better way of proclaiming his independence of mind than by playing for cobnuts in the street."

"That's just what I mean. The wise man will play marbles, or the trombone, to free his soul from the prison-house of commonplace, of fixed ideas. We in the East suffer from a rut peculiar to our environment, a rut of fleshpots and soft living that brings its penalty in gradual mental atrophy. In the ordinary course of existence we are attacked by fatty degeneration of the thinking apparatus; what we require, my friend, is a Sandow system for the mind. And so, people like you and me take instinctively to houseboats and wandering amongst aboriginal things, as a dog eats grass, to ward off insidious ruttishness. And by so doing we fall into the rut of restlessness."

"Well, there, at least, the dust will not choke us."

The K.C. got up, knocking the last ashes from his pipe. "If the end and reward of life is sensation and the delight of living," he said, "let us beware of ruts. Lots of people are dead without knowing it. But this is a queer time and place for us to be discussing our philosophies. Just look at the stars!"

The night was wonderfully still. Across the water the jagged battlements of the dead city loomed fantastic and ghostly in the moonlight. And, with the message of the myriad shining worlds, and the protean music of the clean north wind, all our talk, the echo of our little lives, everything except the beauty and mystery of the sleeping earth, dwindled to its proper insignificance.

·CHAPTER·IX·
OF·THE·ETERNAL·FEMININE

"Seul le Reve interesse
La vie sans Reve, qu'est-ce?
Moi, j'aime le Princesse."

LOINTAINE.

Y original intention was to discuss "Woman's place on the Houseboat," but on mature reflection I have changed my mind. I wish neither to raise false hopes nor to give offence. Wilden, whose instincts remain those of the untamed hunter, abandons something of marital reticence when he says bluntly, as he did when we were discussing the matter a week ago, that she has no place there at all. To which the Admiral agreed.

It was after tiffin, which may account for it. We had walked the Hsi-tai marshes all morning in the crisp November sunshine; but snipe had been scarce and wild, so much so that the Admiral, who prefers dry-fly to wet-shooting, proposed that we should go for a sail in the *Mighty Atom*. A good soldier's wind was blowing and the lake was covered with white, brown, and blue sails innumerable, butterflies dancing on a field of azure and gold. Seen nearer, they became deep-laden mysterious Argosies, of gleaming amber, that swept by, silent, save for the drowsy murmur of their bellying sails and the velvety rhythm of rushing water; boats of every size and shape, hurrying purposeful, on urgent business of barter. From all quarters they come, into all distances they go, down the long gleaming creeks; only their sails visible above the higher dykes. And with it all, scarcely a sound upon the face of the waters or from the low-lying fields.

We had left the *Saucy Jane* at her moorings, the Major and I, and had gone aboard the *Mighty Atom*. After an ineffectual protest by her lowdah against purposeless labour, we had sailed out of the creek and half across the lake before tiffin was done. Thereafter, we had spread rugs on deck and lay basking in the sun, at peace with all the world. It was the Major who then, by an incautious reference to the delights of sailing in feminine society, evoked the wrath of Wilden and much subsequent argument.

Before going further I may as well explain that if the Admiral shared Wilden's conclusions, he arrived at them by routes less frank but more gallant. Also, I may describe the man. His commission as Admiral (of the Swiss Navy) was originally conferred in good faith by a newspaper reporter in Detroit, and accepted by that hospitable city as readily as by Danton himself; his ignorance of nautical matters is rivalled only by his *bonhomie*; and after all, as he very wisely observes, until the Swiss Navy requires a more efficient head, why should he give up the command? In the meanwhile he has qualified for possible emergencies by frequent cruises in the *Mighty Atom* and by completing the education of a cook whose dinners have long been famous in the East. On all ordinary matters his views are of the positive order, his Epicurean philosophy attaining to the heights of dogma; but as regards the fair sex he is wont to say that, with his liberty, he has preserved his illusions and an open mind. It is in argument that I like him best; utterly disdaining theories, he fires his emphatic facts at you like pistol-shots, summing up the matter in a fiat;

thereafter, should you persist, he will attack your mental state, your education, birthplace, and what not—clearly demonstrating from your deficiencies of body and mind the truth of his conclusions. And all with Gargantuan laughter and much popping of corks.

Wilden was lying in the bows, keeping a lazy eye open for ducks, when the Major made that incautious remark. He got up, put his gun safely on the roof, and squatted next the Admiral.

"My dear Major," he said, "that's the worst of you sentimental Irishmen. You're never content to let well alone. You won't believe that perfection hasn't yet taken up her domicile on earth, so that when you get a good thing you must spoil it by sighing for something better. Now, as to your last remark, didn't the preacher say there is a time for everything, a time for taking and a time for leaving behind?"

"Or words to that effect," said I.

"There are dishes one doesn't eat with a spoon," observed the Admiral judicially; "everything in its place."

"Quite so," said Wilden; "and the proper place for the hand that rocks the cradle is on dry land, under a rooftree. Domesticity is one thing and love-making another, but they're both foredoomed to failure on a houseboat."

"There have been honeymoons," ventured the Major.

The Admiral chuckled. "As long as society continues to insist on the isolation of the temporarily insane," he said, "they must go somewhere. We have neither Brighton nor Boulogne, and the spectacle of love routed by seasickness is too painful to contemplate. So they do the best they can, poor things, and speaking more from a general knowledge of human nature than of the immediate subject, I should say that most of them are extremely glad to get back."

"We are not discussing the holy state," said Wilden. "The question before this meeting is the position of the fair sex in relation to houseboats. Try and look at the thing rationally. It doesn't follow because a woman happens to be fond of a man that she should want to go to his club or play polo with him any more than she wants to smoke his pipes or wear his hat. Now, did you ever know a woman who was any good up country, who really liked the business, and didn't make herself jolly uncomfortable pretending that it was her idea of fun?"

"There's Mrs. Manton," said I impartially, "and Mrs. Threddle. . . . The first is the solitary exception that proves the rule: I'm free to admit that she seems to enjoy herself and can walk across country without being a nuisance and frightening every bird within half-a-mile. Yet even she brings along a collie that runs in and wants to fight your dogs at their work. As to Mrs. Threddle, it's only a mistaken sense of domestic duty that leads her astray. She goes in holy terror of being mobbed by the Chinese, comes back with a cold in her head and blistered feet, and then tells all her friends how jolly it is, how dear Fred wouldn't enjoy it a bit without her, and all the rest of it. There's nothing harder to deal with than misguided sentiment of that kind."

"It seems to me," observed the Major, "that I've known Mrs. Wilden and the kids to have a pretty good time in their own way up country."

"Now, Major, don't pretend to be dense. Christmas outings and children's picnics are another story. A man isn't necessarily a brute because he's got a family. This discussion began by your lurid imagination revelling in the vision of petticoats on this boat."

"Keep your ideals," remarked the Admiral; "but keep them at a distance."

The Major smiled as one who can afford to pity his fellow-creatures.

"I don't think even my imagination would revel in the vision of a lady on board such a boatful of chivalry as this. It seems to me," he went on reflectively, "that whatever ideals you fellows may once have had have been drowned in your brimming flesh-pots. Observe, I don't say that a man should necessarily want to take his nursery up country or that a houseboat is the ideal place for courtship. What I do say is that unless a man is a worse misogynist than any of you, there are always moments when the ordinary human man's mind completes the picture with a woman's face."

"In other words," I suggested, "the day being fine and snipe scarce, your artistic temperament is gently stirred by romantic surroundings, and you are disposed to exchange the three of us for one sympathetic person of the other sex. And quite right too —"

"Oh, it's easy enough to twaddle; but you know what I mean."

Wilden chipped in again, "Yes, I think I know the sort of picture the Major has in his mind's eye, and it's all right in its way. The only trouble is that it won't stand up against the hard facts of real life. Of course it's delightful to dream of sailing about like this with the only woman on earth — to exchange the ardours of the chase for transcendental idealism under a blue sky. But by the time you've got her here and taken her safely back again, you'll wish you had worked out your ideals on a yacht near the Bund."

"*Dulce est desipere*," said I, "but there's certainly a good deal in the *loco*."

"Even I," sighed the Admiral, "have often reflected in my melancholy way how jolly it would be to come back, after a long tramp, and find the boat bright with flowers, a dainty tea-table all ready, and behind it, in soft chiffons and lace, the woman you'd like to see there, sweetheart or wife, as the case may be. It's a picture which undoubtedly appeals more to the artistic and æsthetic side of me than that of Wilden in his old dressing-gown, smoking a pipe on his bunk. I can imagine cosy little *tête-a-têtes*, for instance."

"Pretty dreams," said Wilden; "but, as a matter of fact, you've tried it, and you know how the real thing works out. If the dear girl goes out with the guns you've got to reckon on a crowd of natives following you all day, attracted by the strange she-devil;

what with looking after her, and answering artless questions, there isn't much time or opportunity for shooting; and when she gets back to the boat she's too tired to sit up and do the pretty polite. On the other hand, if she stays on the boat all day she's bored to death by tea-time, and expects you to prop up your eyelids somehow and amuse her all the evening.

"*Faut souffrir pour être beau,*" said the Admiral.

"Personally," continued Wilden, "I don't come up country for grand opera or *grandes passions*. You can't have everything, Major. Why not make up your mind that the object of this sort of thing is simply to brush off the cobwebs of pidgin, to get away from tea-parties, dress clothes, and all the other silly parlour tricks we have to play; you can't do that and bring them along with you too."

"All of which," said the Major, "means that you are a beastly egoist. If you want to wear sweaters, play cards all the evening, and fill the cabin with smoke, you can; but that does not prevent the existence of a higher order of intelligence."

Now, I knew what Jim had been thinking about, and was able to sympathise with his point of view. But I didn't want the argument to descend from the general of our talk to the particular in our minds, so I made a flanking movement.

"It seems to me," I said, "that for an idealist it is not fitting to put the bodily presence before the joys of imagination. Why should you want the imperfect reality aboard, Major, when we can all dream blissfully of our ideals of perfection?"

"Why should you take a whisky and soda," said Jim, "when you can think of Pommery?"

The Admiral is never slow to seize an idea of this kind, and the boy speedily emerged with drinks. I ventured on a quotation.

"This insatiate and greedy desire of corporal presence doth somewhat 'accuse the weakness in the jovissance of soules,' it was a wise man who said that, Major; jovissance, as he knew it, and as most wise men have known it sooner or later, is chiefly a matter of imagination."

Jim was getting restive. "If the old buffer meant to say that he would as soon dream about a girl's hand as hold it, he was either a fool or a liar."

"Major," remarked the Admiral, "I'm afraid you are only a poor materialist after all."

"That," said Wilden, "is expressing it crudely. Putting it philosophically, you might say that when the irresistible Life-force commands the blind earth-worm to fulfil its destiny, no amount of wise jaw can stop that worm."

"As to that," observed the Major, "I have never met a woman who talked such rot as you fellows."

"That settles it," said the Admiral, "we'll have a ladies' picnic next week."

Just then Wilden sighted duck ahead (which, as he observed, were more in his line than hens) and the eternal feminine gave place to immediate realities. But that night she hovered again, over our last nightcap, on board the *Saucy Jane*. The wind was howling over the marshes, with a sound like the wailing of lost souls for ever driven through darkness.

"Just listen to that, Jim," I said; "there's poetry and mystery in that, but it's the sort of thing that makes one grateful for good bunks and baccy, and the other prosaic things of life."

"Those fellows talked awful rot to-day," he observed irrelevantly, "but you knew what I meant. Even old Rex there can indulge in his dreams."

"You were perfectly right, Jim, and so were they. It's all a question of the point of view — the eternal struggle of the realist against ideals. You've got to remember that there's always something 'shame-faced' and sheepish about your Anglo-Saxon discussing his emotions or his soul; it's part of the national instinct and training to pretend he has neither. In time he comes to a dull acceptance of the small beer of life as part of the sorry scheme of things and refuses to contemplate the possibilities of nectar. But even he dreams of it for all that."

"I suppose so. But he won't confess it even to himself. He puts his dreams away in the innermost vault, forgets what they look like, and then goes back to the serious business of his existence, collecting bits of metal or mud."

"Jim," said I, "you're getting sentimental. Let's go to bed."

As we turned in, the voice of Wilden came fitfully from the other bank (he always sings when the dogs are being walked), and the words came weird and unreal against the background of the darkness and desolation of the midnight marshes.

> And mine it is to follow in her train,
> Do her behest in pleasure or in pain,
> Burn at her altar love's sweet frankincense
> And worship her in distant reverence.

"I really believe," said the Major, as he pulled the bed-clothes over his chin, "that the British race has put all its available stock of feelings into maudlin after-dinner songs. That's the fellow, mind you, who objects to the idea of women up country!"

"Not the idea, Jim, it was the corporal presence. The limitations of time and space. . . ."

"Oh, shut up." And Jim, without further words, in the childishly sudden manner he affects, went off to sleep, doubtless to sail again over shimmering blue waters towards the sunset, listening to the soft voice, and gazing into the unfathomable eyes of his Lady of Dreams.

Dear Lady of Dreams! To each one of us, so long as the soul within us lives, she comes at times, opening the gates of Heaven, if only for a moment. For days and years we may tread the dusty road of life, unthinking, and then, suddenly, at a turning of the way, we find her waiting; and all our burden of weariness drops from us straightway, as we lose ourselves in the music of her voice, telling of joys and wonders unforgotten. With some, her favoured ones (we call them poets), she lingers, leading them through fields of asphodel to fairy melodies — and in their songs we catch the echo of her glorious message. Most of us she guides but a little way, yet long enough to make us forget our heavy dust-laden feet, to show us the glory of the distant hills, and send us, singing bravely, forwards. Seldom (such is the weakness and isolation of our poor human souls) may we drink a deep draught of Being from "the well amidst the waste"; rare glimpses only do we catch of that inner life of which she tells. Beside a death-bed, or when we see the love-light dawn and glow in another's eye, the veil is swiftly lifted, and far out into the infinite void we hear the beating of majestic wings. At such moments she is with us, our Lady of Dreams.

She walks, as Atalanta walked in Calydon. The strength and beauty of the pine-clad hills is in her footsteps; in her hair the sunlight gleams as on amber waves. Her eyes are wonderful, now dancing bright as northland stars, now deep and clear as some fir-shaded mountain-pool. All things beautiful and cleanly and sweet are hers to love: children and flowers and the song of birds, ripe autumn fields and hearts of simple men. And because hers is the knowledge of all time and worlds, because she understands all Life's sorrows and perplexities, she has no anger, but only pity, for our sins and foolishness. Therefore to her, in certainty of sympathy, we tell in unuttered words our heart's desire, afall, and the deep places of our being are made whole.

In solitude, wherever the kindly earth speaks to us of Beauty, she comes on magic wings, bearer of comfort, and at her passing we look forth with new eyes upon the world. Something of her magic lingers henceforth in the faces of familiar friends; the echo of her voice in simple household words. If we will but listen, hers is the voice that speaks in the thunder of the surf, in the deep silences of the woods, and in the thrush's throbbing song. From the uttermost depths of disillusion she calls us, our Lady of Dreams, to lay at her feet our faded wayside flowers and our rue. As a kind nurse to tired children she brings consolation and healing, because in her are all the ideals of joy and beauty vainly sought in all our uncounted, unremembered lives. Happy is he to whom she comes in time of need, our Lady of Dreams; happier still he who until his journey's end shall seek her, ever undismayed, amidst the world of men.

·CHAPTER·X·
·OF·
·DUCKS, RAIN·
·AND·
·OTHER·MATTERS·

"Who loves to live i' the sun,
Seeking the food he eats
And pleased with what he gets,
Come hither, come hither, come hither:
Here shall we see
No enemy
But winter and rough weather."

SHAKESPEARE.

BITTER wind was blowing from the north, and there was a crackle of thin ice at the edge of the paddy fields and dykes. To eastward the first faint lines of light were breaking the thick-packed banks of cloud, broadening slowly and tipping their dark edges with saffron and pink and pearl. Behind us the world lay still brooding in darkness, filled with the grey melancholy which haunts the hour before the dawn. Slowly, as the light grew, houses and trees stood forth like ghosts, and the walls of Soochow, half-a-mile away, took form, grim and silent, against the skyline. We stood under the lea of a big grave and waited. A hundred yards away, in the unploughed paddy, we could hear the faint fluttering and babble of feeding duck; the morning flight would soon begin.

It was a favourite spot of ours, this, between the feeding-grounds and the Great Lake. Hither, when the north wind blows, mallard flock at dusk with widgeon and pintail and teal; year after year, in January and February, impelled by phantom voices from the past, following the long trail of heredity, and at dawn they flight southwards. Sometimes we come here at sunset, especially when the moon is nearing the full, but this morning I had overcome the Major's chronic objections to early rising, and by six o'clock we were out. It was bitterly cold. Hugging the shelter of a protecting sycamore we blew on our fingers and waited, while old Rex, whining gently in protest against our inactivity, snuggled his head between Ah Kong's knees.

"Major," said I, "it's beastly cold; but they ought to be moving soon."

Jim's reply was irrelevant. "I was just thinking," he said, "that it's just getting on for midnight in London town. The band must be tuning up for supper at the Savoy. Can't you see it all, Phil? Those tired foreign noblemen in the plush clothes, collecting hats at sixpence each; in the corners the children of Israel at their coffee, and, in the distance, the red-shaded lights and the tables glittering in silver and white? Can't you hear the rustle of silk skirts and the sob of that ugly gipsy's violin? It's only just a little way over yonder, just as we left it, and the sun will look down on it all in a few hours. It's all there, the rush of life, the music and the women, the pick of the best on earth; and here we stand like idiots, freezing to death on a Chinaman's grave."

"We might be doing much worse, old chap. It's this sort of thing that makes the lights of London look so jolly bright for a time when we get back to them. There's many a man in town tonight who'd change places with us and be glad of the chance."

Jim, lighting his pipe, struck a match on the tombstone at our feet. The laconic inscription winked at us between the puffs.

"It's a queer business, anyway," he went on. "Observe: here, since the days of George the First, Chang Li-ping, erstwhile Sub-prefect, has slept in peace (provided the Taipings didn't make fuel of him), and many later Changs have burned their joss-sticks on his mound and then crept under it themselves, without a sight or sound of foreign devildom to disturb their celestial peace. And now, here we come from the ends of the earth, digging up their bones to make roads for our fire-wheel carts, shooting guns over their ancestral heads, and shocking their indignant shades with talk of strange sing-song houses overseas. Phil, the gods of the East are dying. Old Li told me so only yesterday."

"The East will get others, Jim. And they will not be ours."

Out of the grey dawn and above the voice of the north wind there came a whirr of wings, faint at first, but rushing swiftly to a clear crescendo.

"Look out," whispers Ah Kong, eagerly pointing; "have got duck come; largee piecee," and a pair of mallard, flying fast and low, come straight over the edge of the grave. So close are they that the purple and bronze of the drake's wing send a swift message of beauty to the mind dormant beneath instincts of destruction. Terror lies in the sidelong glance of the dark eyes, in the lilt and swift upward curve of their flight. Ten yards away and one loud hopeful quack expresses their pent-up feelings; another ten, and they collapse, suddenly overtaken by Destiny, as the guns speak out.

At the first shot a mighty rushing of wings rises from the nearer paddy. We catch a glimpse, a glint of brown and grey, as a bunch of teal sweeps over the farther dyke. From all sides comes the warning quack of mallard, circling like restless ghosts over-head. To the left a flock of widgeon comes hurtling by, leaving three of their number behind. As the light strengthens the flight begins in earnest, and for twenty happy minutes we are in the thick of it. Many birds, after each shot, pass wide to left and right, but the grave is a good screen, and those that follow keep their ac-customed line, some even swerving in, decoyed by the fluttering of a winged bird in the paddy. Teal and mallard suffer especially from this fatal curiosity; drop one of a bunch, and the others, describing a wide circle, will frequently swoop back, singly and in pairs, low flying over the dykes.

The last of our bag was a pair of geese that came looming up unsuspectingly out of the distance, leisurely flapping their way to the lake after the night's feed. Ah Kong, keeping watch, gave warning, but there was no time to change our No. 6; nor was there need, for they came so straight upon their doom that, passing overhead, they got our first barrels at twenty yards and died straightway in their tracks. Rex, released from durance, brought them in, his whole body stiff with pride of the chase, his face puckered up with canine mirth, and snorting joyously through his nose. Then came ten minutes of retrieving wounded and dead birds (how curious is the apathetic surrender of the larger ducks and geese as compared with the dogged instinct of preservation and cunning of a wounded teal!), and Ah Kong shouldered a heavy game-stick as we filled our pipes. And so back to breakfast. The short promise of the dawn had died; east to west the sky was murky grey, and the rain had set in steadily evidently for the day.

On our way back to the boat a curious incident occurred, one of those things which make natives believe in foreign devildom. As we came round the corner of a fir-planted mandarin grave a cock pheasant rose straight ahead; going his best he was just reaching the shelter of some trees when Jim fired, and the last we saw of the bird was a head-over-heels collapse. At the corner where he fell Rex got the scent and followed it into some cover. There, amidst the graves, we came upon an old woman gathering fuel; she had seen no bird, she said; the collie could find no sign of it, and Rex could not pick up a line. It was only a little clump of trees, and all around lay the bare fields; yet we searched in vain.

"He didn't look like a runner," said Jim. "Hallo, what's the matter with Rex?"

The dog had given it up as a bad job some minutes before and had followed Ah Kong, who, with the curious hang-dog manner which natives in foreign employ assume when talking to their countrymen, was still questioning the old woman. Suddenly Rex began to display most unusual interest in the old lady, smelling and pawing at her skirts. Ah Kong seized the situation at once; a rapid altercation followed, and then, with all the *sangfroid* of a conjurer and something at the same time reminiscent of the contortionist, the old sinner dived into her own recesses, so to say, and produced our bird, tied by one leg to some unidentified inner garment. The thing was done with a sad dignity that made us almost apologetic; but something had to be said.

"Miserable and worthless one," I said, "why did you try to steal our pheasant?" Rex, with the bird in his mouth, wagged a vociferous tail.

"How did I know it was your pheasant?" she answered; "I caught the bird running in the wood. But I give it to you because your dog has a devil-gift of mind-clearness and knows secret things. Take him away." So we took him away, and, as we went, the poor soul observed audibly that she had known this pheasant since its youth up, or words to that effect, and that it did not belong to the men from overseas.

The *Saucy Jane* lay moored near the great stone bridge, whose fifty-three arches, the natives say, are never more than fifty-two if you count them from south to north. Its Chinese name is "The Bridge of the Precious Girdle," and the story goes that in the good old days when Chinese officials were really the "fathers and mothers" of the people, when they cared, and paid, for public works, and before squeezing had been raised to a fine art, vast sums were spent on the canals, bundings, and bridges of the great trade route between Soochow and Hangchow. (That this is true we know who have seen the crumbling ruins of all that stupendous masonry.) But for this bridge either the funds or the good intentions gave out, so that for two years it remained unfinished; therefore the tow-path ended in space, and thousands of toilers, in sight of their journey's end, had perforce to "eat bitterness." Then, travelling on Imperial business, came a Great Man (so great that they who tell the story to-day have forgotten his name), who, seeing the unfinished bridge, waxed indignant and sorrowful. Forthwith he saw the Governor and the Treasurer, and finding them without funds (there was no lekin in those good days) he gave them his own girdle of turquoise and rubies and jade; and so the work was finished. It is a pretty story, and it gains in effective contrast with the methods of to-day. There stands the bridge, murmurous as of old with the shouts and songs of coolies bending to the tow-rope, smooth-polished by the unnumbered feet of all those who have crossed it and gone their ways; but the iron-work has been sadly pilfered, many of the stone lions have been thrown down or defaced, while here and there a melancholy wreckage of coping-stones and railing hangs perilously over the water. And although these are the days of Young China, and re-form and sovereign rights, the common people's highway is still nobody's business.

There is good snipe-ground near the Bridge, and golden plo-ver frequent the waste places of the "Settlements," so that, as we trudged towards the boat, there were two voices within us: one the call of the wild, the Spartan cry, the voice of the hardy sports-man — a voice which meant breakfast in damp clothes and a day on the narrow dykes with the rain in our eyes, but withal the screech of snipe rising from the lotus-ponds and the joy of a fast bird well dropped. Also, there was in the air, despite the rain, a first faint message of spring, a suggestion, as of distant music and colour, somewhere behind the veil of grey. But the other voice sang luringly of soft things; of baths and breakfast unhurried, of tobacco and books in the cosy cabin of the *Saucy Jane*, with the rain pattering on the roof for greater comfort.

To be quite honest about it, after a mental struggle in which the sight of Rex's drooping tail and muddy coat had their effect, the Spartan voice allured me less than that of Sybaris, but I would not have said so for worlds. I would leave that to Jim — knowing his little weaknesses — and thus preserve my own "face," while acquiring some merit for making graceful concessions. We all do this sort of thing at times.

Breakfast was laid when we came aboard; there was a savour of frizzling bacon and coffee that tickled the nostrils most gratefully; compared to the dreary dampness of everything outside, the cabin certainly was a very pleasant place indeed.

"Well, we've made a fairly decent bag," said Jim. "Lowdah, come and pull off my boots."

I was scraping the mud off mine at the gangway in a rather ostentatious way, while Ah Kong was busy drying Rex with a wisp of straw, speculating, as I knew, on the chances of a long day at dominoes with the lowdah and the cook.

"Not worth while changing for breakfast, old chap," I remarked casually. "We'll be out again in an hour." But I felt the rain trickling down the small of my back, and the thud of Jim's boots on the cabin floor was like music in my ears. Heroism was foredoomed (so be it), but the soul of me was glad, and that comfortable lying knave, conscience, made no sign.

"Not much," said Jim. "As long as this rain goes on, the snipe may rest in peace so far as I am concerned. Don't believe in making a toil of pleasure. Be aisy, man; we'll move the boat up to the Custom House and look in on old Merryman at tiffin time. It'll be an act of real charity to him, and you can let him expound his latest theories on the reform movement. Anyhow, no paddy fields in the rain for this child. We've got plenty of books."

"Jim," said I, "you're as bad as one of your Chinese recruits. Here we come, a hundred miles or so, to shoot snipe . . ."

"Poppycock. We came to enjoy ourselves, and I mean to do it. Now, just take your boots off, have a bath, and content yourself with a sense of futile virtue."

I had played the Spartan, and honour was safe without more words, and so the boots came off. And then it was that Ah Kong assumed the part that conscience had not played and deprived me of acquired merit. As the second muddy boot hurtled out on to the deck he looked up. The anxious look of a minute ago had

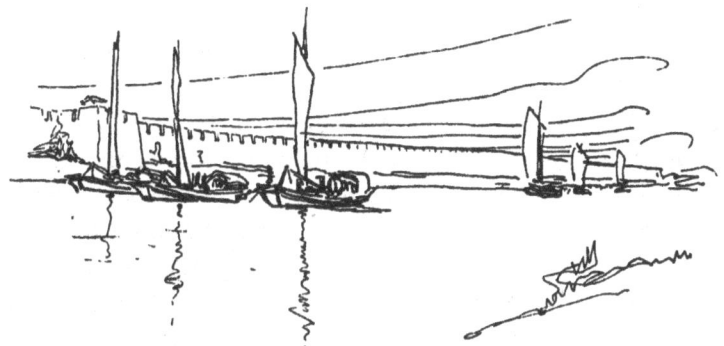

"Under the old grey walls of Soochow."

given place to one of virtuous sorrow.

"Master no shootee more?" He asked it with an implied reproach unmistakable. "Countryman talkee have got plenty snipe
just now."

"No, Ah Kong. Have got some pidgin inside city. Come back
shootee this evening."

He looked at me and said nothing; but when it comes to saving one's face, it is hard work fooling a Chinaman.

As we sat over our leisurely breakfast the boat moved, with
the slow and silent motion of the yuloh, along the canal and under the old grey walls of Soochow — Soochow, once the Paris of
China, belauded of Marco Polo, thrice sacked in the Taiping days.
On the tow-path half-a-dozen miserable specimens of sodden
humanity pulled doggedly towards the city gate, but there was
hardly any other sign of life. Here and there a boat, propelled by
invisible hands, shot past us in silence, but most of the river-craft
lay huddled for shelter under the high banks, and all the life of
the fields had taken refuge in the houses, which stood out, like
weary sentinels, amidst the waste of rain-swept paddy. Even between the walls and the Canal, in that No-man's land where the
beggars and rag-pickers of the city have their motley homes of
old boat hulks and matting, the only living things visible were a
pig, some hens too hungry to abandon the search for food, and
an old woman patiently struggling with wet straw to boil her rice

pot under the shelter of a grave.

"Jim," said I, as we lay on our bunks and soothed our Capuan souls with Craven mixture, "let's leave old Merryman alone for to-day. We'll go up to the P'an Men and then, if it clears, we'll take a walk through the city, look up Wimple, and hear what he thinks of the boycott in these parts. Then we can have the boat meet us over yonder by the camp, and shoot again in the afternoon."

"Right oh!" said Jim. He was in that blissful state of mind which would have made him say "Right oh" to any proposal which would leave him the immediate certainty of half an hour's undisturbed idleness. But I know he does not love Wimple.

So the boat lapped lazily on past the lonely Custom House towards the P'an Men, the busiest of all the gates of the city, the place to which the Chinese officials said the railway line must never come — until they had bought up all the land near the terminus; past the Foreign Settlement, so carefully located, where no trade can ever come near it, in the usual "place apart," most closely resembling, in its carefully marked out town-lots and grass-grown roads that lead nowhere, the delectable City of Eden; past the latest encampment of foreign-drilled braves who, even in the rain, cease not from their martial bugling, apparently the only feature of our military system that the Chinese really appreciate and enjoy. All over the country you will find them, singly and in squads, these soldiers of the coming military power, sturdily practising, by the hour, the war-calls of Europe. Here at Soochow the tuition had originally come from France (*via* Japan, no doubt).

> Mademoiselle, avez-vous du tabac
> Avec une pipe comme ça?

The old familiar notes, blown lustily by a bucolic brave holding the usual umbrella in his free hand, seemed to come from some weird haunt of the utterly incongruous. What, in the name of all things outlandish, is the phantom voice of the Little Corporal doing here in the rain under the walls of Soochow?

Jim looked at the matter differently; the sound stirred his military instincts, and the instincts of the British officer may be generally described as a forward policy whose objective includes the entire habitable globe.

"If they must learn bugling," he said, "which is all damned nonsense until they've learned drill and discipline, why can't they stick to one kind? I've only heard one real Chinese bugler; he was a little Mahommedan sergeant in the Weihaiwei regiment, and to hear him play 'Lights Out' or 'Puddings and Pies' was a treat. I remember once . . ."

I created a diversion, drawing his attention to the Japanese Settlement, where, in one corner of its deserted space, a few braves were drilling (without umbrellas) under the stern eye of an instructor from Dai Nippon.

"Aye, Phil," he said, thoughtfully addressing the window-pane, "it was the little foxes that ate up the vineyard, wasn't it? I believe there's a good deal of sympathy possible between us and the Japanese; we are proud of him as a fighting man, and he likes us for being fairly truthful, and for some other things; but even in the happiest of families the fool brother gets more kicks than ha'pence, and that's what I don't quite like about this alliance. We're the fool brother, and every Jap in the country knows it."

"Do you think he'll make warriors of our Celestial friends, Jim?"

"That's another story. China's a big country, big enough to hold many tribes and tempers, and I've no objection to his being drill sergeant so long as it's a square game. All we want is a fair field and no favour, and I wish we were quite sure of getting it."

"Yes, we kept the ring for them."

"And the stake was the open door. But it looks as if, when they keep it open, there's going to be a door-keeper, and the Japs will be admitted half-price. If they do, it will be our own fault, the fitting penalty for national imbecility and ignorance."

"Surely, Jim, it's a question of economics? We declined to fight Russia for the open door in China, because the British taxpayer didn't want to part with another penny in the pound for a trifle like that. So Japan did the job for us, and thus the British public can go comfortably to sleep again, after reading in *The Times* that, thanks to our gallant little allies, the Far East is henceforth, as Providence meant it to be, our oyster, and will yield up to us its fatness without the aid of any cutlery or energy of ours."

Jim snorted. "Yes, that's the way John Burns and Churchill talk, as if trade and taxes were the only things worth thinking and living for. Can't they realise that the moral effect of that Japanese friend of ours over yonder, drilling his fellow-Asiatics, must be felt all over the East, to the Indian Ocean and round the world again? If England wants to claim any open door or share of her heritage in Asia she must keep her end up. It's that, or go."

The discussion might have gone on, although I secretly agreed with Jim, because there was nothing better to do, also because I like to see him excited, and this is one of the few topics that draw him. Just then, however, there was a hail from the tow-path, and the boat stopped. A bedraggled and muddy individual, with an oil-paper umbrella, was telling the lowdah, in most excellent vernacular, to let him come aboard. It was our friend the Reverend Mr. Wimple, of the Soochow Mission of Latter-day Saints (U.S.A.), semi-political adviser of the Governor of Kiangsu.

·MISSIONARIES·
·MANDARINS·
·AND·
·MORALS·

CHAPTER XI

"First observe the man: then preach the law." — *Buddhist Text.*

THE gang-plank was put down, and Mr. Wimple came aboard, chaffing the coolies. I heard him tell the lowdah to cast off again as he was going with us to the P'an Men, and I made a mental note of the curious fact that the high nasal accents of ordinary American speech are softened, if not lost, in talking Chinese, and that herein lies a new argument, possibly useful to Roosevelt and other philanthropists, for intercourse between God's own country and Asia.

He came in cheerily, depositing his umbrella in the coal-box. "Ugly weather, gentlemen, ain't it?" he said. "The sort of thing that encourages the irreverent folks who think that Providence might be more thoughtful without being less good." He sat down by the stove, his clothes steaming gently, and helped himself in an absent-minded way to one of Jim's cigars. We bade him welcome, not so much because he needed it, as from fixed habits of hospitality. "Thank you," he said, "it's no day for walking; so, when I saw your boat, I thought you wouldn't mind taking me as far as the P'an Men. Are you gentlemen going into the city?"

Jim was signalling a frantic "No," but as I find Mr. Wimple a rather interesting study, I said we were—that, as a matter of fact, we were going to see him and ask the latest news of the provincial capital. "Well, that's lucky," he said genially, "I'm just going along to see old Liu, the Chih Hsien, on a little matter of land business—you know they're making trouble now even about Mission property. We'll all go together; the business won't take ten minutes, and then you gentlemen will come along and have a

"Mr. Wimple came aboard."

bit of tiffin with me. It's all on your way if you're going back by the Settlement, and Mrs. Wimple will be mighty glad to see you."

I had heard indirectly of Mission property business at Soochow; there was a good deal of it handled by godly folk before the Foreign Settlement boom came to its untimely end, and now the railway had provided new opportunities. I said we would go, but Jim dodged the tiffin with a ready lie.

"Thank you," he said, "we'll walk through the city and help you to frighten old Liu. But I promised Merryman we'd tiffin with him."

Wimple is not a type, though by no means an isolated specimen, of the results of American missionary enterprise in China. He is rather one of the peculiar products of Western morals applied, on misguided principles, to the Far East. I remember well travelling out with him on the Pacific Mail that first brought him, one of a batch of seventy youthful enthusiasts, to convert the heathen. Till then, he had been a backwoods teacher in Dakota, saw life through the distorted medium of an undigested Pentateuch, and drank out of his finger-bowl. A year later I came across him preaching at a street corner at Soochow, in execrable Chinese, on the efficacy of faith as distinct from works, and distributing leaflets against the opium habit. That was six years ago; since then he has been led to believe that his mission lies with the educated and official classes, in the conversion of 'this *great* people' from the top downwards, and incidentally it has come to pass that his labours have gradually become more secular and less dogmatic. It has even been rumoured that the vineyard is going to lose a labourer, and the yamens gain thereby another unofficial adviser; this may be so, but for the present Wimple still figures prominently in the social and religious activities of missionary work, and the worthy citizens of the United States, who acquire vicarious virtue through his soul-saving efforts, are privileged to pay for them and for the comfortable existence of Mrs. Wimple and her steadily-increasing progeny; his reports on the infant-school of the Latter Day Saints, replete with appropriate references to the good seed and the needs of the sower, are models in their way. An able man is Wimple, and no doubt his intelligence has revealed to him a truth (which many worthier souls will never realise) that his earlier enthusiasms were possibly due only to ignorance, and that, against the ancient social and philosophic system of China, our creeds and sects wage war in vain.

Since the gloriously futile effort of the Crusaders to convert Asia, with battle-axe and Bible, to Europe's conception of an Asiatic creed, there is perhaps nothing in all the history of religions on this planet so pathetically hopeless as the misdirected energies of certain kinds of Christianity in the Far East to-day. Nor can you readily find a more glaring record of cynical pagandom than in the political purposes to which the governments of Christian States have put the gospel of peace and its messengers. Wimple and his kind are a by-product, the inevitable result of education wrongly applied; because of their prominence with the mandarinate for background they attract undue notice even when (as in Corea) they set a kingdom by the ears. But setting them aside, looking only at the results of Roman Catholic and Protestant mission work, bravely and conscientiously done by hundreds of devoted men and women, who can honestly say that our 'furor' of proselytising is good either in its methods or its ends?

In this matter we have assumed, *ab initio*, false premises — each of the conflicting creeds to which the perversity of word-haunted priest-led men has brought the simple teachings of Christ justifies its attempts at 'converting' the Chinese on grounds of moral and intellectual superiority. In this the "good Christians who sit still in easy-chairs" in Battersea or Boston may be reckoned blissful and blameless perhaps, because of ignorance, but no man who has lived for years amongst the Chinese and observed their habits of thought carries any such conviction to cheer his daily round. If, from sheer force of habit and fixity of purpose, he is able to do so for himself, he will most vehemently deny justification to other godly men, his neighbours; and thus the House of Wisdom is divided, filled, like the Temple of old, with the noisy arguments of the doctors, while the patient heathen passes by, either indifferent to the clamour, or wondering, in his instinctive agnosticism, that there should be so many divergent roads to Heaven.

The Chinese are essentially a practical race, and any system of ethics or morals that we preach to them must appeal, in the first place, to their reasoning faculty; it must also be made to harmonise with certain fundamental principles of life and living which, transmitted through countless generations, have accumulated all the force of instinct. As a race, they intuitively judge the tree by its fruit; works, not faith, justify the exponents of any new gospel of peace. For this reason the medical missionary and the Little Sisters of the Poor are the successful evangelists of China; for this reason also the lesson taught by the allied armies at Peking in 1900 has sunk deeper than any preaching into the hearts of the people; they know, and will not forget, that there it was an Asiatic army, and not those of Christian Europe, which practised gentleness and compassion, soberness and self-control in the midst of savagery; and the knowledge often outweighs our teachings and our texts.

At first glance it would seem that China offers an ideal field for mission work; that the material surroundings which fetter the soul of this people call urgently for a creed which shall open up a spiritual horizon, a larger life. But because the Chinese are a thinking race we cannot bring to their edification the men or the methods which we employ for African savages, nor can we expect them to recognise in our shrieking theologies the simple message taught to Asiatics long ago by the Sea of Galilee. Mr. Charles Booth, writing of the irreligion of the London poor, finds one of its chief causes in "the persistent and undignified struggle between competing religious bodies, rising into almost open warfare for possession of the field." The same cause, amongst others, underlies the failure of religious work in China; "Not peace, but a sword" is the missionary's reply, and the sword is accordingly an ever-present result of his labours — the sword of savage mobs, avenging some real or fancied interference with their established ways; thereafter, the sword of earth-hungry powers avenging the messengers of peace. And anon the missionary returns, under military escort, all unconscious of the grim irony of his position, preaching again the message of forgiveness and peace to an indemnity-paying people. "Little children," he says, "love one another," and next day he earnestly denounces his brother.

If, by virtue of some Utopian scheme, such as Chang Chih-tung's dream foreshadows in China's latest treaty with England, the Christian Churches could be led to agree either to divide the field or to substitute one single human gospel for the dry bones of conflicting dogma; if, for the Babel of doctrines poured forth by Wesleyans, Primitive Methodists, Baptists, Nestorians, Episcopalians, and a score of others, we could give these people a simple creed informed with the fellowship of man rather than with intimate knowledge of the road to Heaven — then the unction of good work which many comfortable Christians overseas lay to their souls might be nearer attainment. It is as easy in Peking as in London to talk of the ultimate efficacy of bread upon the waters, but if the history of missionary work in China can teach anything, it is that the casting must be warily done, and that it was one gospel, and not a dozen, which was to be preached unto all the world.

These things were in my mind as Wimple chatted cheerily in the cabin of the *Saucy Jane*, telling of the social life of the Soochow missions, their literary gatherings, their endless warfare of words, and the fierceness of Roman Catholic competition. The man was earnest enough; his heart was in the day's work, whatever it might be; yet as he talked on, and as Jim sat there, a grim figure of stolid endurance, the feeling that gradually shaped itself in my mind was one of the futility of all those purposes which we three severally represented in the complex riddle of our cosmos. Here was Wimple, representative of a race of conscience-ridden hustlers, preaching his distorted version of an Asiatic religion to Asiatics — a militant exponent of the ways of peace; Jim, peacefully teaching these same Asiatics how to kill each other (and us) most scientifically; and I, endeavouring, like thousands of other born Britons, to earn by a lifetime of exile the means to die decently in mine own place! And I could not help wondering what these 'heathen,' over whom we are all so busy, think of our civilisation and its ludicrous results as presented by ourselves.

We got out at the gate and trudged eastwards, through two miles of narrow lanes, to the house of old Liu. The rain was still coming down steadily, and except in the main streets where the provision dealers are, the city was almost lifeless. Underfoot, the ragged pavement was slippery with black mud; overhead, water dripped from gutterless roofs and sign-boards. Under old marble bridges, by the decaying piles of the canals, an unwonted current was stirring that black ooze in which the burghers of Soochow wash their vegetables and clothes; the Paris of China was submitting to unusual ablutions. We walked in single file, dodging an occasional laden coolie, making way for chair-bearers, beggars, and dogs, Wimple telling us the while many things of the national movement, as conducted here by Young China, and Jim cheerily congratulating any begoggled students we met on the attractions of the provincial city. He calls that cultivating friendly relations with the native.

Old Liu was an acquaintance of mine—a Chih-hsien of the ancient classical type, fat and wheezy, ignorant of everything except the art of squeezing; a very Solomon in the matter of wives, and much addicted to quotation from the Four Books on matters of propriety and virtue. We had one taste in common—snuff-bottles—a fact which had relieved the tedium of certain negotiations about the location of the Soochow Settlement in 1895. With Wimple he appeared to be on terms almost affectionate, received him without ceremony, and repaired with him to the privacy of an inner room where, judging by his fat chuckles, the business was not without its humorous side. Meanwhile, Jim and I sat sipping jasmine-scented tea in a pavilion surrounded by the fantastic rockery work that Chinese scholars affect to love.

"There," said Jim, pointing to old Liu's waddling back, "you have the real incubus of China. There isn't the slightest use in providing the people with Bibles or rifles while these mediæval blood-suckers are let loose on the community. All our diplomacy and treaties must be waste of time as long as we come up against these word-spinning vampires."

"How are you going to get rid of them, Jim?"

"Not my business, I'm not a diplomat. But it's got to be done some day; there have been lots of chances. The whole show could have been cleaned up in '60, or in '98, and again the other day, when the old Dowager made a run for it. Why not begin by limiting the number of officials, weeding out the bad ones, and putting all the 'expectants' to some compulsory form of honest work?"

"With a British sergeant in each village, Jim? Don't forget that Little England's had enough of the white man's burden already."

When Wimple came back (with Liu's flabby paw on his shoulder) we were still discussing the insoluble problem, and as we walked from the Yamên to the bright mission compound close by, I asked him what he thought of it.

"Wal," he said, "it's a big proposition, and wise folks, like Sir Robert Hart and me and the Chinese themselves, aren't in any particular hurry over it. You may bully the East, but you can't hustle it, as Mr. Kipling says."

"No," said Jim, "but we were talking of reforming the official system."

"I've heard it said that a people gets the government it deserves," observed the missionary, "though it does look as if some countries had bad luck. But, speaking seriously, it seems to me there are only two ways about it. One's force, and that's an expensive method, besides making a mess; the other's education and missionary work, and that's certainly slow."

"But don't you think," I asked, "if the mandarin system could be gently persuaded to change a few of its wicked ways, things might be easier for these poor people and, incidentally, better for the foreign devil who wants to sell them piece goods?"

"Speaking unprofessionally," said Wimple, "there are several practical ways of improving the conditions of life for the Chinese; you could stop early marriages, for instance, and keep the population within feedable limits; or you could introduce cremation and so increase the cultivation area; or you might abolish pigtails, and divert the time wasted in unnecessary head-shaving to productive labour. In the course of my experience I've discussed these things with many intelligent Chinese, and they all admit the existing evils, but perhaps they'd as soon have them as some of the things we've got and which we don't seem to be able to get rid of — dumping, you know, and canned meat, and dynamite and new women, and ward politicians."

"Let's stick to the mandarin," said the Major. "Can nothing be done to him without horse, foot, and artillery?"

"Looked at from Moscow, or even from Minneapolis," I observed, "he has his good points."

"The trouble with foreigners," said Wimple, "is that they don't understand the classical mandarin, and so they don't know what to do with him. The Chinese people have got the thing pretty well seized up; the official after all is one of themselves, and he knows just how far he can go in monkeying with the taxes or the public rights. But the foreigner, who gets most of his knowledge of Chinese life from the *hsien sheng* or the compradore, looks upon a peacock-feathered Taotai as the mysterious embodiment of all the Asia he doesn't understand — and he behaves accordingly."

"That's true," Jim admitted, "and the mandarin is always coming up against the European with his own people's sympathy behind him because all his new squeezes are levied indirectly, and either connected with trade or identified with foreign indemnities."

"It seems to me," said I, "that the first thing required is to have all Consuls and diplomats specially trained in the methods and ideas of Chinese officials. That's what made Parkes a success; he had seen the Board of Punishments from within."

"That's right," said Wimple; "ordinary diplomatic experience in Constantinople may be very valuable, but it's worse than useless at the Waiwupu. There's mighty little that Consuls or Ministers can learn about Chinese officials anyway — it isn't in the books, and they never get the chances we missionaries have. Now, have you gentlemen ever noticed anything peculiar about foreign officials doing business with Chinese?"

"Reminds one of marionettes," said Jim, "and you've got to avoid the champagne."

"Wal, I don't suppose you've ever thought it out, but I have, and as you've asked my opinion about reforming the mandarin system, I'll make you a present of one practical idea. Just you get rid of the Chinese official dress, put them into frock-coats and top-hats, and after that it's 'easy street, and home.' I've always had a pet theory of my own about the hypnotic influences of the P'utzu, and last winter I wrote it out for one of our Literary Sociable evenings. They liked it well enough, and some of the folks wanted to print it, but I thought the Board might think it a bit frivolous for a missionary. It ain't really, and if you'd like to read it . . ."

I said we would.

"Wal, come right in and I'll get it for you: it may perhaps help to explain, Major, why the Caucasian's a failure at diplomacy in China. You're sure you won't stay to tiffin? We don't often have company, and Mrs. Wimple'd be real pleased to see you."

But the Major was not to be beguiled, so we went our ways, and Wimple promised to send his paper down to the boat by a coolie, who would bring him back some of our duck.

"He's a humorous cuss," said the Major, "and he knows a lot about the Chinese. I'm not so sure that there isn't a good deal in his idea of top-hats instead of peacocks' feathers — and yet the Japanese . . ."

"They had education under the hats," I said, "and patriotism under the frock-coats. But the imitation was a blunder all the same."

I read the paper to Jim after dinner. There was a good deal of padding in it and many local allusions, but it shows such knowledge of the subject as a whole that I feel justified in reproducing the pith and substance of the thing.

·CHAPTER· XII·
ON·THE·HYPNOTIC INFLUENCE· OF·THE ·P'UTZU·

"And the mean man boweth down, and the great man humbleth himself: therefore forgive them not." — *Isaiah* ii. 9.

IT is a phenomenon persistent in Chinese history, observed by all foreign students, and noticed with complacency by native writers, that the wisdom and diplomacy of the Empire have invariably risen superior to defeat of its naval and military forces, not only nullifying the enemy's success, but frequently deriving solid advantage from the subsequent negotiations. The phenomenon itself is undeniable, as the records of previous dynasties fully prove (*here the author quotes learnedly from the "Mirror of History"*). If we study the subject since the time when the British began bringing civilisation (and opium) to China — which is the beginning of modern history in this country — we find that every defeat inflicted by Europe on the Celestial Empire has been followed by the diplomatic collapse (generally gradual, sometimes sudden) of the victors.

Remember that in the past fifty years China has been mauled five times, her capital twice sacked, and her fighting capacity — or rather her capacity for not fighting — has been much the same all the time; yet how much forrader is Europe now, after the Boxer protocol, than she was in 1860? Ask the diplomat? he'll tell you times were never so bad in his business. The merchant? he is getting down close to bed-rock. The missionary? he's going to be regulated out of existence. Another defeat of China by the armies of Europe, and Western civilisation can pack up and get out, which is just one more instance of the general contrariness of cause and effect in this country.

Newspaper people, and the retired consular folk who pose as authorities on the Far Eastern question, have explained the thing in their own way, of course. They're paid to do it, and they must live somehow. Some of them will tell you that it's the benevolent toleration of the West for this ancient civilisation; others put it down to the international jealousies of the Powers, and there's a whole lot of talk about *vis inertiæ* and the capacity of China as a passive resister. You might as well explain a Mahatma by the rule of three. Some — and they are getting nearer the mark — say that the solution of the mystery lies in a peculiar quality of the atmosphere or dust in Peking, some soporific or flabbifying germ which speedily imbues the most intelligent and energetic of diplomats with the apathy of a dormouse and the complacency of a door-mat. A poet, who subsequently went to sleep himself, once expressed this opinion in some spirited lines: —

> As if the mouldering walls
> Of that Peking which typifies decay
> Shut out all purpose, shutting in the man,
> As if each roof in that foul street where lodge
> The envoys of proud states, had thrown the shade
> Of apathy on those who dwell below.

But no explanation that any of you have heard of really meets the case. The slightest knowledge of humanity will lay out these journalistic fallacies, and the man who ascribes altruistic motives to Governments in these mailed fist days is just talking. As to passive resisters — well, history shows that they have generally resisted themselves into oblivion or comfortable servility; there is no case on record of passive resisters behaving like the Empress Dowager and the Waiwupu, and living to a ripe old age. The Peking germ theory looks all right at first — I believed in it for quite a while myself — but there's a vital flaw in it which strikes you sooner or later, and that is, that a good deal of Chinese diplomacy isn't done in Peking, and yet the results are always the same — the defeated Yellow Man comes up smiling, to stand flat-footed on the stomach of the conquering White. It was perception of this flaw that led me to the solution of the mystery.

And when you think of the money and lives that have been spent on civilising China, all in the hope of getting them to wear our dry-goods while they live, and go to our Heaven decently when they die, it's a mystery that really seems worth more attention than it gets. It certainly deserves a select committee far better than most of the things Mr. Roosevelt worries himself about, and Mr. Rockhill would do well to look into it and leave the foreign relations of China in the Middle Ages to any sinologue that's got nothing better to do.

And, like all great truths, it is very simple. The secret of the unvarying success of Chinese diplomacy lies in certain occult and hypnotic influences of the P'utzu, worn in the manner prescribed by the sumptuary laws of Hung Wu, the first of the Mings. They look innocent enough, don't they, these artistically-embroidered squares? Many of you ladies use them for tea-cosies or cushions (just as some men wear a scarabeus of Old Egypt for a scarf-pin) without an inkling of the deadly work the thing has done in its time on a Prefect's chest or a Taotai's back.

Hung Wu introduced his methods of government at a time when black art was a live business in the Far East. A good deal of it subsequently found its way to India, and reached Europe by way of Arabia, in time to make things quite interesting for the Middle Ages — (*here follows a learned discussion of occult science, as practised by the sect of the assassins, Esoteric Buddhists, the Borgias, and the Society for Psychical Research*).

Besides being an adept in hypnotism, Hung Wu was a student of history, and therefore had doubts as to the permanence of political institutions in China, that is, the China he meant to leave to his successors. Also, like Lord Curzon, he believed in keeping the military power subordinate to the civil. So, with unholy incantations, he devised the P'utzu, and decreed that every official, civil and military, should wear them on their official robes. To the casual glance of the uninitiated they look as harmless as doyleys — sort of prehistoric postage stamps — but as a matter of fact Hung Wu put all he knew of devil pidgin into them, combining all the ingredients of mesmeric terrorism into a nicely graduated series, calculated to catch the eye of a blind beggar. And they have done their work ever since.

I've worked out a theory of hypnotics from a careful study of the patterns on P'utzu, with notes of the relative potency of each combination and observations of results from personal experience — but this isn't the place for them. It would be difficult to explain to you exactly why a white crane standing on one leg on convoluted clouds, with a red sun in the corner, gets in its work quicker than a wild goose with a background of serrated waves, but it's a fact. And old Hung knew what he was doing when he gave the military officials P'utzus that looked all right — beasts like Sime's, very fierce and funny, but which can't stand up against any of the civil birds when it comes to deadly radiations. He knew, in the first place, that a military official would always be too far off in case of danger for any hypnotic influence to be effective; and, secondly, that it didn't matter about the army getting beaten so long as the civil officers of the state could hypnotise the victors into a state of abject apology, which they have done ever since. So he bespattered the military with unicorns, seals, and rhinoceri, whose value, for mesmeric purposes, is trifling. With the civil order he was careful down to the ninth button; never put in a bird that didn't mean business, filled in every corner with mystic scroll-work and secret diagrams; so that in dealing with novices the Mandarin Duck is almost as terrifying as the Golden Pheasant. I once saw a French Consul utterly routed by the Egret of a *liu p'in hsien* — sheer case of unreasoning panic.

Of course the Chancelleries will scoff at all this — they always laugh at any idea that wasn't born in a Legation, which accounts for their chronic smile. And maybe some of you may have your doubts at first — I don't blame you for hesitating while you work it out. But just think of all the cases you've known — doesn't it meet them exactly and explain the whole thing in a way that satisfies pure reason? Of course it does.

Have you ever seen a Taotai or a Chih-hsien go out to talk to a mob when there's a row on? It's an instructive sight. He doesn't do any talking just walks down the street, with a peacock in a necromantic attitude on his chest, and the crowd melts away. If he went in his chair he'd be pulled to pieces — but the P'utzu works like the charm. And Hung Wu knew his business when he put one behind as well as in front.

Have you ever seen a mandarin in a ball-room in England or America? I have; in fact, it was the way the women behaved to old Wu Ting-fang at Washington that set me on the track of P'utzu hypnotism. I'm told it's the same all over Europe; handsome, well-educated, decent women, the sort that we have to approach on our marrow bones, tumbling over each other and making themselves ridiculous for a glance of His Excellency's eye or a touch of his long-nailed fingers. I heard the other day of a leader of Boston society that ran around like a chicken with its head off, because some of Tuan-fang's mission had accepted her invitation to dinner. And I've seen first season buds sitting out in conservatories with — well, let that pass.

And it isn't as if they didn't know all what they're doing. They know all right. The woman who marries a Chinese Secretary of Legation in Paris or Vienna knows all about the other three wives, and mother-in-law, and the sort of a ménage she's getting — but the P'utzu's too much for her, and she just goes dazed to her doom.

Now think it out for yourselves — test my theory by your own knowledge. Wouldn't the reception given to Imperial Chinese Commissioners or Ministers in Europe or the States be very different if they left their clothes behind them — I mean if they wore clothes like ours! Of course you may say that we grovel because of the general splendour of their attire, their brocades, and furs, coral buttons and velvet boots, and that the P'utzu is only part of a sartorial magnificence which makes us feel ridiculous, and behave like poor relations, in their company. Well, that might be a point for argument with people who have never lived in China, but out here it certainly won't wash. Think it out for yourselves, I say, and you'll soon come to see that the theory of strong hypnotic emanations from the P'utzu is the only one that accounts for the extraordinary behaviour of Europeans in dealing with Chinese officials. You've all felt an unaccountable flabbiness, a tendency to self-abasement and idiotic antics in the presence of Chinese officials — men that you often knew for no better than they ought to be, or than yourselves; you've tried to get over it or to account for it, and you've failed. But just make those same literary prodigies take their coats off and you'll understand where the trouble lay. A good many swaggering fathers and mothers of the people would be underground if they did business in their shirt sleeves, or whatever a Chinaman wears under his illustrated cover.

Take any case that occurs to you — a riot compensation claim, a lekin squeeze, or a land case. We know all about them. The foreign press make a fuss, vengeance is vowed, and the air is thick with all the trouble that's going to happen. Then a special Deputy is appointed to discuss matters with the Consul. You know what happens after that; every one of you has got the performance in his mind's eye. Down comes a Taotai or a Fan-tai, waddling in the plethoric fat of professional wickedness, a creature whose 'squeezing' is the talk of half a province, and whose only education consists in having learned by heart a lot of poppycock and then forgotten it. This monstrous survival of barbarism, who couldn't answer the questions of a kindergarten class, comes to discuss the case with the representative of Western civilisation, with a man who very possibly can boast of generations of educated and God-fearing ancestors behind him—and what happens? Old Hung Wu's necromancy comes out on top every time. That poor foredoomed Consul fixes his eye on the malevolent P'utzu bird and the game's up; he becomes an incoherent, posturing automaton, feebly imitating the foolishness of Chinese social etiquette, meekly listening to the sleek Confucianist's farrago of twaddle and bluff, forgetting everything except the unholy fascination of the P'utzu.

Of course, as in all cases of hypnotism, the effect is greater on some minds than on others. With women, and Frenchmen, and sinologues, it amounts to mental collapse; children and dogs, on the other hand, are comparatively immune. But I don't think I have ever met a case of a white man who could face a P'utzu and preserve all his self respect; the subtle influence of the thing invariably compels him to appear more or less overpowered by the Yellow Peril's condescension—to walk mincingly, drink vile champagne, and quote inane phrases from the *Kuan Hua Chih Nan*. And, mind you, the effect is permanent; once the eye of the P'utzu bird has entered a man's soul, he is mentally crippled for life. Which explains why you often hear respectable men, otherwise sane, loudly boasting of their intimacy with Chinese officials, as if they had achieved something wonderful.

I do not say, you will observe, that every mandarin is necessarily either a rogue or untruthful—the unexpected still happens, Heaven be praised!—but the pernicious influence of the P'utzu is the same, no matter what may be the character of the man behind it, and it reduces the European mind to a state of gelatinous subserviency.

Cast your memory back over a few of the cases you have known, where the white man has come forth with all the righteous indignation of a just cause, and collapsed ignominiously for no apparent reason. Not to go too far back, think of the 1900 Protocol with the victorious troops in the streets of Peking and their diplomatic representatives confronting a lot of P'utzu-plastered Boxers. You know the result. Think of Sir James Mackay and Jenks, and Sir Robert Hart and Teddy Roosevelt—I could quote a hundred more,—all the men whose great minds and good intentions have lately wilted under the baneful eye of Hung Wu's black-art birds!

One of the most remarkable cases I ever saw myself was at the funeral of the Viceroy Lui K'un-yi at Nanking. There were eleven Powers represented on that occasion, represented by Consuls in cocked hats and civil dignitaries of all sorts, with a fine assortment of naval and military officers—a show that would have been quite imposing in any European capital, but which, in the streets of Nanking, looked magnificently out of place. I assure you when we mustered at the Yamên, surrounded by thousands of squalid natives and all the tawdry pomp of a Chinese funeral, it was one of those international displays that one only sees in the Far East; and there were some white men there who had handled affairs and men all over the world with credit to themselves and their countries. Well, first of all we filed past the sorrowing relatives. They were in white sackcloth—no P'utzus about—and that part of the ceremony was dignified and impressive with a certain patriarchal quality of its own. Later on, however, when the *cortège* was formed, and especially in the evening, when a banquet was given, the P'utzus were let loose on that ill-fated band of representatives, and the rout was complete. I don't think I ever saw anything quite so ludicrous and humiliating. Chang Chih-tung was in the middle, with a golden pheasant on his chest, receiving obeisances, and the havoc that necromatic fowl made of the cocked hats and epaulettes was appalling. But every P'utzu had a foreigner or

two following it, as Trilby followed Svengali. I got entangled in
the suite of a silver pheasant myself, with an Austrian captain
and a German Vice-Consul. (*Here follows a description of several
historic instances illustrative of the author's theory.*)

Having discovered a truth, the next thing is to apply it — and
here the application is obvious. All we've got to do is to arrange
that the Waiwupu and all provincial officials doing business
with foreigners shall henceforth be persuaded to wear frock-
coats and top-hats. We might give them back all the Boxer
indemnity to buy a complete modern outfit, and it would be
cheap at the price. If, deterred by the sight of the Japanese in
European clothes, they kick at frock-coats, let them choose their
own style and their own patterns — but the P'utzu ought to go.

Of course, as I said before, diplomatists will laugh at this,
but sooner or later some one with less prejudice or more sense
than the rest will give it a trial. And the Consul who first makes
a mandarin do business with his coat off will never let him put
it on again. Until then, we shall all go on shouting aimlessly
into space, ignoring the cause of all our failures; and not until
the simple truth is realised will any of our Treaties be of the
slightest use.

Perhaps it will never be realised — there's nothing so conservative as diplomacy, nor so unwilling to listen to anything outside of its own traditions. In that case the P'utzu will swagger
down the corridors of time, for ever getting in its deadly work
on the unsuspecting foreigner. If so, I would support, as an alternative remedy, the proposal of my friend M'Alpine of the
Scotch Colporteur Society, an eminently practical man. He rec-
ommends replacing the present expensive and ineffective Diplomatic Body by an ingeniously constructed set of clockwork
figures with appropriate gestures, phonographic apparatus,
and uniforms complete. The set of twelve (of best materials),
in charge of a Scotch engineer (himself, I think), to be worked
at a total cost of not more than £3000 a year, the figures to
be taken to the Waiwupu free of charge, singly or collectively

according to political emergencies, at least once a week, and the interviews duly recorded and preserved. On this interesting suggestion Mr. M'Alpine will read a paper at the Society's next meeting. (*Here the author goes off into missionary topics of no general interest.*)

·PREPARATIONS·
·for·a·
·GRAND·SORTIE·

CHAPTER XIII

"Now may we
Be each as one that leaves his midnight task
And throws his casement open; and the air
Comes up across the lowlands from the sea."
The Sea Gypsy.

OWARDS the end of November the devout lover of houseboats, his appetite keenly whetted with brief excursions into the nearer hunting-grounds, sets about him to devise ways and means for a cruise of two or three weeks. The matter is by no means simple: first, there is the question of leave, the pacifying of taipans and the goodwill of Penelope, left to face her household cares alone at a time when these are not of the lightest. With M'Nab, for instance, it is an ever-recurring grievance that the best of the shooting comes precisely at that season when his olive branches naturally expect him to play a central part in the preparations for Christmas, and the ingenuity with which he compromises with Mrs. M'Nab and his conscience does equal credit to his heart and head. With the Major, untrammelled by domesticity, and enjoying large opportunities of furlough, the question is simple; all he needs is to find two or three congenial souls and to agree upon the route. So also with Thurlsby — whose gentlemanly calling insists that litigation shall cease while he rests at the appointed seasons. On these two I can therefore generally reckon. For myself, it has happily been established and recognised that these three weeks devoted to the pursuit of health are absolutely necessary to restore the ravages of protracted brain-work, and the matter has long since passed beyond the regions of official or domestic discussion. I believe my wife has told Mrs. Wilden that I always come back from these trips vastly improved in temper and cheerfulness, and she went so far as to suggest that this might be equally beneficial to Mr. Wilden.

As Wilden is notoriously restrained from junketings and jaunts by a velvet hand in an iron glove, I don't suppose the suggestion did much good. Anyhow, when the Major and I invited him to join us last year, he agreed readily enough, and two days later cried off on the plea of pidgin. I told him to promise Mrs. Wilden that we would be back the day before Christmas, and advised seasonable largesse in advance — but to no purpose. It was against him, no doubt, that the year before he had spent Christmas day somewhere up the Pen-yû creek with a jovial crowd instead of in the bosom of his family, and his story about being stopped by a block of rafts had failed to bring him absolution.

For nearly a month Thurlsby, the Major, and I had talked over the coming trip, casting about for an eligible fourth and discussing our destination. In this way one can get a good deal out of a trip long before it begins. With a map of the country, a tin of Craven mixture, and liquid refreshment à discrétion, I know of few pleasanter ways of spending an evening. Whole worlds of hope lie before you, the joys of anticipation keener than those of memory are yours; while, at the touch of imagination, the unknown lands ahead grow rose-coloured and alluring.

First of all there is the choice of the shooting-ground; next, the plan of campaign, which includes division of duties, commissariat, and equipment. To any one who knows anything of houseboats and the idiosyncrasies of those who travel in them, I need hardly say that in these topics alone lies matter for endless argument between *habitués* and friends — argument profitable and pleasing enough as a pastime, but futile in the matter of any definite conclusion. We certainly had come to none, after four specially-devised symposia, not to mention much desultory talk at street corners and in the Club bar.

Take, for instance, the choice of ground. Thurlsby, with the solemn manner which he brings to bear on questions wherein opinions may differ even when they involve no points of law, would spread the map out before him and invite our serious attention. Now Thurlsby has one or two special weaknesses up country. One is, that if ever he has found decent shooting — it may have been ten years ago — in any spot he wants to go back there regardless of the fact that game has its migrations, and that to give a place a good name is enough, in these days, to clean it out. Then, too, he is partial to his creature comforts — his well appointed cabin and the enamelled bath with hot and cold water laid on — and deprecates exchanging the *Heart's Desire* for the uncertainties of any native craft. All of which means that, keen sportsman though he be, Thurlsby's choice of a hunting-ground is apt to be limited by these *faiblesses*. As for Jim, his Celtic temperament inclines him to listen eagerly to every man's Munchausen tales, and his views vary therefore with perplexing rapidity. On two points only is he definite — two things he wants — a rubber of "bridge" after dinner and a reasonable prospect of bamboo partridge; these things granted, he amicably accepts all other conclusions. As for me, I confess to a disposition for pastures

new, and especially for hill country. I long for the broken sky-
line, mountain sides purple at dusk, sunlight and shadow, and
the song of murmuring waters in the glens; I want a change from
the mud-flat land of Kiangsu, with its everlasting paddy fields
and creeks, its kitchen-garden cultivation, its interminable vista
of graves and sheltered hamlets, each an exact reproduction of
all the others. So that, when it comes to the grand sortie, I vote
stoutly for the hill country of Chêkiang.

It was a week before the start, and we had found neither
the fourth man nor our marching route, when a god came to us
from a machine, a globe-trotter from the P. and O. — Lambton
to wit, who gravitated to our party as naturally as woman to
a mirror. He seemed to come to us out of space, heaven-sent,
unto this appointed end, one of those earth-wandering Esaus
that only the Anglo-Saxon race produces, and in twenty-four
hours he was running the whole business with the indisputable
authority of an old campaigner. He had just come from tiger-
shooting in Siam, and was on his way to look for Reeves' and
golden pheasants in the upper Yangtsze — but he took in our
picnic as epicures take an olive between champagne and claret.
That he had never shot bamboo partridge was reason enough
for joining us.

He had brought a letter of introduction to Jim from a brother-
warrior in the Straits, which told of great shikar with seladang,
and asked Jim to put him on to something good. So Jim, after
a discreet and satisfactory inquiry about bridge, put him on to
us. In five minutes the party was complete. We dined together
that night, the map was produced with the smokes, and in half
an hour our plans were settled. Thurlsby was eloquent in praise
of Huchow and the Meichee country, Jim told us stories of big
bags that had just come down from a party at Chinkiang, and
rumours of some marvellous great deer in the hills near Ta-
tung — but Lambton, looking at the map with an unbiassed eye,
pronounced for the Chientang river. Were there not deer and pig
in the hills, wild-fowl and geese on the broad stream, pheasant

and partridge in the valleys? I had some photographs of the upper reaches, and these, combined with Lambton's opinion, converted the K.C. before we got to our second whisky. To-morrow,
with the *Heart's Desire* looming up reproachfully on his mental
horizon, he would, no doubt, have misgivings; but to-night, as
we discussed the hiring of boats, and many devices therein for
dogs and men, he became enthusiastic. So the start was fixed;
Jim, by reason of his bachelor state, having the freedom of his
cook, was appointed commissariat officer; Thurlsby agreed to
supply and equip eight picked beaters, and to arrange for boats
and towage to Hangchow; Lambton, having time to spare, was
to look after the liquor supply, ammunition, and general req-
uisites; while I, boasting the acquaintance of a junk company's
manager on the Chientang, undertook to engage the river-
boats, and arrange for porterage from the Grand Canal through
Hangchow city to the river.

So the plan of campaign was laid, and, as we four stolid Britons sat yarning over the map, Jim's unromantic dining room
was filled with the sorcery of the silent places of which we
spoke, the sights and sounds of the great outdoor world. Stirred
into mysterious life at the sight of a few familiar names, red
lines and blue blotches on a clumsy map, the magic alchemy of
memory summoned within those four walls a thousand echoes
from the past — ours were the keen unsullied air of hills that
guide blue waters to the sea, shimmer of morning sunlight on
fields bejewelled with gossamer; shouts of beaters in the copses, where fir and bamboo gather to harmonious shades; heavy
scent of bracken, where pheasants lie close at mid-day, — a scent
which for me always brings a swift message of autumn-tinted
English cliffs, and a boy ferreting gleefully, amidst the tall ferns,
for ever and ever.

Ours were joys of prowess in bygone days — not diminished
by lapse of time — chances and strange happenings of the chase,
with many opinions and inventions. Some of Thurlsby's stories
we knew of old, but Lambton had not heard them, and there is

an etiquette of restraint on such occasions which we observed. So we wandered in fancy over the land, the blithe call of the wild in our ears, slaying once more the ghostly birds and beasts of past sorties with much content. That Lambton had stories to tell we knew, but to-night he was sternly practical — note-book in hand he insisted on solid information and cold facts, leading us firmly but gently from our hills of fancy to the Chientang river. So Jim and I got out the log-book of a trip two years ago — a trip where the bag of geese had been so heavy that we ceased from pursuing them — and he took down the dates and figures as stolidly as a broker takes quotations. Then he inquired tenderly after our tastes and habits in the matter of drink, recording them carefully and without that criticism which the matter invited. Finally, he noted our various suggestions as to general impedimenta, of the things each man should bring and those to be bought or hired. Between Thurlsby's boudoir apartment and Jim's barrack-room notions he struck a happy medium, adding some sensible ideas from his own stock, so that under his masterful hand order and precision gradually took form and substance out of chaos. The man was a Kitchener, wasted by accident of birth and patrimony — a specimen of the resourceful practical type of Briton that finds and founds our Colonies, or wanders into the uttermost places of the earth — men usually lost to service of the Empire by reason of the stereotyped futility of our military and political systems.

Jim had got some patent barrack gear from the stores in the autumn, dodgy, collapsible devices of strange forms; things that posed as card-tables and arm-chairs by day, and promised to become washstands or beds by night; also a rubber bath that folded itself into a cardboard case no bigger than a map. They were all Wolseley's, or French's, or Buller's, and Jim was certain that they were just the thing for boat furniture. Also he had a field tent — two men's load — which was sure to come in handy somehow. Lambton wasn't enthusiastic about these triumphs of military ingenuity, and I noticed that his list of gear included things that implied want of faith, but he said the tent would be very useful as an overall for the boat in case of bad weather; for the rest, he thought you could knock up nearly all the necessary fittings of a boat with a few planks and some rope. Jim smiled in a tired sort of way, and said we'd be very grateful for his gear before the trip was over. Thurlsby, impartial and superior, merely observed that he would bring his own camp-bed, and could sit on it in case of need; and suggested a couple of tin bath-trunks as convenient things for carrying dog biscuits.

Last came the official list of dogs, and Lambton must have had some doubts as to the prospects of the chase if he believed all the things we said about our own and each other's kennels. The K.C. believes in Shuster, his thick-set German pointer, as he does in Magna Charta, and when Jim began by asking him if he was going to bring his sausage-dog, there was a brief and brilliant exchange of courtesies.

Lambton, upon our better acquaintance, showed me the entry in his note-book recording his impressions of the dog inventory, as freely stated. It read thus:

Mr. Thurlsby's "Shuster" — German pointer — steady worker — requires to be carried home in a basket.

Same owner's "Di" — setter — good at quail, but prefers working covert with the beaters.

The Major's "Peter" — spaniel — fat and wheezy — alleged cure of recent attack of mange not generally credited.

Same owner's "Damit" — Irish setter — generally works out of range — keen on domestic poultry.

Same owner's "Pat" — Irish retriever addicted to fighting — good at water and does *not* eat wild-fowl.

Mr. Phil Marsden's "Rocket" — half-breed pointer — suffers from dysentery — partially deaf, but generally finds his own way to the boat.

Same owner's "Nelly" — pointer — good on partridge, but prefers retrieving sticks or stones.

Same owner's "Rex"—spaniel—fast and independent in covert—
when following deer or hare generally lost for some hours.

"You fellows need all your own dogs," he said, "and I'd rather not borrow any of them. But if you know of any one who's
got a couple of decent animals that I could beg or hire, just a
spare beast or two in case of accidents, I'd go round and have a
look at them."

Jim knew several—two that belonged to a police inspector,
and Wilden's brace of spaniels—all very useful. Then there was
Willoughby's retriever, not half a bad dog when you got into
his ways.

"Isn't that the dog Willoughby lent to Major Appleton last
year," asked the K.C., "the one he sent back by river steamer
from Wuhu without apologies or thanks?"

"Ay, that's the dog. But Willoughby had forgotten to mention
his little peculiarities. He was a very good dog in some ways,
but he had an irresistible penchant for tame ducks, so that Willoughby generally had to lead him on a chain through villages
in the creek country. Ignorance of this fact cost Appleton four
dollars and a good deal of trouble on the very first morning, for
old Bos—that was his name—got into a large flock, and brought
in six before they collared him. Then, too, he was a good retriever, but as jealous as a woman, and would fight any other
dog that tried to bring in a bird anywhere near him. Appleton
said he hadn't come up country to go off by himself every day,
so the end of it was that the poor beast was shipped back in
disgrace. All the same, as dogs go, I've seen worse."

"Bos isn't in the picture," said Lambton. "I wouldn't mind
the duck mania so much, but a fighter isn't curable in one trip.
Never mind, I think we shall do with the lot we've got, and if
not we can beat up another couple by advertising."

So, after solemnly drinking success to the trip, we made our
way homewards through silent streets, infinitely superior to
their material world of go-downs and sordid trades. Before us

lay the wide prospect of the Chientang river, its snow-tipped hills and pleasant valleys. We could afford to be sorry for these pitiful city dwellers, and to wish for them a better measure of wisdom.

·TO·THE·CHIENTANG·RIVER·

CHAPTER XIV

"Truly the light is sweet, and a pleasant thing it is for the eyes to behold the sun." — *Ecclesiastes*.

BRIGHT frosty night early in December, the soft influences of the Pleiades and belted Orion shining out a welcome and a promise; a pale new moon dropping swiftly to the horizon, her silver song faint in the glorious shouting of the stars, and on the river a whispering north wind, filling the sails of ghostly junks. Across and far down the stream the blue and yellow lights of the long water-front; behind us, the Bond with its pulsating traffic of humanity, great houses, with their thousand eyes like an encircling line, guarding the human ant-heap of the Settlements. This was the picture as we foregathered at dinner-time to the boats. The *Heart's De-sire* lay moored to the jetty, nose up stream; through her cabin windows a glimpse of the dinner-table, of which Thurlsby is so justly proud, in the air a gently-tickling odour of baked meats, heart-warming harbingers of good things to come. Beyond her lay the *Saucy Jane*, her upper deck laden with the Major's camp-kit and the commissariat; her fo'castle resounding with hideous turmoil of dogs, in which the voice of Pat, ever belligerent, grew shriller as the coolies intervened. And beyond the *Saucy Jane* lay the launch, sturdily puffing huge clouds of Japanese smoke to warm itself for the run to Hangchow, 140 miles away.

And so, when the Major has bidden an affectionate (though duly *nonchalant*) farewell to Miss Betty, when the last instructions have been given, and Thurlsby's boy in a bustling ricksha has brought the last consignment of things forgotten, the cry is "all aboard." A little knot of Nancy Lees and brother-sportsmen stand to wish us god-speed and good-luck; their waving hats and handkerchiefs pass swiftly into the night as we glide out upon the river. And then we stand awhile at the bows, the nipping, eager air tingling in our veins, and watch the lights go by, listening to the glad music of rushing water, tasting the fine savour of the night, revelling like schoolboys in the prospect of the days before us. Thus, no doubt, the World strikes a 'ticket-of-leave-man' on his first morning out.

Begone dull care for three immortal weeks! No more, for one-and-twenty blissful days, of bricks and mortar, of soul-sapping routine or Society's anæmic conventions. Back now to the land, to man's forfeited estate of freedom; whither neither 'chit coolies' nor Reuter's telegrams can follow, where the slings and arrows of outrageous pidgin cannot assail us. For the next three weeks let the whole fabric of civilisation be shattered and totter to its doom; it is naught to us. Let Wales beat Scotland at football, China reabolish corruption by Imperial Edicts, Roosevelt propound once more the ridiculous equality of all men, and the House of Lords rush headlong to its fate – we shall not know or care. In the World, but not of it, henceforth until we see the smoke of the Settlements again; and at the thought, in my mind's eye, I catch a glimpse of the uncounted millions out yonder who live and die happily unconscious of all the earth-shaking matters that so greatly perturb us. But Jim is singing lustily a Berserker song; this is no time or place for philosophy: so to dinner and port wine and bridge, and then, over sociable reminiscent pipes, perhaps a night-cap or two, for to-morrow will be a day of idleness.

Of the journey to Hangchow I will not tell, for it is told in the books of the Globe-trotters. All night and all day we steamed through the rich river-lands of Kiangsu, the rice and mulberry country of Chekiang, through the close-packed narrow waterways of Kazay and Kashing, down the long reaches of the Grand Canal, whose time-defying masonry speaks of glories long departed; through villages pulsating with life; past forlorn places, where the ghosts of Taipings and Imperial 'braves' walk unappeased, seeking their tombs; ancient walled cities, silent as their dead. In the Tamen Creek, a famous hunting-ground in the days before the great plain was reclaimed, we went ashore, to still the growing clamour of the kennels and to stretch our legs. A two hours' walk along the banks, the pack ranging wide and free, accounted for five pheasants, a brace of partridge, three hares, and a Mandarin drake, so that Thurlsby located the spot (by the numbers on the telegraph poles) for future visitations. Thus, with a sense of virtue, we came before midnight to the Hangchow settlement (that triumph of the Chinese mind over Japanese matter), and anchored on the farther side, remote from the wrangling of junk masters and the barking of the pariahs that frequent the landing-place by the Custom House. And in the morning, before the first stirring of life on the *Saucy Jane*, there appeared a button-tipped emissary of my friend the junk manager, announcing that all was ready. Next, from the *Heart's Desire* came the voice of Lambton, denouncing sloth and giving orders for the trek; so, having roused the denisons of pantry and kitchen from their lairs, I turned my attention to the serious task of getting Jim out of his bunk.

For an easy-going man the Major shows particular obstinacy on this question of getting up; in the absence of bugles and other helps to military discipline he revels in luxurious ease, like any *merveilleuse*. From the blanketed depths of his chrysalis state he likes to discuss comfortably the ethics and philosophy of early rising, expounding the nothingness of time and the foolishness of haste, while, with the contemplative eye of an alligator, he watches the preparations for breakfast; and, because misery likes company, the sound of his contented gruntings, while I shiver over my shaving, becomes a cause of offence. In the matter of arguments and ingenious excuses he has become, from long practice, so expert that discussion is a burden; I have long since exhausted all the subtle devices by which a man may be artfully lured from his bunk. Dog-fights on deck and reports of duck ahead he ignores; shots fired on the bank move him only to mild inquiries as to their results, while in altercations with natives or the crew he gives me *carte blanche* to act for him, proffering sleepy suggestions. If the weather be fine he will generally unroll himself as the savour of coffee comes from the pantry, but on rainy mornings vigorous measures are necessary. To let the camp-bed down suddenly by one end disturbs the chrysalis; thereafter, cold water applied to the unprotected parts induces life and movement. Lethargy leaves him with the bed-clothes; protesting prodigious plans of activity, he carols like a lark to the sound of splashing waters; and at breakfast, which he eats with his loins girded up, he will ask you to observe that he is ready before every one else and expatiate on the wisdom of taking things calmly. Next morning, *da capo*; so that the daily raising of this military wreck becomes a business of stratagems and much thought. I tried once to shame him to a sense of the selfish wickedness of sloth, but the result was disappointing. Jim's exculpatory theory is that a fellow should never get up until the other has done dressing; otherwise, he says, you get in each other's way, and then both snap and growl, not meaning to be nasty, of course, but because the chill hasn't been taken off things. So he sacrifices and effaces himself while I take the chill off. On the occasion in question, however, my own particular virtue of

activity was disinclined to assert itself, because of an unmistakable lethargy of the legs begotten of a long and empty-handed
tramp the day before. Probably it was lack of vitality that disposed me for once to resent Jim's arguments as things of monstrous injustice. So when the boy had brought tea and let in the
light of day, I proclaimed the equality of all men on houseboats
and my intention to give him precedence in dressing and the
dog-walk on the bank. Jim's interest was aroused to an extent
rarely induced at this time of day; he rolled over, swathing himself more tightly in the blankets, and seemed to be really relish-
ing the flavour of this new and original idea. No doubt his legs
were also reluctant to move, and so, firmly declining to assume
a position which he described as mine by usage, merit, senior-
ity, and special qualifications, he proceeded to argue the matter for an hour, at the end of which time he became gradually
incoherent, and finally dropped off again to profound sleep. I
did the same — and at tiffin-time we compromised by getting up
together. Jim said it was one of the best mornings' sport he had
had — and the result of it is that he now enjoys uncontested right
of eminent domain of his bunk until I have taken the chill off.

Curious, when you come to think of it, how great a part in
this absurd life of ours is spent in getting ready for bed and then
getting out of it again; how, with one accord, when the light
has gone out of the day, poor tailor-made humanity must drop
all its buzzing business and chances of joy, must strip off all its
brave trappings and wrappings and creep between white sheets
of oblivion. That every time this planet revolves, we must re-
hearse, each for himself, the great mystery of silence that lies beyond; this, I say, is a wonderful thing. For I can imagine a world
peopled with forked radishes very like ourselves, all of whose
little days should be given to the uninterrupted fulfilment of
the purposes of existence (whatever they may be), who would
not need to be wound up over every twenty-four hours by this
soft-handed brother of Death. A world without beds or pillows,
or weariness or waking, seems to me as properly conceivable

for the temporary home of intelligent puppets as this whirling absurdity in which each creature exists by eating its fellows. All our fine writing about sleep, our reveries and croon-songs and *berceuses*, all this chorus of gratitude for oblivion, makes really a very pretty indictment of the scheme of things created, and I, for one, admit to a sneaking sympathy and admiration for that Baltimore lady who, having realised that going to bed is an inevitable part of our ludicrous existence, decided to simplify matters by remaining there for the rest of her days. This is at least logical, whereas Jim's attitude is simply irritating.

On this occasion, however, under the stern hand of Lambton, he made but little argument—our pet domestic weaknesses have a horror of strangers—so that, before the sun had raised the edge of the soft white veil lying on the paddy fields, we were having breakfast, with a pandemonium of packing raging from stem to stern. And wherever the fray was thickest, wherever dogs and men and shapeless masses of gear were inextricably mixed, thither came Lambton, and chaos melted before him. Even Jim, surveying the turmoil from a safe seat on the ice-box, was pleased to express approval.

Getting to Hangchow city by water (there is no land route) affords a very typical object lesson of the ways for which our Celestial friends are peculiar. In any other country the provincial capital would either have been built at the end of the Grand Canal, or if, because of ancient necromancy, it had to be miles away, there would at least be a road wide enough for cart traffic. But at the back of the Chinese economical system lies the hoary axiom that the wayfarer is common prey, the trader lawful plunder, so that communication with a great city is arranged chiefly with a view to the levelling of successive squeezes on merchandise and man. (Which, by the way, was the reason why, until the Boxers made their upheaval, the Peking Railway stopped five miles outside the gates, why other railways will stop short of many other places, and why steam navigation is discouraged on inland waters; for which dull matters consult the works of

The Western Lake Pagoda, Hangchow

travelling M.P.'s.).

And so it is not so easy to get to Hangchow even by water, for at the end of the Grand Canal you must unload everything into small boats, owned and controlled by predatory tribes, which boats, with all their contents, are pulled over rough locks, by other birds of prey, to narrow waterways beyond. Whether you take this route depends a good deal on the weather, and on what part of the great straggling city you want to reach – the alternative being that you and your belongings are carried from the Kung Chen bridge by human beasts of burden through an interminable wilderness of smelly streets. So narrow and so ingeniously strewn with obstacles are these slimy purlieus that no vehicle, not even the degenerate ricksha of Nanking, could ply there. And so, all day long, an endless chain of coolies comes and goes on the stone-paved alley-way that connects the outer world with Hangchow (Messer Marco Polo's "City of Heaven"), poor staggering derelicts, doing in their thousands the work of one locomotive, because a thousand lives are worth less than a donkey-engine in the Flowery Kingdom.

My friend the junk manager had arranged for our kit to go on by small boats as far as possible, and thence to the Chientang river by porters; for us there were sedan-chairs, flimsy things covered with shiny green cloth, whose attendant scarecrows, three to each, were waiting for us on the bank. By ten o'clock the last motley cargo of coolies, dogs, and impedimenta, had started, Ah Kong and Gehazi bringing up the rear, and as we mustered on the Customs jetty, the *Saucy Jane* and the *Heart's Desire* turned their noses towards Shanghai and slowly disappeared. Thurlsby said he realised what marooned people must feel, and commented critically on the appearance of every native boat in sight. Also, at the hybrid shop near the bridge, where a Cantonese retails the things which 'foreign devils' eat and drink, he bought several tins of Keating's, with the air of one who intends to meet his fate as a gallant gentleman should.

The entire population of the Hangchow settlement turned

out to see us start, as to a festival. The crowd was not oppressive, consisting of seven Europeans, one Japanese lady, and two melancholy-looking dogs, but it was hospitable after the manner of all the remote places where white men exist to teach the Chinese the hard lesson of honest administration. They gave us drinks, offered us all manner of assistance and good advice, begged us to stay a day or two and try the shooting near the Settlement, and asked about every one they knew from Canton to Corea. When, driven by Lambton, we eventually started, they stood in a brave little group and cheered. And my mind went back instinctively to Mark Tapley and the thriving city of Eden.

There is something more than a resemblance to that delectable city "as it appeared on paper," in the foreign Settlements devised by the Chinese since their war with Japan in 1894: the plan is identical, from the laying-out of broad roads that lead nowhere to the sale of town-lots where no town can ever be. Hangchow is perhaps the most interesting example of that form of political activity which the Chinese Government has devised, in these latter days, to adjust the clamorous views of the patriots to the necessities and rapacities of the Button'd man. And when one remembers that the city (*entre autres*) was opened to the trade and residence of foreign merchants, as part of the purchase price of peace, fourteen years ago, the actual result as it confronts one to-day is not without a certain humorous quality. It is a quality which no longer appeals to the enterprising individuals whose names adorn the boundary stones, standing like sentries at the corners of these melancholy swamps, individuals who, by the eye of faith, saw here a new Shanghai and paid for the land accordingly, but it is there all the same. To the Mandarin, riding snug in his sedan-chair, the result of these activities of the foreign devil must be a subtle jest, of very delicate flavour. Come with your armies, your consuls, your missionaries, and your machines; bombard us and destroy, and go your ways with more solemn treaties, if you will—and behold the result! There lie the marshes, familiar haunt of the heron, as they lay on the day when Nieh Chih Kuei congratulated the Japanese (and himself) on the assured prosperity of the new trade-centre. The much-vaunted roads, proof of local municipal good faith, can still be traced by the lighter green of their rank grass; quail and hare use them gladly as basking-grounds on sunny days.

In addition to its crop of boundary stones, the Settlement boasts the usual public buildings necessary to the complete isolation and repose of the foreign trader. First, there is the Custom House, surrounded by quarters for the staff; ungainly structures that loudly assert the presence of the white men and remind Young China of that birthright of well-paid billets which shall presently be the reward of patriotism. Seen thus, flaunting their bold chimneys and curveless lines in derision of all *'feng-shui,'* these excrescences are instinct with the challenge of nonconformity. In the city, hushed up in crowded streets, they might have been forgiven, but here, conspicuous against the bleak back-ground, they simply proclaim to every junk-man on the river, to every farmer in the fields, the message of those ways which are not as the ancient ways of this people. Setting art and fitness aside, it is always a matter for wonder to me that our missionaries and merchants have been unable to live in something less aggressive than the dwellings they erect in inland places. All of which is a useless digression.

"On the tow path"

Beyond the Custom House is a police station, another proof of Chinese activity on Model Settlement lines — the fact that there is no population to police being a matter of secondary importance.

There is a European Superintendent and a squad of native con-
stables who mournfully parade the water-front, accepting their
uneventful, useless profession with Oriental stolidity. Finally, at
the corner of the Settlement nearest the city, whence all its teeming trade must pass to and from the city, there stands a building within whose unpretentious walls lurk mighty forces, the
Lekin office to wit. Here, in the hands of mild, goggled *shupan*
and elusive runners, works the vast noiseless machinery which
throttles trade from Harbin to Hainan; one tentacle of the insatiable octopus that battens on all merchandise that travels by
land or by water, enormous, unassailable, defying all weapons
and words of diplomacy. Of the secret parts of this machinery
we Europeans know as little to-day as we knew forty years
ago; of the collection and divisions of the spoil we shall remain
complacently ignorant to the end. Wherever it is to the interest
of the Celestial system that we should remain unenlightened,
there are we surrounded with darkness impenetrable; no better
proof of this than the recent solemn discussion and restoring of
lekin-abolition in our Treaties. All we know of this thing is its
result: we see it throttling one trade staple after another, we see
its rapacities extending, and we know that neither by railways,
inland navigation, nor any other subtle device of the white men
can those rapacities be checked, for lekin will only die with the
passing of the Mandarin. And those people who talk hopefully
of conference and commutations, of the Mackay Treaty, and Pro-
fessors of Political Economy in Peking—well, may they live to
see their dream come true.

For the time being, the foreign merchant, enjoying by Treaty
the benefits of trade and residence in this provincial capital of
Chekiang, must be content to dwell in the marshland set aside
for him where, so long as the police and lekin stations do their
duty, no Chinese trader will ever come to disturb him. Thirty-
seven years ago it was recorded in one of the white man's paper
victories that the area of the Settlements was exempt from lekin,
and many a paper battle has since been waged to maintain that

position. This modest little station on the edge of the Hangchow is the last word of China on the subject; as for ours, you may see it across the river yonder, the house where a British Consul lived during the foolish days of hope, and until realisation of this subtle joke enabled the Treasury to effect another laudable economy by removing him.[1] And the same grim jest has been perpetrated with equal success in every one of the newer Treaty Ports, so that, good reader, when next it is triumphantly announced in the House of Commons that Fat Sham or Ping Pong-foo has been opened to trade, by reason of the efforts of the Liberal (or Conservative) Government, you will understand this to mean that unhealthy spots have been set apart for the foreigner — commercial isolation camps — at a convenient distance from these enlightened cities, in which, under no circumstances, will he be permitted to buy or sell. And yet there are people who profess to see no humour in politics!

I was discussing these things with Jim, wherever the traffic allowed of conversation, as we trudged the first mile or two towards the city. He takes but faint interest in the murkier problems of Chinese economics, but à propos of lekin, he told me of one of his former pupils, a philosophical young warrior who, in due season, ran to fat and conceived a strong distaste for lethal weapons and the possibility of going to his grave for any phantasy or trick of fame. So he discarded the arts of war, acquired a pretty Soochow girl en secondes noces, and got himself appointed to one of the lekin stations on the Quinsan route. There Jim saw him, long-gowned, begoggled, growing pumpkins on a trellis, studying the classics by night, and the art of squeezing by day; living by the water-side in a ramshackle place, half-yamên, half-harem, amidst a perpetual wrangle of boatmen, runners, dogs, and the general public — and all on the princely salary of 30 dollars a month. "It was a rum thing to find him there," said Jim, "for all the world like a bit out of Analects, with 'Buddha's fingers' on the table, and a bird-cage over his front door; because only two

---

[1] He has lately gone back there — another joke.

years before he had been a fiery reformer sort of fellow, with his pig-tail under a Japanese cap and braided trousers — but I suppose the classical instinct is latent in their system, like cat-hunting in a terrier."

"Yes," I said, "it's wonderful how quick the Western-learning species reverts to the Confucian type — there's no Conservative so bigoted as your converted Radical. Did he tell you anything about the economics of lekin?"

"Not exactly — but when I asked him how he liked the job, and what were its prospects, he led me to infer that they were something better than those of a military man, apart from the fact, grateful to his philosophic soul, that he now runs no chance of perishing untimely for other people's foolish ideas. What he said was 'that it wasn't the salary, but the income' that made the attractions of a lekin station."

'Not the salary, but the income' — a neat way of summing up the hoary system which China invented (like everything else) centuries ago, and which American Mayors have now adopted with the necessary modern improvements. 'Tis a good word.

Walking on flagstones, slippery with immemorial slime, through narrow streets (where tubs of fish, piles of vegetables and old clothes encroach upon the right of way) did not appeal to Thurlsby as congenial exercise, and when a dog, bolting from a pork-shop, ran between his legs, he gave it up and we took to the chairs. By a succession of miracles we reached the city without killing any of the old women and children upon whom our coolies rushed with blood-curdling noises, and in a little while we came upon the rear-guard of our transport, a tatterdemalion sitting placidly by the road side with one of Jim's patent convertible articles slung on one end of a pole, and a bag of dog-biscuits on the other. A little farther on we saw Thurlsby's dogs ingeniously moored to our kitchen stove outside a wine-shop, flanked by a miscellaneous assortment of bedding and provender; and for the next hour the flotsam and jetsam of our porterage greeted us, lending a certain home-like and familiar aspect to street corners and tea-houses. Jim, anxious for his Lares, said he felt like sailing through wreckage. Lambton, whose commissariat instincts were outraged by this casual procession of our goods, was for collecting and driving the stragglers before us; with difficulty I persuaded him not to hustle the East. The methods of Chinese transport are chaotic to any eye but that of faith, but their results are good, and I knew well that every one of these hundred and fifty waifs would turn up at the appointed time and place without loss or damage of a single package. When you bear in mind that many purloinable things are packed in loose bundles and netted baskets, and that a carrier's labour earns something less than a pound a month, you are bound to admit that the Chinese system of collective responsibility produces in the mass a very decent substitute for honesty.

Through the city at last, out of its eastern gate to more suburban alleys; mulberry gardens, fir-shaded graves, and the houses of rich gentry; finally to the turmoil and traffic of the Chientang river, where the paper and timber merchants' hongs stretch for miles along the high-walled bank. Here the chair coolies were paid off — the equivalent of 1s. 6d. a man for the twelve miles — and choosing a spot on the wall least frequented by dogs and beggars, we sat down to smoke until the coming of the transport. Lambton, like a benevolent conjurer, produced sandwiches and a capacious flask; the sun shone warm on our backs, and our souls were at peace. Below us the broad stream lay crowded with strange craft innumerable — sampans, slipper-boats, cargo-wallahs, and passenger junks, of curious designs and rigs, unlike the deep-water types of the Yangtsze, but the same, no doubt, that carried the river's trade when Hangchow was the capital of the Tang Dynasty. The tide being out and the stream low, boats were discharging their cargoes into wooden-wheeled carts, drawn by slow-moving oxen, through the shallows; passengers were coming and going between the junks and the shore on planks raised above the mud by trestles. Bright sunlight everywhere, and the unceasing din inseparable from the Orient's struggle for life.

Far away to the south we could see the river gleaming at the foot of purple hills, the hills amidst which we too were to go joyfully; and the sight consoled us for the increasing attentions of the loafers whose friendliness, combined with great personal uncleanliness, eventually made us evacuate the position. So, the junk manager having turned up opportunely, we proceeded to inspect the boats.

There was one for us, a great unwieldy-looking thing that reminded one of the Canton flower-boats and Noah's Ark, as depicted on Bryant and May's match-boxes — a boat that drew less than two feet of water, with a crew of five coolies and a lowdah, and a big mast forward of the cabin and two long sweeps astern. The cabin, boarded and roofed with oiled pine, was divided off into cubicles, one of Noah's inventions no doubt; back of the cabin was the lowdah's lair, a darksome cubby-hole, stuffed with bedding, facing a primitive kitchen of the native type. The crew, we were informed, slept in the murky depths beneath the cabin floor, a piece of news which Thurlsby received without demonstration of delight.

Two other smaller boats, thatched with rough matting, were the Ark's convoy — one for the dogs and cook, the other for the dog-coolies and beaters. There was good kennel-room for the pack in the square foreholds, and a bundle of rice straw, bought from a floating haystack along-side, made them look inviting enough for any tired dog.

Lambton was, of course, ordering people about (putting things ship-shape, he called it), and had speedily removed the cubicle partitions from the port side of the Ark, thus making space large enough for four camp-beds, the dinner table, and other pieces of resistance. He located a bathroom next the kitchen, and for each man a cubicle on the starboard side for the storage of kit and gear. He had found a Chinese pen and ink, and was busy writing up his assignments of places and their uses after the manner of the Ordnance Store Department, when Jim,

A BOATMAN OF THE CHIENTANG RIVER

philosophically basking outside on the spare straw, announced the arrival of the first of the transport corps. Thurlsby, obviously dejected by the inspection of the Ark, observed that the wretched creature probably was the only survivor. Anyhow, there he was, a human scarecrow coming along the wall at a good dog-trot, cheerily swinging a tin bath and my kit-bag through the crowd. We cheered him as one man.

And after him, by twos and threes, they drifted in, until in half an hour they had all come safely to the shore, where their burdens were dumped in a line at the foot of the wall, tallied by the Man with the Button, and pronounced correct. It was a long line, and the sight of all this monstrous collection of worldly goods made one wonder whether these poor beasts of burden, knowing nothing and needing nothing of the thousand things essential to our existence, were not perhaps happier than we. Looking at the matter in this light, it certainly seemed ridiculous that the needs of four men should involve the expenditure of energy represented by that interminable line of tatterdemalions.

At a word from the Man with the Button, the line shouldered its poles, each man depositing his load under Lambton's masterful eye in its appointed place; and as the sun dropped to the level of the roofs above us the last man filed out with his dole of cash, the gang-planks were handed in, our moorings slipped, and we dropped out into the stream. Thereafter, much bustle of bags and coolies, unpacking and sorting of gear, until, as the twilight faded and the young moon's faint rays glimmered tremulous on the water, the Ark's interior presented a comfortable and business-like appearance. With rugs and mats on the floor, Jim's tent spread on the roof; blankets slung to catch the wind that came shrewdly through many a gaping creek in the planks, with lamps swinging fore and aft, and oil-stoves cunningly disposed, even Thurlsby admitted that the result was grateful and comforting. And when, as we sat at dinner, the tide came in, with a great clamour and turmoil arising from the boats along the wall as the bore rushed past them, our crew, howling like the rest, hoisted anchor. We were off, and not a man of us at that moment would have changed places with Mahmud on his golden throne.

Ah, those are the meals to remember! Meals eaten with light hearts in goodly fellowship. Take all your banquetings and feastings of uncongenial souls, eating indigestible food to the glory of society, and give me some good honest food with a decent glass of wine, in the places of contentment and good cheer! Not many such are vouchsafed to us, as things are ordained, but when they come, they leave memories that linger fragrant as jasmine and lavender. I think each of us four hardened individuals felt this, grateful to the gods for the hour and the scene, as we smoked our pipes on the fore-deck after dinner, listening to the gentle lap, lap of the water under the bows, and to the crooning song of a coolie in the stern, and watching the pearl-grey and silver track of moonlight on the dark stream.

Nobody wanted to talk — this world of river and hills, these murmuring voices of wind and waves, the real world which we forget in the huckstering caravanserai of men's making, it claims, when we find it suddenly again, a tribute of silence that we pay instinctively; our idle talk is hushed, under these stars, as in a cathedral. Jim indeed made an attempt at conversation, asking Thurlsby whether his conception of immortality included the possibility of excursions from Arcturus to Sirius and beyond, and if so, what sort of society he expected to find there; but he was not encouraged.

As we turned in, after a libation to Diana, I summoned the lowdah, christened Noah by common consent, partly on account of his ship's build and partly because of his unmistakably bibulous features. To him I gave orders for the night, to sail as long as the wind lasted, and if it gave out to yuloh till daylight. Fuyang, our first hunting-ground, must be in sight by breakfast-time; after that his merry men might sleep the clock around. Noah grunted. I promised largesse if we got there in time; if not, revilings and a fine. Another grunt. He must keep touch with the other boats, never allowing them out of sight. Another grunt. Did he quite understand? "Yes," he grunted. So we turned in.

·DISCIPLINE·
· ·ON· · ·
·BOARD·THE·ARK·

CHAPTER XV

"Item: that the fleete shall keep together and not separate themselves asunder, as much as by winde and weather may be done or permitted." (From the Ordinances instructions and advertisements of and for the direction of the intended voyage for Cathay, compiled by the right worshipfull M. Sebastian Cabota, esquire, 1553.)

T midnight I awoke; for a moment all the subtle atoms and essences that make up the living Ego, the legion forces of consciousness and memory, refused to return from their wanderings in the great Shadow Land; it needed the familiar rumble of Jim's snore to restore the realities of time and place. At that stertorous summons each particle of grey matter stood smartly to attention, and the citadel was manned against the terrors of darkness. Swiftly, then, the captain of those mysterious hosts reassured me of my pin-prick place in the Universe. Next came the reports of outposts, restoring communication between yesterday's rear-guard and the advanced line of to-morrow. So I sat up in bed, listening for the song of the wind in the sail or the squeak of the yuloh on its pivot. There was no sign of life or movement on board, neither murmur of gliding water nor splash of pole from the bows. We were at anchor, laid snugly by in some sheltering backwater; every man on board was asleep.

Slipping on a dressing-gown and Mongolian socks, I groped my way to the stern. A spluttering lamp tied to the rudder-post showed the yulohs drawn in-board and idle, the sail was down, its cordage creaking in the breeze, which came gently whispering across the river on its way to the south. The other boats lay moored a length astern. The tide had ebbed; phantom junks, silent and mysterious, were gliding down in mid-stream. It was an unfamiliar and unfriendly world, under the thousand glittering eyes of night.

Noah was in his bunk, deep buried under a mass of greasy quilts, a samshu bottle on a shelf near his head exhaling its fragrance as the key-note of a fantastic medley of stinks.

"O son of a turtle," said I, " get up!"

I said it once, — I said it twice, — I went and shouted in his ear, but he slept as sleep the drunken or the dead. So I pulled off the quilts. He gave a little quivering sigh, like a tired child, and rolled over on his stomach, as one who protects something precious. Then I prodded him with the first kitchen implement that came handy, which happened to be the toasting-fork. This stirred him, at last, to incoherent speech.

"Head wind," he grunted, "ebb tide. There is no help for it, you can't go on to-night." And swiftly clutching the bedding he rolled it tightly round him, with his back to the wall, looking out upon me with a goblin blood-shot eye that blinked horribly in the flickering candle-light.

"Thou lump of baked mud, predestined to re-birth as a pig, get up!"

I reviled him, argued and threatened, — he tucked himself the tighter in his wrappings, and finally addressed himself once more to sleep. So I found a jug of water and poured it down the back of his neck. That did it: with a yell as of ten thousand scalded cats, Noah arose. In five minutes three of the crew had tumbled up drowsily from the depths; two manned the yuloh, one went forward to pole, and we were under way.

I mention this incident because it reveals several truths useful to houseboat travellers: firstly, that if you sleep at night, the lowdah will assuredly sleep also; secondly, that while lowdahs as a class are truculent and depraved — for reasons already explained — a drunken lowdah is the very devil; thirdly, as was said long ago by an early British diplomatist who had mastered some of the secrets of the East, these people yield nothing to reason, but everything to fear; and, lastly, that there is nothing so terrifying to a Chinaman as cold water applied to, or near, his head.

The jealous care with which the Celestial guards his pigtail from water is a peculiar characteristic of the race, which the Rev. Arthur Smith has neglected to explain. The fact is due, no doubt, to some deep-rooted instinct, some remote aversion of organic memory; be that as it may, its results confront us every day, in the umbrellas and enormous hats of husbandmen, in the effect of a shower on the most excited mob. 'Tis a subject which deserves the attention of the Royal Asiatic Society.

Noah was not a fair specimen of the Chientang river men, who, as a class, are good-humoured philosophers and well disposed. They have a certain sturdy independence of bearing, not ungrateful in a land where servility largely prevails; towards officialdom and politics they are cheerfully indifferent, unless their time-honoured rights are infringed or there be talk of steam-launches invading the river. It is a boast with these water-men that their forefathers have sailed the Chientang junks since the days of the Yuan Dynasty, and they would have you know that the Manchus are usurpers. But the Throne's affairs are not theirs, and so long as the tax collector is reasonable and trade brisk, they are not concerned with questions of State. As for the foreigner, if he be a missionary who bargains like a native and travels in a hurry, let him use his own boat; but sportsmen are notoriously squeezable, heaven-sent givers of largesse, whose boats move leisurely, with long days of rest—and therefore welcome. They have something of the sporting instinct, too, these sturdy oarsmen, and no little knowledge of the habits of water-fowl, and if you treat them well (which only means as fellow-creatures) they will tell you where to look for feeding geese, and work the boats warily into range of duck and teal.

Having removed Noah's blankets as a precautionary measure and heard him, horribly muttering, give orders to yuloh till daylight, I went back to bed. Once warmed to their work the coolies stuck to it cheerily, knowing that to-morrow would bring idleness and sleep. The lowdah's grievance was evidently not theirs. It was grateful and comforting to hear the steady swish of the long stern sweep, the low voices of the men, and the faint tap, tap of the lowdah's pipe; to feel the gentle rocking of the boat; to snuggle down in the blankets with a sense of virtue and duty nobly done. Every now and then, from the pole-man in the bows, there came a weird cry (long-drawn and quivering in the silence, like the voice of some lonely ghost seeking its mate), and from our boats astern, or from others out in mid-stream, came faint tremulous replies. Thus, on the Chientang, they make the world-wide instinctive appeal to Æolus, attuned by centuries of experience to the local ways of the Wind god, as all men have done from the beginning of time whose ways have lain upon the waters. It was good to lie there in the darkness, to feel oneself again amidst the old companionable gods whom we have slain with machinery, to hear the words of men who still speak of Poseidon and Pan and all the tutelary spirits of the woods and hills, even as they spake who followed Ulysses of old upon the wine-dark seas. Good to drift back even for a little while, out of our clock-work modernity, to this forgotten backwater where the voices are still heard that whisper down the ages—voices that remind us of things our souls knew long ago when the world was young.

Our boatmen keep their watches by the stars, or by some occult mechanism in their stomachs; and they changed them with man-of-war precision, three men on and three off, day and night. Those who came off duty would slide down into the bowels of the ship, and, sitting round a sooty, spluttering lamp, smoke rapid pipes and talk for half an hour before curling up to sleep. The smell of those pipes, of that evil lamp, and of close-packed humanity was wafted from the depths, a pungent and abominable incense of labour. Through cracks in the flooring one could see, amidst the gloom and smoke of that cockpit, the little group, squatting on their haunches, a Rembrandt vision of Oriental faces in deep shadow, and from their drowsy talk came shreds and patches of the little things that make the sum of their little lives — Liu San's luck at dominoes, the quality of Noah's rations, the chances of wind and weather. The relations of these men with each other and the world in general were instinct with a certain rugged gentleness and courtesy, by no means the least of the benefits that the race-mind has acquired from centuries of Confucianism. Their virtue of chronic cheerfulness was less easily accounted for — probably an accidental foregathering of good-humoured souls, possibly a local benediction for merit acquired by virtuous forebears. Seldom have I met men so visibly contented upon such small provocation; it was a thing to inspire wonder, and a lingering desire for the prescription. From the rowers in the stern came songs before sunrise, songs all day long, droning recitation, and high-pitched falsetto tales of love and war; from the rice-pot there came ever the cracking of new and flavoury jokes. There was one fellow in particular, a squat, merry-faced Sancho Panza, whose stock of Rabelaisian stories was apparently inexhaustible, and whose poling was done to an accompaniment of songs and war-whoops most original and invigorating.

His mahogany complexion was mottled and pitted with small-pox, and his friends — he seemed to know every man, woman, and child on the river — called him "Bean-curd." As I drowsed off to sleep, he was explaining, amidst frequent tappings of pipes, the organic disturbances and horrible results that usually follow the sudden application of cold water to the human body, especially in the case of drunkards, and he cited a case that had occurred in his wife's mother's family, where a sleeping watchman, thus rudely awakened, had run naked through the land for more than a hundred li, and thereafter persisted in considering himself a tortoise. It was evident that any signs of eccentricity on Noah's part would be readily discounted.

Lambton sleeps, as he does everything else, thoroughly; therefore he had heard nothing of my midnight discussion with Noah. But at daybreak he was up and about, and from the borders of No-man's Land I heard him warmly inviting Jim to come and walk the dogs along the bank; to which Jim replied that it was bad for animals to be disturbed in the middle of the night. Then the gangplank was let down, and we heard a cheery whistling above our heads, getting rapidly fainter. I gathered that we were skirting a hill, which meant we had crossed to the east bank of the river. The whistling died away in the distance, and we lay cosily wondering where we were, and how long it would take to get Jim to breakfast. Suddenly we heard Lambton's voice in the distance, shouting words in-

"Bean-curd."

distinct, but of unmistakable wrathful purport; a moment later I was on deck and saw him at the top of a small hill waving excited arms in the direction of Hangchow. But the hillock was at a bend of the river, and our view was confined to a projecting spur, where the fir trees stood close-packed in shadow, covered with glistening fairy lace of silvery strands. I recognised the spot—Li Shan—and knew that, from his perch, Lambton could see the valley of Fu Yang to the south on the opposite bank, some two hours' journey up-stream. And I rejoiced at having kept Noah up to the mark.

But, as the Latins discovered long ago, the best laugh is that which finishes the story. Lambton, stalking moodily downhill and getting within range, announced his intention of keel-hauling the lowdah and then going back to bed. Coming close, he explained that our convoy — dogs, beaters, and all the necessary impedimenta of the chase — were nowhere to be seen. The best thing to do would be to sail back and find them. This was one up to Noah.

As Lambton jumped aboard, Thurlsby emerged in a purple dressing-gown embroidered with white storks, and I told them the tale of the night. It was clear that Noah had taken his revenge by allowing the other boats to part company, a thing contrary to his sailing orders and all recognised usage among lowdahs. Unless prompt and stern measures were taken, there would be an end to discipline for the trip; we should be at the mercy of this cross-grained wine-bibber. This being unanimously carried, after a brief council of war, Gehazi was ordered to summon Noah from his lair. Rubbing bloodshot eyes, and blinking at the light, he squirmed his way forward, and, being evidently nervous, gave himself courage, after the manner of his kind, by taking an intelligent interest in the horizon and noisily abusing Bean-curd, who was swabbing the deck.

In disciplinary cases it is usually best to deal with a Chinaman through another, superior to him in rank and if possible not of the same province; for thus, in the eyes of his fellows, he loses more face, and what is more, he cannot snatch the fearful joy of pretending not to know what you are talking about, a dodge which even Viceroys do not disdain, on occasion. So Gehazi was appointed Inquisitor, duly prompted, and bidden to speak fiercely.

Noah, with the crew looking on, and well aware that much face hung upon the issue, tried all the usual tricks — at first he affected surprise, looked around for the missing boats with a sympathetic eye, and protested his innocence as that of a man far famed for honesty from his youth up. Had he not carried missionaries, and was he not the possessor of a certificate of character from Dr. Main, whose name was better than silver in all that land? Reminded of his sailing orders and the undeniable fact that beaters and dogs are necessary for shooting, he disdained responsibility; were there no lowdahs on the other boats, and had we no servants to tell them what to do? Because he had made a bargain on their behalf, must he be answerable for all their offences? And from so monstrous a suggestion of injustice he rapidly generated wrath-matter (for the gallery), and, becoming truculent, told Gehazi that a lowdah of thirty years' good repute was not to be thus bullied, — had he not already been despitefully used? — and if there was to be any more trouble, the foreign gentlemen had better get another boat. He was becoming noisy when Jim quietly intervened.

"Gourdful of bad samshu," he said, " you have received $25 bargain money, you are guaranteed by the junk company, and there are Prefects at Fuyang and Hangchow — it was your business to see that the other boats did not drop behind. You are no lowdah, but the son of a sodden mud-carrier. Are we to go back and lose a day because of your drunken foolishness?"

Noah, abashed by straight talk, suggested we should await the coming of the boats. There were birds, he said, in the hills.

"Yes, we will go up the hill," said Jim, "but you will sleep no more to-day — you will go down river with two men and bring them quickly. And if they are not here by mid-day you will lose a day's hire. Now, mud-turtle, be off, or you spend to-night in the nearest yamen."

With a little gentle persuasion the thing was done, and Noah disappeared down-stream, in a sampan rowed by two coolies, whose object would naturally be to get back to their own rice-pot as soon as possible. The boats turned up before noon, and, satisfactory relations having thus been established on rational principles, Noah's behaviour for the rest of the trip was that of a sadder but much wiser man. Ignorance and vacillation (which are the component parts of our political benevolences) merely incite the Asiatic to his lawful prey. But deal with him firmly, in all justice, and he gives up monkeying with his destiny and yours.

So, waiting for the convoy, we spent the morning on the Li Shan. Pheasants were scarce, for here the hills run right down to the river, with little intervening cultivation and few of those wooded groves and oases in the open where the birds love to lie in the heat of the day. The hills were high and thickly wooded, stretching back to the south and east, a very goodly sight for eyes weary of horizons unbroken; a country where, if local reports speak true, leopard and deer and pig abound, and where to camp out would be a delight. The hill-men are brisk, sturdy folk, kindly spoken, with a something of frank independence, as if to be raised but a few hundred feet from yonder crawling ant-hills of the plain were enough to endow man with a new backbone and the eye of speculation. In all their little valleys water-wheels were turning to the music of fern-fringed waters, making the coarse buff paper in which shop-keepers wrap their parcels from one end of China to the other; on every hillside clearing, on threshing-floors, and on the grassy banks of ancestral tombs it lay drying, each square sheet separate, in sunny patches, testifying to the untiring industry of this race and its pitiful ends. A thousand years ago they made the same paper in the same way by these murmuring mountain streams.

To tramp the woods without beaters or dogs was healthy exercise, but the bags would not be the heavier for it, so we made for the river where, in the scrub and thick cover at the foot of the hill, we found bamboo partridge. They were plentiful enough, lying in coveys at the edge of the covert, and by taking turns to flush them from the inside, we got some lively sport and five couple of the little brown birds. But the hillside being the only retreat, the coveys flushed like Roman candles, skirted the bush for a few yards, and then turned sharply in again, so that the only chance was to stand back and wait for snap-shots. At this game Lambton speedily became an expert. To know where the birds are likely to be, how the covey will spring, and how far you may let them go, are things which come by instinct to the man versed in woodcraft.

At noon there was a shouting in the distance, and our malingerers sailed round the bend. Then, in a little while, Ah Kong and his fellow dog-wallahs, with great yapping and turmoil of the joyful pack, came to meet us. Of course there was a story, most circumstantial, of a broken yuloh, to save Noah's face; but we paid no heed.

Before a good northerly wind we bowled along to Fuyang, where a long valley, dotted with copses, stretches far into the hills—hills covered with bracken and low scrub such as pheasants love. Here, at our landing, we sprang and killed a deer from the first thicket, a brace of pheasants from the long grass on its sunny side, and a couple of snipe from the paddy field in which it stood. And here for two days we scoured the low hills, after beating the copses of the valley, revelling in the glorious sunshine and the silent underwoods, all red and gold under the first touch of frost; and the bag already made a brave showing at the stern of the beaters' boat.

On a long trip, where transport to one's base is uncertain, the cleaning and hanging of game is a matter which requires more care than it generally gets. To keep birds in good condition they should be cleaned at once, stuffed with dry charcoal, marked with the date of killing, and hung in the shade. Chinese sportsmen send their game to market packed tight in the hold of a dirty boat, with the result that it comes to table at best tasteless, at worst savouring of things unpleasant, so that epicures speak evil thereof, comparing it unfavourably with the hand-reared fowls of England. But cure and hang your birds properly, and they have a flavour as subtle and aromatic as the best fowl that ever lay on a poulterer's slab.

Another word to the wise. Let not the cook in cleaning pheasants or deer make away with that most succulent morsel, the liver. The meat of red-deer, as a standing dish, is uninteresting, but (I have said it before) it makes excellent food (with rice) for the dogs, and is therefore valuable where beef and mutton cannot be bought. But the liver is a delicacy which the Chinese fully appreciate, most edible and toothsome, so that unless you insist upon its preservation, they will tell you "have makee throw away." Also I know of no better dish for breakfast than pheasant liver on toast. Wang-li, the cook, knows my penchant in this matter and is complaisant, but the average menial will either trust to your forgetfulness of bird anatomy or sturdily protest that pheasants have no livers worth mentioning, and certainly none worth eating.

One item in the bag, a civet cat which, fleeing before Shiela and Rex, emerged untimely upon Thurlsby's gun, was not hung in our larder, but at the farthermost point of the dog-boat. Lambton, with the cheerful help of Bean-curd, thick gloves, and a rope, skinned it on the bank at sunset; but the smell of that feline was upon him and on the dogs, an all-pervading and persistent smell that afflicted our nostrils for days. So strong was the effluvial memory of the beast that, when the dog-boat was to windward, it drowned the flavour of our post-prandial tobacco; but Thurlsby, regarding it already as a disinfected and decorative hearthrug, declined to throw it overboard. So it remained; but a close season for civet cats was voted *nem. con.*

From Fuyang we worked up-stream to Liuchia Chwang (hamlet of the Liu family), where thick woods skirt the foot-hills, and where a thick undergrowth of bracken, scrub, and heavenly bamboo affords ideal hunting-ground for partridge. Here Peter, Rex, and Lambton's spaniel (hired from a sporting tax collector) had a field day, which laid them out for forty-eight hours (Peter was duly carried home in a basket slung on the beaters' poles), and fifteen brace of birds were brought to bag, each one representing glorious moments of expectation, successful stratagem, and triumph. In addition to our half-dozen beaters, most of whom were unconscious of any purpose or method in their work, and blundered about erratically in tolerant good-humour, there were wood-cutters abroad, and children attracted by the chance of picking up an empty cartridge, so that promiscuous snap-shooting was out of the question and our chances considerably reduced. And the birds were certainly less plentiful than of old; this is bound to be (as I have told you in another place), because the new-fangled ways of Young China have created a demand for game on the menus of their fashionable restaurants. Here, in the heart of the woods, we met several trappers, and realised that the bamboo partridge's habit of lying close and flying low make him an easy mark to the skilful netter. With a little ground-bait at the edge of an isolated clump of cover, these men will sometimes snare half-a-covey at one stroke. A few years hence and we shall probably find no shooting except in a few deserted places, remote from railways and the pernicious effects of universal education — such as Mongolia, or Ireland, or Saghalien.

Towards sunset Jim bagged a fox, and thereafter there emerged from the underwoods a grass-cutter, loudly wailing and exhibiting a pellet wound in the calf of his leg. It was only a scratch, but a crowd gathered as if by magic, sympathetic and garrulous; so the victim, accompanied by all the house of Liu, was invited to the boat, where Jim anointed the wound with listerine and cold cream then, with largesse of a dollar and two cigars, he departed amidst his admiring friends. Whatever may be the opinion of the Chinese as to the doctrines and general doings of the white man, they have an implicit belief in his virtue and skill as a healer. This is the result of medical missionary work, and it is no small thing. Wherever you go, amongst the junk-men on the river or in the villages of the outlying hills, these people will tell you of marvellous cures of the Hangchow Mission Hospital, of the wondrous skill and sovereign remedies of the good doctors who visit the out-lying stations. This touching confidence of theirs in one undeniable virtue of the foreigner will bring women to you with their sick children, and men with their tales of woe — pitiful visitants and most embarrassing. Jim's knowledge of first aid to the wounded, and the houseboat's medicine chest, often served their turn; his consultations on the tow-path were frequent and interesting; and by the end of the trip he was beginning to take himself seriously as a practising physician. So was Bean-curd.

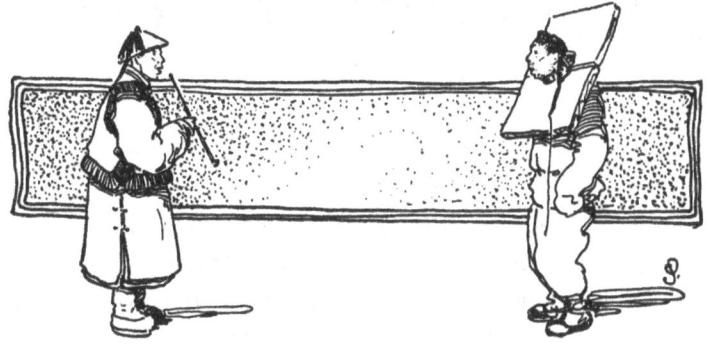

·OF·RIVERSIDE·MEMORIES·

CHAPTER XVI

"And now we breathe the odours of the glen,
And round about us are enchanted things;
The bird that hath blithe speech unknown to men,
The river keen that hath a voice and sings."

O'SHAUGHNESSY.

NEITHER you, O patient reader, nor I desire any detailed itinerary or account of this or any other of our journeyings. *Les jours succèdent aux jours:* they are gone, each with its chances and changes, like unto the rest. Sunrise and the joy of a new day; a muster-call of dogs, beaters, and carriers on the tow path, so many hours of steady tramping, so many birds bagged, or haply missed; lunch in the sun-flecked shade of a pine grove, followed by a pipe smoked in silent rumination on a soft bed of ferns. On again, slower now, working gradually round to the spot where the boats' flags stand out above the river-bank, till the sun is gathered to the purple peaks and the evening mist floats on the water like a veil of milky gauze; back to the boats, as the dusk falls, through farms and villages where the smoke of the rice-pot rises, with message of comfort to meet the toiler homeward bound. Each day is like the rest; each evening brings the same ineffable luxury of hot tubs, tea, and meditative smokes, the same delight of drowsily stretching tired limbs in idleness Olympian, until a tickling fragrance from the kitchen culminates in dinner. Each night brings the same good cheer, rosy-hued plans for the morrow, and the deep dreamless sleep that comes of doing fit things. And so the day is done, gathered into the unfathomable depths of Time, leaving only fragrant memories that shall he with us until we, too, pass out into the shadowy bourne that lies beyond the sunset.

I might, of course, set forth each day's journey, with maps, and give you a *résumé* of local industries, a comparative analysis of dialects, and a scientific summary of the day's bag. This, with the aid of other men's writings, would be easy, and in accordance with the usage of book-making in China; also, it would materially assist me in the provision of the intolerable tale of words required by Mr. Arnold to complete this volume. But I promised you at the outset that herein you should find little geography and less science, and I keep my word. I will tell you only of things that stand out against the background of memorable days, as trees against the sky-line of a hill. Memorable days — ay, but already, under the stealthy hand of knavish Time, their charm is informed with a collective quality, hazy in outline, subtle, elusive. There is fragrance in it still, as in a jar of pot-pourri, but the essence of each individual flower is lost. Really important people (Prime Ministers and *prime donne*) keep diaries to prevent such pathetic evaporation of marketable memories.

Let that pass, — to my tale. At Wang Shapu, a country of low rolling hills covered with oak scrub, we bagged sixty pheasants in two days and did some goose stalking in the open, to the ruin of our clothes and the unmistakable amusement of the geese. But the particular mental picture which I garnered in that spot (I cannot think of it calmly even now) is of my lonely self on the brow of a steep hill, a brace of pheasants dropped sixty yards below; Nelly pointing steadily just ahead, Ah Kong and the beater on the other side of the hill, and down there a Chinaman calmly retrieving my birds under my very nose, and making off with them to a village some two hundred yards away. I never saw those birds again, and therefore — such is the way of man, with pheasants or females — I shall remember them with regret, long after every bagged bird is forgotten.

To do the Chinese peasant justice, he is usually a decent fellow in this matter of retrieving, especially in country where foreigners do not shoot too often. To have one's bird deliberately lifted in the open by the Lord of the Soil was a new experience, another pernicious result, no doubt, of the "sovereign rights" movement. As a general rule, unless you happen to be in a district where so-called sportsmen have irritated the natives by tramping through their crops, the countryman will take a kindly interest in your proceedings, advise you where to find game, and help to retrieve a lost bird. And should you express appreciation with a ten-cent piece, you will be none the less welcome when next you pass this way.

It was at Wang Shapu, at our anchorage under the joss-house, that Gehazi, in all innocence, threw Thurlsby's front teeth overboard — two pearly incisors on a gold plate, which lay by night in a tumbler of water by their owner's head. It was dark that morning in the Ark. Gehazi saw only what he mistook for the remains of a whisky and soda. Anyhow, the teeth went overboard, and the horrid fact was discovered only when Thurlsby awoke half an hour later. By that time Lambton had got the boats under way. When the K.C. realised what had happened, words failed; there he stood, in his pyjamas, grievously stricken, a mute appeal for help and sympathy in the gaping void of his upper jaw. I don't think any of us had ever appreciated before the value of dentistry to the modern man. And what made it worse, in the face of distorted misery so acute, was the irresistible tickling of the ludicrous side of the tragedy. Jim's facial contortions, intended to express sympathetic grief, reminded one of those Japanese rubber masks where the tragic and comic blend in a hideous grotesque.

To proceed, in the face of so grievous a catastrophe, without attempting a rescue was out of the question, so the morning was spent in search for the lost treasure. Happily there was not more than four feet of water at the fatal spot, and Bean-curd's trained eye eventually caught the gleam of gold "in the waves beneath him shining," and, stripping with the swiftness of a conjurer, he retrieved the precious object. Thurlsby received it with a smile the like of which his clients and colleagues of the Supreme Court have never seen.

That night I heard the incident discussed by our beaters and the crew over their rice-bowls, and Ah Kong, whose prowess as a *raconteur* evidently pressed Bean-curd to emulation like any *trouvère* of olden time, told a wonderful story of the ways of white men and their many inventions. The utterly fantastic details of his tale threw a new light on his powers of imagination, and I made a mental note of the fact for future use. But the story, as he told it, was not without a certain humorous quality.

Nearly all foreigners, he said, towards middle age resort to the aid of skilled physicians to replace, as Thurlsby had done, worn-out portions of their anatomy. The Chinese had no such devices: even a wooden leg, if a man have need of one, he must buy from the European. Well, he, Ah Kong, was once up country with four foreigners in the Changchow district (he gave all their hong-names, and explained how they earned their rice), and they had stopped one day to watch an acrobat contortionist at a village fair. One of the village elders, talkative and friendly, asked the foreigners whether such feats could be seen in their honourable country. Mosely, the tea-man (there was no mistaking Ah Kong's description of *him*), replied that a contortionist could not earn a living in England because all Englishmen could take themselves to pieces. And with that he scooped out his left eye. The crowd, forsaking the acrobat, gathered close to see this marvel, whereupon each of the foreigners took off and exhibited some portion of his anatomy: one his hair, another his teeth, and the last man his left arm. The headman, sore amazed, asked whether the white man's stomach was also removable, to which Mosely replied that it was, but only in the early morning. That, with certain necessary omissions, was the story; whereupon, led by Bean-curd and supported by the whole strength of the company, there ensued a most edifying discussion on the comparative anatomy of white men and yellow. Its details I must leave to the night wind that heard them and sighed; to the pale moon that nestled her face behind fleecy clouds.

Now it is a fact that these four men, even as Ah Kong described them, do actually exist in the flesh; but it is a thousand to one that they have never been up country together (Benton, the man with the wig, doesn't shoot), in which case my young friend must have invented the whole story, simply to impress his yokel audience and to score off Bean-curd. And yet we still wonder at the primitive lies with which these people regale us every day!

At Liu Kuang-tao, below the rapids, we left poor old Rocket, a victim to dysentery: his grave stands on a wooded knoll overlooking the river, and his dogged soul, if there be any justice in the scheme of creation, is in Elysian fields where game is plentiful. Poor fellow, the hard work and cold had aggravated his chronic trouble, and although we dosed him with condensed milk and brandy, his mortal coil could not stand against it. But the courage and spirit of the beast! Even on his last morning, hardly able to stagger ashore, how his eye brightened and his tail wagged at sight of the gun! To hear his pitiful little whine, as we went off without him, sent a lump to my throat. Poor old Rocket—sleep well! Many a good day have we had together, and if, when my turn comes to creep underground, my duty has been done as you did yours, we may meet again—who knows?—in hunting-grounds more celestial. Also—if the Buddhists are right in their conception of the scheme of immortality—you may yet wield the gun, while I, in expiation, range patiently ahead.

Just below Liu Kuang-tao we came across a family of peripa-

tetic wild-fowlers, three brothers, with their promiscuous assortment of women and children, natives of Kiangpeh on the Yangtsze,
whose ancestors, it seems, have plied this trade from time immemorial. Their boat was narrow and low in the water, in shape like
an elongated slipper-boat, with a monstrous-looking swivel gun
projecting from its bows. This archaic weapon was practically all
barrel, — a rusty gas-pipe barrel over twelve feet long, about 4-
bore, with a ramshackle shoulder-piece where a stock might have
been. Its charge of villainous saltpetre and miscellaneous iron-
ware (nails, slugs, and scrap heap refuse) was rammed down by
the man in the bows, who apparently attached little value to life,
and the blessed thing would kill, they said, at 150 feet and more.
Our followers showed unmistakable respect for these practical
sportsmen, — men who could, and did, make shooting pay, — and
I heard Bean-curd explaining to Ah Kong how that a wild-fowler
from Kiang-peh, by reason of long practice and inherited virtue,
can see as well on a dark night as common men by day. Their
modus operandi is the same as that of punt-gun men all the world
over: a stealthy approach to duck, close-packed on open water,
or to geese on the riverside feeding-grounds, and a careful shot
into the darkest part of the mass. These men know every inch of
the river, the winds that bring birds down to the mud-flats, and
all the mysterious habits of wild-fowl, and they make good bags.
The headman told me that it was considered bad business to let
off his ancient piece for less then ten head, and the average would
be considerably over this. The noise of the gun being great, it does
not do to repeat it very often, as the birds are easily frightened to
the inland waters. Bright windy nights are best for duck on the
river, but most geese are bagged on the flats, just before dawn.

Three families of these prehistoric sportsmen, it seems, divide
the river between them, by the sort of prescriptive right which
grows naturally in China, and their bag is sold to a goose-eating
clientèle, which has also grown up all along the river, as well as to
the markets of Hangchow and Shanghai. Seeing that the mouths
of our crew watered undeniably at sight of the geese in the punt's

forehold, we bought three, at the equivalent of eightpence each as korban for the crowd: two shillings' worth of pure joy. Our own bag of wild-fowl, up to date, had been small, consisting of one goose, a few duck, and a dozen teal, inland wanderers all.

Above the rapids the river runs blue and clear between high hills, at mid-day a streak of dancing light gleaming between the deep shadows of the thickly-wooded banks.

The hills are too steep and too closely timbered for shooting. There is but little current on the stream; with a fair wind you can get through in a few hours, but with a breeze from the south it might take days, for tracking is impossible in many places. Above the gorges the country is much the same as below, low rolling foot-hills stretching back from the river, where game is fairly plentiful. On an island just below the rapids we found woodcock and had good sport, the flushed birds making across to the left bank where Thurlsby lay *perdu* in the cover. On our last day up stream we came within sight of the town of Yen Chou; the country ahead looked inviting (it always does), but the time had come for taking the homeward trail, and we left that country undisturbed.

On that day, scouring a valley above the gorges, we met an imposing funeral procession, with droning horns and wailing pipes, dragging its tawdry panoply of woe along a flagged path amidst the fields, bearing the husk of some departed mandarin to its ancestral resting-place in the hills. All the usual pomp and circumstance were there, strangely incongruous in this remote place, where the north wind's song whispered low and sweet through the pines; all the pitiful insignia of the social atom that had been, whose very name must so soon be forgotten; red boards with high-sounding titles blazoned in gold, umbrellas of honour, and life-size paper effigies, with a stream of relatives and friends following in sedan-chairs and afoot, accompanied by all the rag, tag, and bobtail of professional ghouldom. And loud above the burden of the *marche funèbre* sounded the voice of the mourner, gasping sobs and wailings of women clad in sackcloth, the very soul of human grief, speeding short-lived man to his long home. And as we stood to watch the procession go by, Pat, who had been busy in some thick scrub to our right, gave tongue, and thereat a deer broke cover right in front of the leading minstrels. Jim, the only one who could get a clear shot, fired, and the deer, badly wounded, went away with three dogs in full cry. Then occurred an interesting thing, proving once more how much better is a live dog than a dead lion (or Button-man): for the funeral march stopped abruptly, the coffin-bearers dropped their load, and the women in sackcloth ceased to wail, all eagerly intent on the chase. The departed and all his virtues were forgotten, all the etiquette of conventional grief swallowed up in the impending doom of a fleeing river-deer; and when, 300 yards away, it stumbled and the dogs were upon it, an excited chorus of "ai-yahs" broke out all along that line of mourners. Until the beaters had brought in their quarry they stood there, talking all at once and curiously examining the strange clothes and guns of the men from the West. And then, all of a sudden, the bearers resumed their illustrious burden, the sound of lamentation broke out afresh, and the evening air was filled with the shuddering sobs of afflicted humanity. And as I watched the motley procession drag its serpentine length down the valley, I realised how one touch of nature can indeed make the whole wide world kin, for even so, long ago in Kildare, had I seen another dreary *cortège* of conventional woe, with all its paraphernalia of hearse, mourners, and crape-trailing mutes, forget their business and their affliction while the hunt went by. It is one of the universal weaknesses of humanity, a common instinct of atonement, that we must needs make amends to our dead, the dead who are beyond reach of a kind word, deaf to our kindness and our care, by loud proclamations of unavailing grief, by tardy epitaphs that shall atone for words of comfort unspoken.

In all this region, where the white man goes out but seldom, our boats were the centre of politely inquisitive crowds, our dress, dogs, and domestic economy the subject of interminable discussion. But that which attracted more attention even than our humble selves was the appearance of Ah Kong and his brother dog coolies. Most of our followers were ordinary natives, of little distinction, but the kennel-wallahs were indeed a remarkable trio. For these *poursuivants* of the permanent staff usually acquire a sporting tendency of mind which, with the help of their masters' discarded raiment, expresses itself in their persons. Jim's man had arrayed himself in the complete summer kit of a Sikh policeman, putties and all, crowning the whole with a saucy yachting cap. Thurlsby's sported a striped sweater with tight rowing shorts, wearing his hair like the blades of the Foochow Road, but tucking his pigtail under a straw hat. But all their united glories paled

before those of Ah Kong, arrayed in a Monte Carlo hat, Norfolk jacket, and riding breeches, with woollen stockings of generous pattern (they looked like Wilden's) and canvas gaiters. The majesty of his appearance was undeniable, *hors contours*, dazzling from the outset and growing in splendour, but when, at the end of the first week, one of the gaiters succumbed, Jim's man equalised matters to some extent by carrying an empty binocular case slung in most jaunty fashion. Let it not be imagined, however, that this gorgeous apparel was produced before we were well clear of Shanghai. There, amidst their own kith and
kin, to savour of the European and his wardrobe is a reproach which no self-respecting Celestial would willingly incur; they may go so far as to wear your discarded hats (and not a doubt but that your singlets, etc., are comfortably next their skin), but the donning of Western raiment, *coram publico,* is a thing they leave to those *âmes damnées* of native servitude, the "ridey-boys" of the Race-club. Far afield, amidst the innocent peasantry of another

province, these scruples vanish, and it seemed to me, watching the strut and swagger of these fellows in their borrowed finery, that they hoped to be mistaken for the lordly foreigner, to have their share of the curious awe of the vulgar. I cannot account in any other way for Ah Kong's unusual solicitude for my welfare, shown in frequent offers to carry the gun through villages. Even the beaters, in white sail-cloth trousers and police boots, had their little hours of gratified pride, their little circle of admirers in wayside hamlets.

And the bearing of these varlets, relying on the protection of the foreigner, is apt to be somewhat masterful towards the lord of the soil; 'tis a matter that needs watching. To give an instance. I had wounded a hare one day, and Rex had followed it into a patch of thick jungle which grew round an ancient grave. Ah Kong disappeared after Rex, and in a little while there came from the thicket sounds of falling masonry and splintering wood. The hare had crawled through a hole in the brickwork into the mouldering coffin, where it lay dead amongst the bleached bones of the departed, a gruesome spectacle. By the time I reached the scene, Ah Kong had enlarged the opening enough to allow Rex to retrieve his quarry, which was done amidst much rattling of mortal remains and stirring of grey dust. Feeling like a body snatcher, I rebuked Ah Kong with much strong language, reminding him of the respect due to ancestors and the fate of those that desecrate graves. There was a countryman working in the field close by, and, as we emerged with the hare, he came towards us.

"What will you do, Ah Kong," I said, "if he makes trouble? This is none of my business."

"No fear," he replied. "He no talkee nothing. This countlyman velly stupid. All same damnful savage."

Which (proving true) seems to show that the most venerable customs of the Chinese may be affected by circumstances and environment, and that their morality is tempered by opportunity. And this brings them very near to ourselves.

At Liu Kuang-tao, on our way down stream, occurred a memorable moment with wild pig. Lambton, Thurlsby, and I were at breakfast. Jim had just flooded the hold of the Ark by the usual collapse of his india-rubber bath, and was sitting disconsolate on the flabby remains, when suddenly Bean-curd on the fore-deck shouted loudly for us to bring the guns. Rushing on deck (Jim was there also) we saw, about a quarter of a mile down river, seven black objects in the water. They were pig, said Bean-curd, swimming the river. The anchor was up in a moment, oars out, and the boat heading swiftly across stream to cut them off, visions of roast pork spurring the crew to howling activity. But alas for all fond hopes! Within 300 yards of the porkers the Ark struck a shallow, and the race, so far as we were concerned, was over. Jim, with a towel about his loins, got out his Mauser, but by this time a crowd of Chinese, armed with poles and boat-hooks, had lined the bank so that shooting would have been dangerous. Helplessly we watched the gallant landing of the pigs, a wild *mêlée* of squealing quadrupeds and shouting men, a convulsive maelstrom of blows and grunts, which left three black corpses stretched upon the shelving bank. And as we pushed off from the shallows, the remarks of Bean-curd to Noah on the subject of navigation in general, and drunken navigation in particular, were not fit for the ears of decent men.

And so we made our way down stream, with varying fortunes and much content of body and mind; nothing to mar our joyous days except the thought that each sunset brought us nearer to the end of our sweet liberties, nearer to desks and office-stools, and all the abominable machinery of our money-grubbing businesses. And every night the river gleamed, a pure line of molten silver under the stately-moving moon, and the north wind came gloriously singing through the dark passes of the hills, rustling in the shadowy sails of up-stream junks, speeding the swift wings of the wild swan, hurrying the serried squadrons of geese. I never hear, in the silence of a hushed city at night, the deep note of heron passing overhead or the cry of phantom curlew, but that, in a flash, I am back again in those moonlit reaches of the Chientang river.

Did I understand you to ask, O practical man, the cost of such a trip? A pity, is it not, that we must express the value of all things, even halcyon days, in terms of sordid sycee? Yet such, I will admit, is the net result of all our philosophies reduced to their last word. Well, Jim, who carried the purse and made out the accounts on half a sheet of notepaper, avers that such bliss as ours is within the reach of any man who can afford to pay for it at the ridiculous rate of ten dollars—a pitiful pound sterling—per day; and this might be reduced if you take the common tow instead of a private launch from Shanghai to Hangchow. The price of Noah's Ark, with crew, was $4.50 per diem, and the smaller boats $1.25; a beater's wage is 40 cents (tenpence), and of chickens and eggs you may buy enormous quantities for a laughable sum unless the cook is within range. Bread and meat are not to be had for a king's ransom, for this people knows them not.

But why should we talk of such things? Find them out for yourselves as part of the day's work and play. Take care of your souls; get you to the hills and look down on the green valleys, the laughing waters, the dim soft distances of this good rolling world, and, never fear, your journey's cost will he paid with a light heart.

OF SMUGGLING
& SOME ASPECTS OF THE ART OF
GOVERNMENT

CHAPTER XVII

"All that shaketh does not fall: the contexture of so vast a frame holds by more than one nail. It holds by its antiquity, as olde buildings which age hath robbed of foundation, without loam or mortar, neverthelesse live and subsist by their own waight." — MONTAIGNE.

I HAVE mentioned, I think, that all along that low-lying coast of the Yellow Sea which runs from Shanghai to the mouth of the Chientang river there is a great industry of salt-making; for miles and miles, upon the No-man's land lying between the sea wall and the tide, you may see the salt-pans glistening in the sun and bent figures of men toiling like ants. It is a good healthy trade this getting of brine on the wind-swept marge of the sea, and the men who ply it are a sturdy race; but the salt is not like Tidman's, being a dirty mud-coloured substance at best, for the sea water is so turbid near the mouth of the great river that, even after filtering it through clay, the evaporated residuum retains particles of up-country mud.

Now salt in China is a Government monopoly, which means that the article produced, like Italian tobacco, is very bad, and that a vast horde of official harpies batten and prey upon it, from the time it leaves the brine-pit or salt-pan to the moment when it reaches the consumer. Furthermore, it means that, because the duties and squeezes levied by the Gabelle amount to far more than the cost of production, salt-smuggling is one of the great trades of the Empire, providing employment for a mass of boatmen, carriers, spies, desperadoes, and illicit retailers on the one hand, and on the other for barrier watchmen, examiners, river police, gunboat patrols, Government informers, and many other varieties of armed or buttoned men; so that salt, properly considered, becomes a most romantic and precious commodity. I could tell you many interesting things about it, — of the business relations between the Putung smugglers and the gunboats at Sung-kiang, of the tricks of the Yangtsze river steamers and the remarkable experiences of my friend Chief Engineer M'Cormick; also there is the historic and authentic tale of the preventive service flotilla in and around the Great Lake which, because of too much zeal, had so discouraged the contrabandists of that region that half the flotilla had to take to salt-smuggling in order to justify the existence and protect the livelihood of the other half. But my present business is with houseboats and the villainy of Cyclops, erstwhile lowdah of the *Mighty Atom*, who fell because of salt.

It was a Chinese New Year outing. Jim and I had made up a sortie to Haiyee with Wilden and the Admiral, and had had great sport with woodcock and duck, a northeast wind having brought a heavy fall of snow and driven the birds to inland sheltered places. On New Year's day, after breakfast, we had shot inside the city, and, returning to the boats at noon, were for taking fresh beaters and working across the country towards Chapu. But of Cyclops and his merry men there was no sign; the Admiral's boy and the cook were alone in that deserted ship — and all that we could learn was that they had "makee go buy someting."

On board the *Saucy Jane* everything was in order, the muster-roll complete, and a look of smug virtue on every man's face; but they also vowed they knew nothing of this unparalleled desertion. Concluding that they had gone off to some convivial gathering of relatives or fellow-rogues, we sent out scouts to round them up, and meanwhile made the best of it over lunch. The Admiral's rage had resulted in a fierce generation of wrath-matter, producing at first voluble incoherence and then an ominous speechlessness, from which he only recovered gradually after the third glass of port; but his emotion did not blind any of us to the fact that we could not leave the *Mighty Atom* behind; for to be boatless at the end of a day's trudge is not the most jovial of adventures. So we waited for the return of Cyclops, whiling the hours away with bridge. The Admiral held four aces twice and won steadily, so that his longing for opportunities of personal violence faded softly away. By four o'clock he was inclined to take a lenient view of peccadillos on New Year's day, and when Cyclops and his merry men appeared, followed by an army of salt-laden coolies, it was he who intervened, with reference to the merciful man and every dog his day, when Jim and I were for refusing to let them bring their contraband aboard. Wilden, being a trader, and therefore imbued with sneaking sympathy for any one that defrauds a Government, sided with the Admiral, and the stuff was speedily disposed in the secret depths of our ships. I had often seen salt under the anchor chains of the *Saucy Jane*, but never before had I been a witness and accomplice at its shipment; for these loadings are usually done privily and at night. Both crews were in the deal, as was clear from the way they divided and stowed the cargo, as well as from the conscious sheepishness of all concerned.

So, minus an afternoon's sport and plus certain prospective illicit gains for our crews, we made our way homewards *via* Kashing. The cheerful alacrity of our men next day, afloat and afield, was a pleasure to behold, fully worth their profits on the salt, and Cyclops was positively obsequious in his attentions. I forgot to mention that this worthy got his name because one eye having been gouged out in an animated discussion with some of his Putung friends, the other protrudes horribly, like that of a Pekinese gold-fish. Despite this facial handicap he confronts the world and the river police sturdily, and to us, his employers, he shows many estimable qualities. I say that he shows them, for although at this moment he is engaged in the uncongenial task of making coir mats in the municipal gaol, his place and his old friends await him at the end of the year's durance, the lean year which he is serving for that cargo of salt. And this doom overtook him, as we discovered later, because of his failure to recognise the obligations of honour among thieves.

It was a hireling varlet, engaged for the trip by Jim, who gave him away, one of those Ishmael "boys" that live on short jobs and what they plunder from globe-trotters. I suppose Cyclops wouldn't give him a share because of some unwritten lowdah law on the status of hirelings; anyhow, he made a mistake, for, while we were shooting the long grass stretch inside the city wall, the fellow went off and lodged information at a lekin station. Shortly after our return to the boats a t'ing ch'ai came on board, with the card of one Feng, described thereon as Sub-Prefect and Brevet Assistant Salt Comptroller, by the grace of Kuang Hsü, in the province of Chêkiang, and many other things besides. Mr. Feng, said the Man with the Button, was loth to disturb the honourable foreign gentlemen, but having learnt that their boats were carrying a large quantity of salt, he, being a zealous officer, etc. Of course the honourable foreigners could not know that salt was a Government monopoly or that the houseboat crews were evil-doers, but they must agree that the Emperor's revenue must be protected, etc. And the upshot of it all was that half an hour later we were moored alongside the lekin station, and our salt—we had come to look upon it as ours—was ignominiously carried ashore by the licensed villains of the law.

Having secured their prey, Mr. Feng's myrmidons desired nothing more of us, and there the matter would have ended but for Cyclops and the Berserker rage of the man. He had lost his venture; now, because of a sudden bloodthirsty longing for revenge, he must needs lose his liberty to boot, a thing not uncommon in a race which believes that suppressed wrath-matter in the system will kill a man as surely as poison. We never knew exactly how it happened, or who had betrayed the betrayer; but what we had heard was the yelling of a man in mortal agony, and what we saw was Cyclops with the hireling's head in chancery, trying to get at his eyes before shoving him into the river. Jim, as usual, was on the scene of action before any one else, and Cyclops seeing him coming, abandoned the idea of eye-gouging, and, with one fierce kick in the hireling's abdomen, sent him screaming into the water. Thence we fished him with boat-hooks, and laid him unconscious on the bank; and Cyclops, sullenly satisfied, was seized by a *posse* of runners.

Unwilling to leave the wretch to the unknown terrors of criminal procedure in *partibus infidelium*, Jim and I decided to call on the redoubtable Feng, and give our bond to deliver him safely for trial in due course before the Mixed Court Magistrate at Shanghai; so, sending on our cards by the *t'ing ch'ai*, we put on our longest coats and made our way through dark narrow lanes to the laoyeh's residence.

He was something of a surprise this Assistant Salt Comptroller of Chêkiang, one of the curious phenomena of modern China that make one rub one's eyes and wonder where the whole fantastic business is going to end, and how such remarkably new wine can be contained in the crazy bladders of antiquity. We were ushered through the courtyard of an ordinary ramshackle building into a hall dimly lighted with a ship's lamp; thence, without warning, into a room which might have been transplanted bodily from the sea-view terrace or esplanade of any watering-place in England, a room that made one think instinctively of master mariners and Portsmouth, of white decks and brightly-polished brass. There was the horsehair sofa, the mantelpiece ornaments, the pictures of Nelson, and the "Fighting *Téméraire*." There was the officer's sword, hung between photographs of football teams, and beneath it the photo-album on a brown crewel mat. If it had not been for a large picture of the late lamented Viceroy of Nanking, and the indefinable savour of the East in our nostrils, we might reasonably have expected to hear the call of the newsboy or the muffin man's bell. And as we were trying to adjust this interior to the Celestial scenes through which we had just passed, and wondering whether we had not got into the European harbour-master's house by mistake, Mr. Feng appeared.

I think he was really glad to see us. At least, he said so, and insisted on our staying to dinner. For a man, even an Oriental, who has been four years in the British Navy and passed with distinction in navigation, gunnery, and torpedo work, it must be difficult, at first, to return to the sweet simplicity of native life in a back street at Kashing; and our host had only been here a month. He would get used to it in time — they all do. The impress of the West would fade, and the East claim him again, body and soul, for her own; but, for the moment, he was evidently struggling with his environment and greedy for a talk of the old life. He had meant to stick to the navy, the Chinese navy, and had served for a while on an alphabetical gunboat at Canton. It wasn't his fault that, since the *débacle* of '94, there hadn't been any navy worth mentioning to stick to. All his people were officials, with a fairly good "pull" in Peking; so, when the bottom of his gunboat dropped out on a mud-bank, they had got him this job. He didn't know anything about salt revenues, but his secretary did, and the financial results were not altogether unsatisfactory. After all, one has to live somehow.

As to Cyclops? He didn't know much about the law, but the man was a foreigner's servant, and wasn't there something about that in the treaties? Anyhow, he didn't want to be bothered with the case. If we would promise to hand both men over to the Shanghai Court, he would be delighted never to hear about it. Of course if the hireling died, it might be awkward; but it was our business. The main thing was that we were to stay to dinner. So we left it at that, and orders were sent to restore Cyclops to the *Mighty Atom* and to put the hireling to bed, with restoratives, on board the *Saucy Jane*.

We had a most interesting evening. A pal of Feng's dropped

in, another limb of Young China, a graduate of Yale, who called himself Arthur Lee and brought a banjo. He too was apparently delighted at this windfall from the West; told us he had completed his training as a civil engineer, had worked two years in the Straits, and had recently come back because his father wanted him to get married and had found him a job in the Telegraphs. He was an ardent patriot, of course, and a reformer of the Cantonese school, that is to say, he considered the intelligent youth of that province as pre-ordained to open and devour the Chinese oyster. For our sake and from politeness, he tempered the wind of his enthusiastic remedies to the shorn lambs from overseas; but for the rest, the Empress Dowager, the Court, and the fossilised Mandarin, he included them in a wholesale and eloquent denunciation expressed in terms that vaguely reminded one of the *New York Journal*. And the worst of all the maggots that infested the rotten body-politic were the students from Japan. Listening to this fiery exponent of new policies, one realised that strange destinies are in store for all the uncounted millions that toil on, unconscious of the clash of systems at their gates; one realised too that, simple as it sounds, "China for the Chinese" is not going to be a children's picnic. It will be "Ireland for the Irish" on a grand scale, and without the R.I.C.

They wore no P'utzu, our hosts, and they ate with knives and forks; Feng, clad in a claret silk tunic with his queue curled away under his cap, explained that until lately he had worn foreign clothes, but that, for an official, it wouldn't do. He used them still for shooting, but even this had been imputed to him for sin by the gentry, and a friend in the Fu-tai's Yamen had warned him to discard the breeks and stick to long robes and petticoats. He waxed pathetic at being deprived of trouser pockets; and when you come to think of it, when you remember how vast a part these same pockets play in creating the lordliness of Western men, how they can transform a boy in a moment from infantile indignities to worlds of domination and freedom, how by their virtue commonplace heads of dull families assume masterful ways impossible to pocketless humanity, one perceives that they may be near to a great truth who insist on dress reform in China as more important than the abolition of eunuchs or lekin. Also one perceives — and I commend the fact to Foreign Offices, Members of Parliament, journalists, and all other blind leaders of the blind — that a Government which gravely informs the Powers to-day that it cannot control its provinces when they break treaties or kill missionaries, and to-morrow can enforce its edicts in the matter of pigtails and clothing, is a Government which has by no means reached the end of its resources.

The humble philosophic attitude towards this amazing world through which we pass so quickly, that attitude to which only the Greeks, as a race, have fully attained, would appear to be henceforth hopeless; nevertheless, if East and West are ever to meet, if the scurrying masses and turmoil of white men and yellow are ever to come to a good understanding, the secret of that philosophic attitude must be discovered. And the yellow man is far nearer to it than we, for all our many inventions. With us, the mysteries of the Universe and the eternal questions of our being, the ends and purposes of this brief flitting of men across the painted veil, all the things that matter, are drowned and lost in the Babel of voices that goes up, day and night, from the great market-places which, God help us, we call civilisation. On one side stand the politicians, lawyers, traders, pressmen, and quacks, shouting to half-deafened mobs new tricks to gain a point in the struggle for life, the struggle wherein we all forget to live. On the other, the clamour of the sects, shouting louder still to weary stragglers from the crowd their sure systems of salvation and panaceas against predestined evil, tearing each other to pieces meanwhile for the love of strange Deities of their own fashioning. Everywhere, men, drawn by the Babel, are leaving the quiet fields, the mountain pastures, and the paths of the sea; the roar of the Press grows fiercer, the unceasing whirr and clicking of machines assail the stars, and for the glory of mammon man goes willingly to easeful death, unconscious of all the wonder

and beauty of life. This is the chief result of that material progress which we so fervently commend to Oriental peoples, and which they, having preserved something in their lives of dignity and wisdom, resist with all the weight of passive inertia.

I suppose that what we are pleased to call economic pressure—which in its final expression means greedy men with quick-firing guns—will eventually confer on China our inestimable boons of Parliament, Party Government, Company Promoters, Suffragettes, and all the rest of it—but I take comfort in the thought that it will not be in our time. The soul of China will brood on, unmoved by all the clamour at her doors, while yet a few generations work their unquestioning Stoic way to rest. "All

that shaketh does not fall: the contexture of so vast a frame han-
geth by more than one nail." The feverish fantasies of our short-
lived Western philosophies, the nostrums of all the leaders of our
body-politic, Peace Societies, life-lengtheners and soul-curers,
industrial evolutionists and star-gazing theorists, the East has
heard and forgotten them all long ago. Christianity's centuries
lie strewn with the wrecks of moralities and systems, while the
force that holds China together has been transmitted, unchanging and unchanged, unassailable as a wind-swept rock. Europe
may dominate her, as we have dominated India, by superiority
of mechanical and economical devices, but the soul of the East is
beyond our reach, buttressed and entrenched behind a philosophy beside which all our shibboleths are but vain imaginings.
Take the white man from India to-morrow and the ancient races
before whose eyes he struts and frets would speedily forget him
and all his words and ways; no mark would he leave upon their
creeds, no change in their attitude towards the mysteries of life
and death.

It is our custom, in the interests of what we are pleased to call
the cause of civilisation, to condemn the Chinese system of policies and ethics, and it is the business of our diplomats and missions to endeavour to persuade this people to replace that system
by our own. From the economic and commercial point of view
we may be justified; but if we test their form of civilisation and
ours — as philosophers must do — by the possibilities of happi-
ness obtainable by the largest number of individuals; if we strip
the question of all self-interest, proselytising fervour and cant,
then, it seems to me, we have good reason to desist from disturbing the deep-set peace of the East. If it must be that we continue
to run up and down the face of the earth, preaching to each other
the road to Heaven or the coming of the millennium; if we must
bestir ourselves night and day, shouting the latest answer to the
riddle of life, explaining the Creator's will and the mysteries of
pain and death — well and good. But the East asks for no such futile turmoil of soul; its attitude towards the inscrutable purposes

of the Creator was fixed ages ago, by consent and teaching of its sages, an attitude of patient acquiescence in the human insect's limitations. It is prepared to take the present cheerfully and eternity on trust, and when all is said and done, what more practical philosophy has the West evoked? Does any one honestly believe that it would profit either East or West to inoculate the sons of Han with the moral standards of modern Europe.

But I am wandering from Mr. Feng and Arthur Lee and all the world of things as they are at Kashing to-day, which we discussed amiably with our hosts, over coffee and cigarettes, to our mutual edification.

Feng wanted information about railways and road-making, police organisation, and all the other administrative panacea wherein Peking has been taught to see salvation and the Mandarin sees opportunities; ways and means he touched on lightly, lamenting his countrymen's rooted aversion to direct taxation and the rapacity of the Central Government. Lee, being in the Telegraphs, was naturally anxious to know about physical culture and the organisation of a Volunteer corps, and in return for what we told them of these things they gave us such information as they thought good for us, on judicial procedure, lekin, and the doings of the provincial gentry of Chêkiang.

It is impossible to talk to a Chinese official about the system of administration which he represents without marvelling that a machine apparently so clumsy and defective should preserve such astonishing vitality and cohesion. In European countries such a system could not last a week; at no point of its unwieldy bulk can you find evidence of definite purpose, inter-communication or method; everywhere you come upon rule-of-thumb makeshifts, compromises, and gaping voids. No written law runs through the land, nor any code; edicts are meaningless except where they voice local opinion; even precedents, the unwritten foundation of rough-and-ready justice, are at the mercy of every Yamen clerk. Yet the thing holds together and does its work for a third of humanity without any great jolting or creaking. The explanation lies, of course, in the patient docility — up to a certain limit — of the Chinese people, and the wisdom of rulers who have learned to a nicety where that limit is and who seldom transgress it.

In discussing the government of China it is well to be definite as to what the word "government" means and includes. In Europe the term applies chiefly to the administrative functions performed by the State's executive; in China the State exercises little or no administration. The internal policies of the country are essentially matters of local custom and option; the family, and collection of families, being at once the foundation of society and the arbiter of executive measures. But if government consists in the maintenance of place and power by the exercise of political instinct and the nice adjustment of conflicting forces to produce equilibrium, then the Manchus, with all their faults, undoubtedly govern China. Many of those who criticise the Chinese system fail to realise that an Oriental government may survive without administrative activity, by virtue of that traditional authority tempered by prudence which enabled Moses to be a lawgiver without organising a police force. The rulers of China have learned to know their Demos, and it is for this reason that, despite corruption, internal weakness, and the dangers that steadily menace them from without, they steer clear of many a rock on which modern states have been wrecked, safely guiding their ancient craft by hoary landmarks and craft

of the pilots of long ago.

And then, the Mandarin. He is an official, of course; but the fact does not justify us in expecting from him the function of our bureaucratic executives. For the Man with the Button in China no more governs — in our administrative sense — than does an Imperial edict. He represents, in fact, the privileged class as distinct from the plebs, a class entitled by virtue of birth or intellect to do certain things, to collect certain revenues on behalf of the Throne (and himself), to see to the observance of such laws, written and unwritten, as custom has sanctioned, and to be the untoward and visible sign of the established order of things. But let him go ever so little beyond his prescribed authority, let him attempt any unprecedented forms of squeeze or collective injustice, and the real rulers of the country assert themselves unmistakably, inflict chastisement (with impunity) on the offender, and return quietly to their labours. The Mandarin, in fact, bears to the Chinese people a relation somewhat similar to that which the Irish politician occupies in America, except that, *au fond*, he is in closer sympathy with the masses because of unbroken kinship and tradition. Both are admittedly and frankly corrupt; both owe their continued existence to the patient, hard-working character of the people on whom they live — and both must eventually disappear, as education arouses the nation to a sense of the waste which such a system involves.

Finally, as to parties in the State. Human nature being what it is, it is inevitable in China, as elsewhere, there should be political factions — Chinese and Manchus, Conservatives and Liberals, anti- and pro-foreign; inevitable also that, as with us, the struggle between these factions for place and power should have for its ostensible object the ultimate good of the people, while the real end is the old, old question of the "haves" and the "have-nots" working itself out in the survival of the fittest.

All these things we discussed, in philosophic vein, with Feng Tajen and Arthur Lee, who quoted Herbert Spencer and the Old Testament in effective defence of the Chinese system. It was all rather weirdly exotic, with Nelson gazing placidly on the scene and a gramophone from which Caruso and Melba rent the air at intervals. Towards mid-night we left them, personally escorted by a brand new bobby with an archaic lantern, and made our way through slumbrous high-walled alleys to the boats. There Cyclops greeted us in the cheeriest fashion, and there I saw the hireling playing dominoes with the Admiral's boy as if salt-smuggling and attempted manslaughter were but creatures of the heat-oppressed brain. It is a philosophic people.

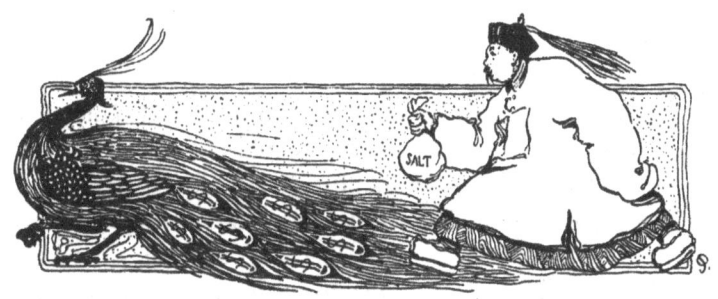

· CHAPTER · XVIII ·
Of · SPRING · SNIPE & THE COMING of the · RAILWAY ·

"Moored to the cool bank in the summer heats,
'Mid wide grass meadows which the sunshine fills."

The Scholar Gipsy.

KNOW some men—old stagers mostly, addicted to their little comforts and preferring warm weather to cold—who consider that the spring snipe-shooting is the best sport of the year. For myself, I hold no such sweeping opinion; all sport is good, all seasons have their merits, and in their changes and differences lie much of the charm that calls each restless Nimrod to his wanderings. No doubt, on a bitter winter's night, when the stove is working badly and the thought of undressing as a prelude to cold sheets makes your teeth chatter, or when yulohing in a damp dingey against wind and rain after duck that are always just out of range, it is in human nature to think longingly of rape-fields shimmering in the sun; of leisurely tramps through sweet-scented fields of bean, where the fat birds rise from their feeding with a lazy squawk; of warm nights on the houseboat deck under the new moon of May.

But then, again, when the May-day sun has shone more fiercely than you expected, when all the available moisture in your system has perspired from you into a mud-swamp, or when the first hungry mosquitoes of the year drive you untimely from the deck to bed, shall you not then take comfort in the thought of bright frosty mornings to come?

There is, as the wise man has said, a time for pheasants and a time for snipe, a time to be hot and a time to be cold; but for mutable man, brief joy-seeking atom, is it not well that memory softens past evils, while Hope glorifies the days to come in disparagement of the present? Else had half the world made shipwreck of its courage.

Nevertheless, if comparisons must be made, there is something to be said in praise of spring snipe-shooting. Imprimis, it combines the ardours of a revival with the joys of a lottery; then it is springtime — springtime when the heyday sings in the blood (ay, even in the blood of Bank managers) a song of half-forgotten dreams. Every creek is sweet with the breath of hawthorn and eglantine; from the shimmering haze of the level distances comes a murmur of familiar sounds that remains for ever in the mind blended with the scent of the rape-fields; clicking of buffalo-wheels, rippling water purring in the paddy runnels, song of thrush from the bamboo grove; expostulating creak of yulohs that cut the jadewater as their boats glide past us in the bright sunlight; and everywhere, like an undertone motif of industry, "the murmur of innumerable bees."

The spring snipe makes his appearance in the regions around Shanghai with the regularity of a Canadian Pacific captain. Scheduled, by the unwritten laws of their destiny, to cross the continent of Asia, from south to north, each spring, seeking the marshy uplands of Mongolia and Saghalien for their breeding-grounds, these vast armies of birds, travelling by night, feeding and resting by day, make their unvarying pilgrimage with an unbroken front, covering many hundreds of miles. Between the 20th and the 25th of April any night-watcher of the skies may hear their first line of skirmishers shrilly calling overhead; by the middle of May the rearguard has passed on, and only rare stragglers remain. A wonderful thing this migration of birds, wherein Rome's augurs found signs and portents, wherein lies awesome speculation enough for any reverend man to-day. Whence grew the law that leads this snipe to make his little life an unbroken summer, that sends him northwards and south with waning and waxing suns? What moons of transmitted memories have taught these birds to travel at fixed dates and by invariable routes? In its regularity and vast distances the migration of the Asiatic snipe seems to me more wonderful than that of our swallows, over which miracle White of Selborne cogitated to so little purpose.

Not the least remarkable thing about the spring snipe is, that, for all his long night journeyings, he contrives by rich feeding and sunny siestas to keep extremely fat, so that even the amateur sportsman perceives that this is not that *Scolopax gallinago*, aimless wanderer, and common snipe, with whose razor-like breastbone we have been unpleasantly familiar all winter. The fatness of the spring snipe is indeed a joy to housewives, associated in the mind of epicures with mangoes and the succulent samli of this season. So fat is he that one wonders how, in such portliness, he wings his way to the northern breeding-grounds, and whether such unromantic *embonpoint* is fitting for birds on their way to courtship and domestic bliss.

The flight reaches the Yangtsze Delta, as I have said, about the 20th of April, but from Wuhu, where the river dips south, the snipe are sent to the markets a week or ten days earlier. With the advent of the first pintailed birds, many houseboats that have lain idle since Chinese New Year put off from their moorings, scattering over the inland waters, from Lokopan and Four Waters to Hsitai Lake and Soochow, and Nimrod trudges through regions of trefoil, low grass, rape-seed, and bean in blissful expectancy of the good brown birds' sudden rising from the wet furrows. There is a man of my acquaintance—Brandon, to wit, a man of more than average veracity—who annually asserts that he has found spring snipe (*Gallinago stenura* and *Gallinago megala*) a week or more before ordinary mortals have heard its familiar squawk. Doubtless there are spots that attract eccentric and adventurous birds, and from a truthful man, who knows the difference between the 14-tail feathers of *Scolopax* and the 26 or 20 of the pintails, I accept these statements meekly. Nevertheless, I would not advise you to tramp the furrows, except for the fun of the thing, or the chance of winter birds, before the 20th of April.

But in the first week of May, what time half the population of Shanghai goes temporarily mad, abandoning its business for four days to watch the race-course performances of Mongolian rats, then any man with ordinary luck should find the spring snipe in their accustomed feeding-grounds. These vary to a certain extent, of course, according to wind, weather, and the height of the water in river and lakes; but whatever the conditions, each year's flight seems to have inherited the accumulated memories, and to have learned the landmarks of its predecessors. This to me, who could not possibly remember how and where I fed on any last year's pilgrimage, is marvellous indeed; but any observing man will confirm it, that to certain spots these birds come, year after year, from the far-distant south with the precision and regularity of a time-table. In August, when they pass southwards again, their habits, modified no doubt by the responsibilities of domestic life, are less dignified and leisurely; no longer (small blame to them) are they conspicuously fat; they stay with us but a little while, appear erratic and restless, and go swirling about (especially towards evening) in sudden wisps and most unexpected places—no doubt the effect of large and undisciplined families.

There is a peculiar charm about these May-day outings—the charm of fragrance and colour spread broadcast under cloudless skies, of lotus-eating noontides, leisurely siestas and bathing in willow-shaded pools, so that shooting becomes an incident, rather than the sole object, of the day. There is something in the air, even before sunrise—a suggestion of silent travail in all these fertile fields, wherein you seem to hear the growth and stir of all their myriad lives. Amongst the reeds the white mist rises slowly, like incense, from the river-banks, and the bright yellow of the rape glistens through unbroken veils of gossamer. One has to admit the innate savagery of man, to explain his desire to slay food, with noise of gunpowder, under such conditions. Thus one meditates, full of intelligent sympathy with the vegetarian movement, until the first bird rises; then certain unphilosophic muscles bring the gun automatically to your shoulder, and you proceed to shoot, without further analysis of the brutality of man, until the sun is nearly overhead. It is clean shooting, and one can get rid of a hundred cartridges in a good morning's work; nevertheless, it lacks, for my taste, the chances and changes, that quality of unexpectedness, which one should look for in sport.

There are other objections to spring shooting. In the first place you and the dogs have to walk through ripening crops, and although you do no great harm to the rape, heavy boots play havoc with the young wheat and beans. Good sportsmen will stick to the furrows, but at times you must cross them, to the hurt of the lord of the soil. Then there are flies, which seem to gravitate instinctively towards a houseboat from the four quarters of heaven — flies and mosquitoes and winged beasts that flop into your soup, or the tresses of Neæra's hair, creatures that buzz and bite from sheer gladness of heart. That flies are inseparable from the ointment of all earthly joys I know, but I can call to mind more than one sultry excursion when the ointment has been completely lost to sight beneath their legion wings. One particular excursion I remember well, for it nearly ended in a catastrophe. It was on the *Heart's Desire*, Wilden's boat, one blazing afternoon in May under the walls of Soochow, and all the flies from a beggar's camp had come aboard. Wilden, a man of resource, has invented a device most effective in catching flies on the ceiling; it consists of an ordinary tumbler with half an inch of whisky in it. This, held directly under the fly, so disturbs his mind that he falls straightway into the whisky, to die a drunkard's death. Well, Wilden had cleared the ceiling of flies after dinner with a view to

a restful morning, and half a tumblerful of them bore testimony
to his ingenious device; but, alas, that tumbler was left on the table, and Wilden, awaking thirstily before dawn, mistook it for his
unfinished whisky and soda. I draw a veil on that horrid scene.
  Then there is the heat—and when the wind is in the west it
can be unpleasantly hot in May. Brandon will tell you that he
prefers the hottest day to the discomforts of winter, to getting
into bed, or out of it, in the cold, or putting on half-frozen boots.
Quot homines, tot sententæ: there may be many to agree with him;
but one may defy cold with oil-stoves, blankets, and hot grog,
while against heat there is no remedy save the ice-box, which
generally fails you in the hour of need. And then the bag, those
savoury birds to encompass whose death we have come so far,
how many times has a sultry day's swift process of decay made
useless slaughter of it all? Happily, this need no longer happen,
for with the coming of the railway each day's bag can be saved
from thus vainly perishing, and decently fulfil its destiny, between the fish and the roast, for omnivorous man.
  With the coming of the railway between Shanghai and Nanking (it has come since I began this interminable book) things
have greatly changed on the river. Places that were accessible
only to the lordly taipan and the fortnight's leave man are now
invaded by the week-end tripper, ay, even by the Portuguese
clerk; you may now see more guns than pheasants in the Pen-
yû Creek; from Chinkiang as a base all the barrier country lies
open. Already the gentry of Quinsan have petitioned that the
gun-bearing foreigner may be restrained from further invasion
of that once peaceful region: from the Chinese point of view the
nuisance is undeniable, and 'twill lead, no doubt, to passports,
licenses, and all manner of horrid regulations, taken from the
best Japanese models. In a country like this, without game-laws
or protection of any kind, the railway that gives native trappers
access to distant markets, and brings guns in a few hours to
regions hitherto unaccessible under a week's trip, must put an
end to all game in its vicinity—but, thank Heaven, the man who

looks for unbeaten paths and solitudes can still find them, and this railway-building fever that has at last overtaken our Celestial friends will help him to do so.

The Foreign Settlement at Shanghai has been called, not without reason, the best missionary in China, and you may see its results to-day in the cheap but cheering imitations of its civic administration in Peking, Canton, and many of the great cities; nevertheless, the railway is a better. For if China is to find herself, if she is to put her house in order, to protect for herself that sovereignty and territorial integrity which our international agreements so glibly guarantee for the time being, two things are essential: firstly, the people, the "stupid people," as the literary expression runs, must be educated to the point of insisting on reform of the system of government, which leaves their country at the mercy of aggression; and, secondly, the reformed Government must be relieved of its peril of bankruptcy, because bankruptcy means the united action of creditors who, so long as the debtor is solvent, work each for himself. And railways (Chinese railways, unconnected with foreign politics) will do more towards these ends than any other for education. The Mandarin of the old school knows this, and for years he has successfully headed off the "fire carriage," denouncing it as a destroyer of men's homes and ancestral sepulchres, working on the people as Demetrius stirred up the Ephesians, and with the same laudable motives. But the people are not so stupid as literary traditions would make them, and a few object lessons, taught in the face of every official obstruction, have done their work. Most of the provinces know now that they want railways just as they want education and the abolition of opium, and, when the people want anything in China, the Government is wise enough to know that they won't be happy till they get it. It is in this formation of public opinion on rational lines that lies China's hope of escaping political extinction.

Your Chinese trader is a traveller by instinct; railways to him mean new fields for barter, interchange of produce between districts that have stewed, commercially speaking, in their own juice since the beginning of time. They mean outlets for surplus labour, markets for surplus produce; they mean post-offices, newspapers, and the voice of the great world beyond. For gentry and local officials they mean opportunities in construction and management, perquisites and patronage. Therefore, though their organisation in Chinese hands is at present chaotic and rudimentary, the idea of railways is popular; every train that carries its load of traders and workers from one city to another is doing the work that is most needed, developing new channels of communication, helping to the exchange of knowledge and ideas, from whence must come reforms.

As far as the development of trade is concerned, or increase of China's producing power by reason of railways, the sanguine predictions of the wise men and Chambers of Commerce were justified, no doubt, by general experience, but they are falsified by Chinese fiscal and administrative methods. As long as the lekin system lasts, every new railway will afford new opportunities for the rapacities of the Mandarin; the lekin system will last, under one name or another, despite pious opinions and treaties, so long as Imperial revenue and the monstrous cost of its collection depend chiefly upon taxation of trade. And this indirect taxation, which simply follows the line of least resistance, will continue so long as the Central Government remains, as at present, without effective organisation and authority to collect direct taxation, that is to say, until the whole body politic is reformed upon economic principles. To-day the air is full of projects of reform, schemes for Constitutional Government, a new Navy, Law revision, and a Budget; but they revolve, like the Socialist movement of Europe, in a vicious circle, without constructive inspiration. For, to arrive at reorganised taxation, without which these schemes are foredoomed, effective authority is essential, and this cannot be established without a reorganised civil service and efficient police, which requires new sources of revenue, and, in the meanwhile, defenceless trade, goods in transit by boat, railway, or cart, continues to be taxed to the extreme limit of its endurance. Herein, again, the ultimate remedy lies in the education of public opinion, but for the moment the lekin system is more firmly established than it was even six years ago, when the Chinese Government and Sir James Mackay made arrangements (on paper) for its abolition.

You will perceive, long-suffering friends (unless you have wisely skipped this chapter), that from the subject of spring-snipe we have come perilously near to the discussion of serious matters. The transition, *via* the railway, was easy, but some of you may consider the trick unjustifiable, remembering the promises I have made you. To be quite frank, I could not resist the impulse, for there has been so much twaddle written by quite prominent persons about China and its Government that a few sensible remarks seemed timely and harmless. Let it pass at that.

To return to the railway. I was at Nanking recently, shooting snipe with the genial Irishman who is building a local line for the Viceroy, from the riverside terminus to His Excellency's Yamen, and there I met one of those excellent, thirty-year-in-the-country, sinological persons, whose business it is to teach the Oriental idea how to shoot, and whose views on Chinese affairs are eagerly sought (and reproduced as original) by travelling M.P.'s. I congratulated this worthy man on the completion of the line and on the impending construction of the hotel, progress which links up Nanking with Shanghai and civilisation, by enabling Cook's tourists to do the place comfortably in forty-eight hours. His reply was curious, opening up a new point of view and illustrating the broadening effect of outport life. "Yes," he said, "it's all very well, and no doubt it will do good. But it has its drawbacks for us who live here. Hitherto, you see, our morning paper has come from Shanghai by steamer, and I am accustomed to finding it on next morning's breakfast table. Now it reaches us in the evening, and I cannot say that I like to read a morning paper at night." Resisting the flippant suggestion that he should put it under his pillow unread, or bribe the post office to hold it till morning,

I sympathised with him heartily, realising at the same time how little we can guess at the far-reaching complex results of our well-meant attempts to amend the established order of things. But if, because of the railway's disturbance of one of his minor habits, this professionally reasonable man conceives a grievance, what must be the pent-up feelings of all that swarm of river-folk whose means of livelihood are dislocated, and perhaps destroyed, by this earth-shaking invention of the foreign devil? All the Soochow launches, stern wheelers, and passenger junks whose business dwindles day by day as the native traveller realises the advantages of speed and comfort; all the riverside inns and petty traders that lived on the water-borne traffic. Happily 'tis a patient philosophic people, living as a rule from hand to mouth, and therefore not averse to new ventures. The South Gate's loss should be the North Gate's gain; besides which (for reasons which you will find in serious works) vested interests in China, excepting those of the Man with the Button, are only locally articulate at best. Therefore it is that under the heaviest dispensations of the Chinaman's Providence, to wit famine, flood, wars and rebellions, they will die stoically in thousands, accusing or attacking no man, inarticulate in the face of the irremediable purposes of destiny. And no doubt they include railways in this category.

Nevertheless, injure these patient philosophic people in a matter where their customs or sense of justice expects redress, and you will find them as excitable and unreasonable as any peasantry in the world. An illustration of this occurred recently, when a young man, the son of a farmer near Chinkiang, was killed by a slow goods train running to Nanking. Following the custom popular in the north he had gone to sleep on the line, the rails affording a fair substitute for the Chinese idea of a pillow; but he had made his bed at a curve, so that the engine was upon him before the driver knew it. The train was stopped and the body taken to the nearest farm-house. Thereupon followed the usual scenes of loud lamentation, accompanying demands for compensation by the family. When such scenes occur after any shooting accident up country, if you do not know the language and "talk reason," the crowd usually seizes a hostage, dog, gun, or even a boat, pending a settlement; in this case they simply put the corpse back on the line and camped around it, beldames screaming on the embankments while their men sat stolidly on the rails demanding five thousand dollars. An hour later the mail train came up, lined up behind the corpse, and joined in the discussion; then another local from Chinkiang. By this time two villages had joined in the argument, which ended only after a detachment of troops had cleared the line. In discriminating between the act of God and the work of man, and determining his attitude in each case, the Oriental is often as obstinately illogical as any Scotsman.

But for all the coming of the railway, there will always be life and movement of boats on the Soochow Creek. It will not share the fate of the Peiho, whose ancient junk traffic passed with the building of the line to Peking. For the Soochow Creek (as the Grand Canal is here known to us) is the main artery of waterborne transport and trade converging from all points from the Great Lake, from the rice regions of Anhui, the silk and paper districts of Chêkiang, from countless towns and villages on inland waters remote from the railway. There will always be sails gliding silently amongst those green fields, white sails and brown and blue, gleaming in the sunlight into the farthest distances, fewer than to-day, no doubt, but plenty of them still. There is little or no current on the canal, so that carriers work with equal profit coming and going, making boat freights for the commoner and durable kind of merchandise lower than anything a railway could offer; and all the wandering petty traders and craftsmen that people these pleasant backwaters, the cormorant men and a dozen other fishing tribes, the shell-gatherers, the pedlars and beggars, these care nothing for your new-fangled methods of locomotion. For them, and for their picturesque apologies for homes, has been the freedom of these creeks since the beginning

"On a quiet backwater."

of time, and here they will be until Celestial socialism suppresses vagrancy and enforces a "minimum wage."

There is something typically Chinese, and something of irony, in the fact that much trade would naturally forsake the river—freight in market stuffs and fish, silk cocoons, tribute rice and other perishable cargo—but for the subtlety of those very lekin barriers and squeezing stations which the railway was expected to wipe out of existence. The *modus operandi* of the lekin spider who sits at the centre of the great web that stretches over the waterways of three provinces is delightfully simple, of that type of audacious simplicity that marks the best efforts of our Rockefellers and Harrimans. Magnificently ignoring the Central Government's interests and obligations, regardless of everything beyond the purview of his own blood-sucking business, he calmly decrees, treatise and conventions notwithstanding, that a rate of lekin should be levied on the railway four or five times higher than that collected on the river. Of course there are powers behind this lekin spider, powers of Buttoned men concerned in the launch trade, of vested interests in high places; nevertheless, it is typical of the country and its unchanging ways, that despite sendings of Imperial Commissioners (lavishly entertained at Gargantuan feasts), petitions of merchants, protests by Chambers of Commerce, and denunciations by the Press, one man's fiat should thus be able to defy all the King's horses and all the King's men, compelling the trade of three provinces to follow his impious will for the better collection of arbitrary and illegal levies. The spider has no armed forces; nothing to help him in this plundering of the community but "olo custom," yamen lobbying, and the long-suffering of a class incapable of collective resistance. It is the knowledge of these things that leads the plain man to wonder by whom, and how, the decrees of China's impending Parliament shall be enforced.

· CHAPTER · XIX ·
OF · GEESE · & · A · DEAD · CITY ·

"That which is dead falls not out of the universe."

— Marcus Aurelius.

A H KONG, in whom the racial instinct of utilitarianism has survived, in spite of five seasons of houseboat wandering and much good example to the contrary, estimates the bag, first in terms of avoirdupois, and then by the market value of each bird or beast. For him geese are better than pheasant or Mandarin duck, and a mallard more desirable than a woodcock; he would rather see a hog-deer swinging aft than half-a-score of partridges. To a people that instinctively reduces all things to terms of food, a good bag is a big bag; and Ah Kong is not peculiar in holding that the returning boat's "face," in the eyes of rivals or strangers, must be greater or less according to the bulk of game in evidence. Several dog-wallahs and lowdahs of my acquaintance are adepts at hanging a small bag so as to create a tolerably imposing effect, arranging it with a view to preserving their dignity when coming to moorings down the long line of boats in the Soochow Creek. One lowdah I knew, who, after following for years the fortunes of a keen shikarri, and thereby acquiring much "face," passed for sordid reasons into the service of a dilettante houseboat owner, a stout and wealthy son of Israel, and thereafter the week-end bag consisted generally of miscellaneous small birds; this fellow used to buy pheasants and wildfowl up country and festoon the houseboat with them, *honoris causa*, when homeward bound. Whether Jacobstein was privy to the business I know not, but in any case he paid, you may be sure, for his glory and those birds.

Ah Kong is at his keenest when there are geese about. Not that he ever shirks a long day's trudge after less weighty game, no matter what the weather; — in all the years of our wanderings only twice have the dogs been left to the hands of a stranger; the first time being on a joyful and domestic occasion when he claimed leave of me on the ground that his wife had "catchee puppy"; and the second being when he spent a week in gaol because of certain unlawful dealings instigated by the said wife's brother, a notorious rowdy of the French Settlement; which has nothing to do with the present narrative.

Whenever a cold snap comes with a north-easter, Ah Kong's fancy lightly turns to thoughts of geese, and he is careful to see that wire cartridges, loaded with treble "A," are aboard. When a sortie impends, he will report "too muchee goose" in the market, and suggest the Pingwu country and Cholin as likely spots. I think that in his mind's eye he sees a memorable New Year's day when Jim and I got amongst them, and made the stern of the *Saucy Jane* to look like a poulterer's shop — one of those lucky chances of the right place at the right time that come to those who wait. It was indeed a trip to remember. We had sailed for a four days' cruise in company with the *Water-Baby*, then owned by Mirabelle, a jolly fat Frenchman whose enormous salary helps the Russian Bank to keep down its dividends. And with Mirabelle was M'Nulty, of the Dock Company, in whom a growing penchant for whisky and anecdotage struggled with the aboriginal instincts of a keen sportsman. On New Year's morning, a fine boisterous wind booming from the sea, we had done some combined stalking in the flat country between Sung-kiang and the coast, where the geese, with vedettes posted, stood huddled together in the open fields, motionless dabs of grey against the brown. With the scanty covert of these parts it is usually no easy matter to get within range of the birds; but either because, to see Mirabelle crawling on all fours, or at full length on his jolly fat paunch, was enough to root any bird to the spot, or because they were storm-tossed and weary, we made several successful stalks. The *modus operandi* was for three guns to approach from different sides, crawling as close as possible, while Ah Kong kept the sentinels interested by fluttering a handkerchief 150 yards away. When the crawling began to converge on the centre, Jim, whose blue nankeens look like a Chinaman's kit, would walk casually towards the geese from the fourth side. As the sentinel's first warning scream sent up every white-billed head in the gaggle as if you had pulled a string, each crawler rose and sprinted his best towards the turmoil of grey wings now beating feverishly upwind; and before the skein could tail out to its wedge-like formation overhead, some of them usually returned, with a satisfactory thud, to mother earth. By tiffin-time we had ten geese and a couple of teal, and Mirabelle, dirty but enthusiastic, was planning fresh exploits for the afternoon.

But, alas! for the transient virtue of man! It was New Year's day and the *Water-Baby's* menu would not have shamed the Café de la Paix. M'Nulty, professing good resolutions, began with whisky, but Mirabelle's example, and the gradual lapse into the convivial sentimentality proper to such occasions, led him to Pommerey and Greno, thence to port, green peppermint, and many professions of love and goodwill to sportsmen in general and ourselves in particular. By three o'clock we had sung *Auld Lang Syne* twice, and M'Nulty had proposed the healths of Robbie Burns, la belle France, and Highland Mary, interspersed with Homeric tales of his own inpecunious and riotous youth. In this mood he and Mirabelle agreed that goose-stalking had no further attractions for them, and they settled down accordingly to a convivial game of picquet. Meanwhile the boats, sailing and tracking, had come within sight of the walls of Cholin; so Jim and

I went ashore, with Ah Kong and a beater, and made our way across country towards the city.

More vividly than the grim vestigia of Pompeii, or than any of our garnered relics of vanished peoples, these deserted cities appeal to the imagination, bringing home to us, as in a lightning flash, all the pitiful passions and destinies of man. Here one's footfall echoes through long streets of desolate homes, and the rank grass grows thick in the forsaken haunts of men; from the embrasured gates, through which half-a-century ago the stream of life flowed fast, the eye rests on the abomination of desolation—paved streets and bridges are there, the outline of houses, temples, and gardens, all the handiwork of a peaceful and industrious people, passing to premature decay. Over all lies a brooding silence; no curling smoke from any roof, hardly a sign of life except a few reed-cutters in the moat. From this grass-grown wall one can picture something of the untold horrors of those days, when the wells were choked with the bodies of women, and there were none to do honour to the dead; when those who escaped the Taipings fell a prey to the Imperialists, and no man's life was safe from Nanking to Ningpo. You can hear the horrid turmoil of the city's sacking, the wailing of children, the shouting of savage men; and remembering that all these things happened, within the memory of man, to a people bred in traditions of unbroken peace, it is not hard to realise that when the few survivors crept back, upon the passing of the scourge, they should place their trust no more in city walls, but prefer to make their homes along the open waterways.

Looking down from the gate, on this bleak winter's evening, it seemed like a city of the forgotten dead; but in spring and autumn there is life and work between the walls, for all the land that is not too thickly strewn with ruins is sown with millet, melons, and lucerne. Nor is the city itself so completely deserted as it seems from the walls. Men live there, a few new-comers unhaunted by memories of evil days, and more will come each year as the pressure of population (eased for a time by that scourge) makes itself felt again. Away towards the North Gate, near a swamp that was once the fish-pond of a rich man's garden, where duck came for shelter in hard weather, I know a small temple from which incense has gone forth into these solitudes for many years. It is only a shrine, probably built by the rich man, to the tutelary spirits of fire and water, and, judging by its state of repair, I imagine that its revenues are entirely drawn from the sale of marsh reeds; but the bonze is a philosopher, of contemplative habit and friendly, with whom Jim and I usually smoke a pipe when we pass this way. As becomes a dweller of these ghost-ridden silences and pastor of a vanished flock, he is of gentle voice and slow speech; caring little for the things that disturb struggling humanity, but very wise in ancient tales, given to much speculation on the elemental mysteries of the life and destinies of man, learned in legend, folklore, and the proceedings of spirits. With ghosts, which naturally abound in his vicinity, he is on friendly terms, professing to know more of their habits than he is at liberty to reveal. And with all this—no doubt as the result of much solitary thinking—he has all a child's curiosity in regard to the inventions of overseas men. He knows that they so use and control the thunder-matter of clouds, converting it into light for their houses, that the storms of to-day are not so frequent or so fierce as in the olden times; that by means of this thunder-matter their carriages move swiftly without smoke, and the words of men are sent in a flash across the four seas; and he never wearies of asking of these marvels. A fitting and proper resident for a dead city this gentle priest with a child's soul, serving his placid gods in the little shrine under the wall, finding consolation of dreams and fearful joy in his evening pinch of opium. He is not ashamed of his smoking, but complains of the high cost of the beneficial drug, to obtain which, I fancy, he must deprive himself and his gods of many better things.

No, friends, I shall not weary you with the whole truth about opium abolition. It would serve no good purpose, for the great heart of England has determined that it is part of our civilising mission to remove this evil, greatly ignorant of the thing itself and of the grievous ills that must follow its sudden uprooting. The automatically self-adjusting conscience which leads comfortable Christian Britons to acquire merit by promoting the spiritual welfare of other nations, is not a matter for argument. Vicarious philanthropy of this kind postulates moral superiority, to deny which is to class oneself amongst those to be prayed for; yet, any man who honestly faces the facts, comparing the gin-beam of pious England with the opium-mote of pagan China, must find it in his heart to pray for a Buddhist mission if only to plead against the Saturday night horrors of our crime-laden cities. Opium, taken to excess, is an evil—granted; but only four

or five per cent of the Chinese people smoke opium, and probably less than half of these do so to excess. And the good sense, the innate thrift, and instinctive morality of the people (which owe nothing to Imperial edicts) are creating a public opinion in this matter, on lines similar to American State prohibition, and equally effective as a social force; with all that, however, there are serious problems that remain to be solved in connection with this abolition of opium, problems of fiscal and agricultural readjustment, and it remains for the rulers of the country to make sure that the chamber swept clean of one evil spirit be not invaded by seven devils infinitely worse. Of these matters Exeter Hall knows and asks little or nothing. The thing is evil—it is on the other side of the World, — away with it! If one might hope that, with the abolition of opium, the Macedonian question, and all the other outlets for our philanthropic energies overseas, the Nonconformist conscience might awake to the immediate need of cleaner, soberer, and healthier conditions amongst our own people, we might sympathise more kindly with this activity *in partibus infidelium*. As things are, I often wonder what intelligent Chinese think of the edifying debates on the Great British People's Licensing and Education Bills?

Which reminds me to return to our geese. It was between the city and the sea-wall, just at sunset, that fortune smiled on us, and the heart of Ah Kong was made to rejoice. The wind was still blowing bitterly cold in squalls off the sea; we had bagged only a brace of pheasants and some teal, and were thinking of making tracks to the boats when a skein of geese came swift and low over the wall, heading straight inland. They were the first of a steady flight that came in twos and threes, as if to a rendezvous. There was cover behind the high graves, and in this wind the guns could not be heard to windward, so the flight kept its line, and for ten minutes ours was a warm corner. There we stayed after the flight was done, hoping for more, after the manner of insatiable man, until the last ray of light was gone and the last bird retrieved. Then, with Ah Kong staggering under the weight of many geese, we stumbled contentedly across the fields towards the houseboat mast lamps glimmering in the distance. Halfway there met us a noise of shouting, and thereafter Mirabelle and M'Nulty, with lanterns and guns and several of the boat's crew; they had heard us firing, as they said, in the dark, and from the fusillade had imagined some horrid catastrophe or piratical attack. And so, as old Pepys would say, right gladly to dinner.

Mirabelle, weary of M'Nulty and picquet, had been out with his spaniel at sunset looking for quail on the grassy slope of the city wall, and the voluble account of his adventures lasted half an hour or more. First of all, it seems, he had fired at a bird just as it was topping the wall and the dog had gone after it, as spaniels will, taking the twenty-foot drop with a squeak of astonishment, — " And that was a thing extraordinary, was it not, for when I looked down, expecting to see the poor beast with all his legs broken, behold, *le voilà*, trying to climb up the wall with the quail between his teeth," and the good man sang the long praises of his dog, as all sportsmen should do, deriving vicarious merit and glory from the canine's faithful intelligence.

His next adventure was less glorious than lamentable. Hearing a great whirr of wings in the dusk he had "fired twice upon the brown" — a swift moving shadow overhead — fully expecting a bag that would make M'Nulty repent his sticking to the boat. The immediate result was four crows, reluctantly retrieved by the faithful dog, and for us, much explanation of so undeserved a misfortune. Jim and I sympathised, of course, but M'Nulty, in whom mixed drinks and losses at picquet had produced a reaction of melancholy, observed that Mirabelle was not fit to be trusted with dog or gun after tiffin, and the sooner he realised this the better.

That night we lay close to the city; and at midnight, the wind having dropped and the lights of unnumbered worlds shining clear overhead, Jim and I smoked a last pipe on the wall while Ah Kong walked the dogs. Passing through the idle, battlemented gate that hears no more the closing sunset gong, we looked upon that waste of darkness and haunting silences. No friendly beacon-light in all that was once a city, no watchman's cry to mark the passing hours; here, close to the teeming haunts of men, it was as if time had ceased, as if the last Trump had sounded, leaving a world untenanted and void to carry all its burden of cities, all humanity's pitiful broken toys into the depths of space through æons of silent years. It was more forlorn even by night than by day, this city of the dead, and the distant hooting of an owl seemed as the voice of some poor homeless soul.

"Ugh," said Jim, "this gives me the shivers — come along to bed." So we made our way back to the boat and to the comfortable voices of men.

CHAPTER XX

"I do not searche and tosse over Books, but for an honester recreation to please and pastime to delight myself." — MONTAIGNE.

HE provision of books for up-country reading is a delicate matter. There are, I know, houseboats that take no thought for the business; frankly Philistine boats with sporting owners of the good old British-beer-and-brawn type, who assure you that their whole concern is to walk until they eat and sleep, and then to eat and sleep until they can walk again.

Wilden will tell you in his cheery way that a volume or two of *Gals' Gossip* and a pack of cards are all the literature he needs, and I knew one good man who went up country quite happily for several years with a job lot of old *Punch's* and magazines that he had picked up at an auction. But it should by this time have been made clear to you that for the inner brotherhood of Houseboat Idlers, while the killing of game is the day's chief ostensible end, it is by no means the only object of these our delectable journeyings; and

without good, companionable books no decent man can idle satisfactorily for a fortnight. He may manage to get through his day,
to kill his share of beasts and time, but he will lack the fine flower
of conscientious idling, properly anticipated and equipped.

Now, some men read for pleasure, others deliberately to im-
prove the mind, as a sort of business investment or bread upon
the waters, and others again from a sheer instinct of conformity
to the usages of polite society. Thurlsby, whose profession naturally inclines him to precision and authority, toils steadily, year
in and year out, through the dreary waste of Somebody's "Best
Hundred Books," some of which tomes accompany him on every
trip, Acton's or Lubbock's infallible prescription for the equipment of a first-class mental interior. We have all seen these lists —
they begin with the Bible, Dante, Milton, and Herodotus; go on
to Plato, Marcus Aurelius, and Gibbon; and end up with *John
Inglesant*, translations from Tolstoi and Anatole France. There is
generally a new one published every year for the better bewil-
derment of earnest artisans, who look for them in the *Review of
Reviews* or *M.A.P.* Such things are not for self-respecting Idlers.
They merely prove that modern Man, product of cities and co-
operative societies, remains still true to the primitive type, in
that he moves in herds under the direction of superior minds,
and generally suffers for so doing. For reasonable beings (like
you and me), the fact that any particular hundred books are (or
were) the best pabulum for Lord Acton or Sir Alfred Austin, is
proof sufficient that we should do well to avoid a considerable
number of them. One might just as reasonably be asked to swal-
low the best hundred patent pills, or to listen continually to the
best hundred popular melodies. These quidnuncs who thrust the
"Books that have helped them" at you make no allowance for
the seven ages or the changing moods of men; to hear them talk
you would think that the whole world is peopled with nothing
but respectable middle-aged gentlemen who should spend their
days in patent arm-chairs with book-rest attachments, training
their minds to a fine level of superior stodginess. But for all their

solemn exhortations and their dull shelves packed with uniform bindings, there are yet books of verse beneath the bough, and cakes and ale for those who would rather remember the sound of laughter,—books that one may take on a honeymoon or a house-boat with all propriety and satisfaction.

The selection of houseboat literature, being a thing intended to increase and promote the pleasure of right-minded persons, is therefore a matter of individual taste. Nevertheless, because of the good understanding that pervades the cult and fellowship of Idling, because of our common ways and byways, not all of one man's meat need be another's poison. I am laying down no rules—Heaven forbid—but merely to satisfy your curiosity in a matter quite as interesting as anything else in this book, I suggest certain kinds of literature which fittingly lend themselves to houseboat days harmonising with the spirit of our wanderings.

Reading, as a matter of pleasure, resembles eating and drinking in this, that sometimes we have appetite for a square meal, and sometimes we need only a snack or *hors d'œuvres*. Yesterday we called for strong meats and good red wine: to-day, give us pasties and junkets and ice-cream. In reading, as in feeding, there are proprieties, times, and seasons to be observed; a time for curry and a time for caviare; and the wise man is he, and fortunate, who can adapt his diet to his moods. On a wet afternoon, for instance, when the boat is slowly crawling through some mournful expanse of sodden, gameless country, I do not want to read of things gently melancholy, of life's brief candle, and the vanity of man's desires. That sort of thing appeals to me quite forcibly, and strikes me as appropriate on a bright noonday, or in the siesta hour of a summer's afternoon, when the comfortable warmth and stir of life is all around. Then, to a well-balanced mind, the poet's restless longings act as a corrective to realities, and I can listen sympathetically to the words of men grown wise in contemplation of the woes of humanity. For the same reason, it is in wild outlandish places that I love to read of the lives and sayings of honest, frank-spoken men. On a boisterous wintry night, when the shrill winds are shrieking over the marshes, what better than to curl up in your bunk, and, heedless of those clamorous voices, to travel over the fair face of the earth in company with sentimental Sterne, or Stevenson and his donkey; to pace the Mall with Boswell or jolly Pepys, or to ride through the smiling lands of France with stout Froissart or wise Montaigne. Howl on, wind! Here are human voices of comfort and good cheer, stout hearts whose message has lightened many a traveller's load through lonely places and dark-stumbling nights!

There are times, then, for ancients and for moderns, — times for poetry and times for prose. No sensible or sensitive man reads *Tristram and Iseult* on a full stomach, or George Bernard Shaw on an empty one. In some matters of pure choice we decide for ourselves, according to temperament and the hour, while others are decided for us by the unwritten laws of fitness. Jim, who has curiously fixed habits in the matter of literature, always reads himself to sleep with poetry, which (unless it be Browning or Meredith) is commendable enough and conducive to dreams, even though one may disapprove of fixed habits in such a matter. Before dinner, from a survival of a military sense of duty, he usually reads a Service paper over his vermouth, and, for the rest, the shelf over his bunk proclaims a very catholic if somewhat old-fashioned taste. Most soldiers and all lawyers are old-fashioned in their reading; there is something in the cocksureness of new writers, particularly of the iconoclasts, that offends their nice sense of decorum and discipline. Jim honestly prefers Lytton to Belloc and Dickens to any modern scribe. Kipling and Stevenson he counts among the elect, but for the solemn purposeful works of Mrs. Humphry Ward and Mr. Hall Caine he has, as he puts it, no more use than a dog has for mice. I have sometimes tried to dissuade him from this sweeping intolerance, because art and wisdom and kindliness did not really die with Queen Victoria. I have tried to show him that it is not fair to blame a writer for not being dead, and that while Marie Corelli may very properly be avoided, there are worthy and profitable bookmakers, such as

Conrad or Chesterton, whom to eschew is foolish. But I make no impression on him.

And if you are at all old-fashioned, there is something to be said for such an attitude. For, however much we may be attracted and amazed by the marvellous cleverness of these new lights of the literary circus, however much we may be drawn by the ringing clamour of the market-place, it is to the ancients that we go instinctively

> When in disgrace with fortune and men's eyes.

There is a healing virtue in them, born, I think, of the comfortable thought that all the eternal questions and problems of our harassed modernity are nothing new, and that the best answers were known to those stout old fellows even before they sang or fought their little lives away. Your modern lacks something of this quality. He toils, heartily enough, along the roads we know; his landmarks and adventures might be ours, with a little effort or a little luck, for the seeking; but in his forebears we catch an echo of the myriad sandalled feet of those who made this grim journey between two infinities when the world was young. Their voices bring the dim past close to us, in human comradeship, making of this whirling planet our good Mother Earth indeed, and easing us, if only for a little while, of this close-fitting Time-garment. Which of us but has found a forty-parson power of contentment in that deep-browed pagan, Homer, whose voice rings down the ages as fresh as the winds that blow on the Arcadian hills, that voice to which countless generations have gone for joyful sustenance while all their sages and their saints have passed to oblivion. Boy or man, you can read the immortal story of Ulysses at any time. And of this indestructible flavour are also the Norsemen's Sagas, and the Book of Job, and the *Morte d'Arthur*.

These are regular passengers on the *Saucy Jane*. Others may come and go, but they abide. The Golden Treasury is there also, and a dozen of the leather-bound Temple classics, with sweet Will of Avon, Swinburne, Shelley, and Omar. Montaigne is there, of course, and Stevenson's Essays, with odd volumes of Balzac, Dickens, and Hazlitt; Hans Christian Andersen, Lafcadio Hearn, and Hakluyt's *Voyages*. In this company, I warrant you, any man may travel to the ends of the earth and lack nothing of good conversation. And for serious business literature we have the Badminton books on shooting and Yarrell's *Birds*, by help of which Jim has won many a bet from unsuspecting tender-feet.

These, then, are our good familiar friends, in the sense of whose presence lies comfort, even if we should have no word with them for days, and give our attention to transient and less noble guests. They are there when we call upon them, to enjoy when the mood calls, a very comfortable and seemly company of fellow-travellers. To each man his own friends. I make no pretence of advising you in this matter of the choice of books, but I "extremely bewaile those men of understanding who do lacke the same."

Strange, is it not, when one thinks of the part played by the dramatic, epic, and passionate poets in the life-history of our western half of the world, to realise that this Chinese race has contrived to exist without them through the long centuries, and dispenses very easily with their soul-stirring voices to this day? Strange that so large a family of the human race should have settled down to a prosy philosophy so different from that of its neighbours. True, they reckon verse-making among their literary arts, and the composition of couplets and quatrains as an elegant pastime for scholars in the dilettante manner, even as old Etonians do and parsons of studious habit. You will find their classic, machine-made odes scribbled by pilgrims on Temple walls, and songs after the convivial manner of Li Tai-po in way-side inns; but for the voices that move and hold the hearts of men, the voices of Olympus and Valhalla, you listen in vain. The best Chinese poetry consists of lyrical effusions reminiscent of the *Georgics* — a comfortable well-balanced Muse, very suitable to a people thus orderly-behaved and firm-rooted from its cradle to its grave. But for the deep notes wherein speak the tragedies of life and death, for those trumpet tongues that have called the human beast from his stall, setting his face towards the heights, for the brave songs that have made our old world young with dreams of Beauty, spiritual and physical, these have no place in the Celestial philosophy. The placid road to Nirvana, if you will, and an appreciative eye for sunsets by the way, and the swaying of bamboos in the breeze; but for them no marshalling of captains for crusades, no perilous quest of Holy Grails, no chivalrous idealising of their pleasing but commonplace chattel, Woman.

Of course our friend the Babu, secure in his ignorance and our own, will patriotically prove to you that the *Book of Odes* contains every essential quality and ingredient of the highest kind of poetry. He will remind you that the Psalms of David, and the *Rubaiyat*, so greatly esteemed by intelligent Europeans, are the work of Oriental poets, and he will assure you that innumerable masterpieces, equally admirable, are to be found in the literature of China. Ku Hung-ming, for instance, being himself a scholar and a maker of indifferent verse, who knows his Goethe and Shakespeare-Bacon by heart, and has translated *John Gilpin* into elegant quatrains, will tell you that the divine afflatus of the Greek, Roman, and Elizabethan poets is simply a matter of convention in literary taste, and that the Muses are as much at home, though perhaps less noisy, in the Hanlin Yuan as on the heights of Parnassus, — but then Ku Hung-ming enjoys benefit of privilege as a charmingly original and inaccurate writer. As for the real Babu, being neither flesh, fowl, nor good red herring, but only a by-product and an exotic, he must not be taken too seriously. His voice at the moment sounds shrill above the inevitable clash of systems raging from Calcutta to Canton, but in spite of all his clamour and his undoubted capacity for inciting Demos to violent Chauvinism, he represents no permanent instinct in the national Zeitgeist. At best he is a theorising philosopher and a faddist; at worst a hybrid parasite "that mocks the meat it feeds on." Brought into being by the present craving of the Chinese people for something better than the dry bones of the classical system, educated for the most part by teachers as ignorant as himself, he occupies for the moment an artificially prominent place in the body-politic. Quite incapable (even and especially when educated in Japan) of assimilating that higher form of patriotism, wherein the interests of the individual are subordinated to those of the Commonwealth, without generous impulses of altruism, he loudly proclaims his Heaven-sent mission and his reforming panaceas, and clamours for the granting of a Constitution, which shall bring him in, with his smattering of "Western learning," on the flowing tide of a new dispensation. Meanwhile, you may find his handiwork in political agitation of the baser sort, in mendacious and inflammatory presswork, directed with nice impartiality against everything he fears or resents, inciting to deeds of violence, at the first sign of which he will assuredly betake himself to the nearest and safest hiding-place. Not a pleasant type, the Babu, and dangerous to any form of government, constitutional or autocratic; but apparently an inevitable result of the heady new wine of the West poured into these ancient Eastern skins. He, too, will pass and be forgotten; like the *tricoteuses* of the Bastille, the scum thrown up by days of upheaval and ferment—an ephemeral phenomenon.

Not long since I came across an interesting specimen of the Celestial Muse pressed into service of Babu patriotism. It dates from the time of the American boycott, and affords, I think, a very fair example of Chinese poetic methods as well as of existing political conditions. As regards its subject matter, be it said that China has an undeniable grievance against the materially civilised world in this exhibition of discriminating race prejudice applauded by the very nations that enforce in China the principle of the open door. Recognition of this fact has induced in the American Government a somewhat shamefaced instinct of reparation which finds its expression in conscience-money; but apart from this doubtful benefit, the boycott injured many Chinese without sensibly affecting the volume of American trade. Let that pass: we must needs use such weapons as lie handy. Here, at any rate, is the poem: —

A SONG OF THE SEASONS

The first month of the year is fragrant with the scent of the plum-tree;
On the west side of the World there lies a great calm Sea,
Within that sea is set the land of the Flowery Banner.
The affairs of that land are controlled by the men of the Labour Union.

The second month is beautiful with the beauty of the red apricot flower.
We, men of China, who went forth to labour, suffered many hardships,
We successfully opened many mines of silver and gold.
For the American people we built and completed all the roads whose rails are of iron.

The third month opens with the flowering of the peach-tree;
The men of the Labour Union, forgetting the work we had done in the past, devised other and newer ways;
They consumed with fire the street of Dong Sung Ka;
They burnt us natives of China until the weeping of men and women was indeed pitiful to behold.

The fourth is the month of all flowers and plants and herbs;
As for us, we men of China, we thought upon the bitterness of our lot;
I have been sent into the world by Heaven,
Why should the treatment accorded to dead pigs be meted out to us?

The fifth month is the month of the flowering of the pomegranates;
As for the men of the Labour Unions of America, they carried out the schemes of injustice which they had planned.
On their coasts they built prisons of wood.
In them they confined us, natives of China.

The sixth month is that in which the flower of the Lotus takes its tint of
   red;
After taking us into the prisons of wood which they had built, they
   scorched us with fires of sulphur;
Officials of all grades and students of all ages received the same measure of ill-treatment.
They were treated without mercy.

In the seventh month the hyacinth begins to bloom.[1]
Hardships such as these we have suffered for more than twenty years.
It is a great pity that we men of China, whose number are ten thousand
   times ten thousand,
Four times over, are not equal in value to the half of the smallest of cop-
   per cash.

The eighth month is that in which the cinnamon sheds its sweetness;
Among the members of the Chinese Chamber of Commerce is one
   whose name is Tseng Sau Ching.
This man planned a most civilised method.
He spent money on it, advanced the righteous cause, and his fame has
   gone forth.

The ninth month is the month of the yellow chrysanthemum.
Let us all assemble together and discuss its details.
It is best not to use American goods.
To oppose the interests of America is our best course.

The tenth month is the month when beautiful flowers become green;
We advise you men and women of China,
If you wish to eat your rice for the future in peace,
Attend to and realise the importance of this movement.

In the eleventh month the blossom of the reeds is blown about by the
   wind;

---

[1] Translator's Note: It doesn't.

We, every one of us, must remember and not too soon forget the
Pin-Head Cigarettes and the scented soap of the American Trading
  Company.
Furthermore let us remember not to use American piece goods any
  more.

In the twelfth month the flowers of the "hindl" are many;
All you gentlemen who have listened to my song, be civilised, and
  retaliate.
Do not learn the barbarous ways of the Peking Boxers, or imitate them,
For if we commit any wrongful or mischievous act, we shall "eat our
  own bitterness."

As neat a blending of art with utility, in the Walt Whitman
manner, as any man could ask for. My old writer, it is true, sees
in this gem internal evidence of Japanese origin, and as the thing
was circulated by agents of the Dai Nippon Tobacco Monopoly,
I should not be surprised if he were right. But, even if it be so,
the Japanese scholar has only adopted and followed the petrified
classical models of composition which China gave to his country
in the dim ages.

Before taking leave of the Babu, let me remove a possible
misapprehension. Not all of foreign educated Chinese (not even
all of those "raised" in American Mission schools) are necessarily Babus. There is a large and happily increasing class of Young
China, men of good families, sense, and substance, that now returns from abroad with a thoroughly sound education, an education which enables them to appreciate the qualities as well as the
defects of their own institutions. It is of this class that is being
formed the wedge that shall presently split up the classical system. As a class, however, these men are naturally less hungry and
therefore less noisy than the Babus, who swarm in their clamour-
ing thousands wherever schools, telegraphs, custom-houses, and
other Government offices offer hopes of employment for men of
"Western learning," that learning which they have acquired in six

months' attendance at a mission or Japanese night-class. These men, who are, I suppose, the Chinese equivalent for the street-parading, bobby-bashing students of other lands, are anti-foreign, anti-Manchu, anti-taxes, anti-opium, anti-everything; they have a quarrel with the universe and are not particular at what spot it begins. For their constructive policy, so far as you can get them to define it, consists of vague and frothy declarations of the rights of man and denunciation of tyrants; windy schemes for the millennium and universal content, with much undigested Rousseau and John Stuart Mill, assimilated through cheap and bad translations. These views for you and me; but for the native press and the platform, red-hot Republicanism and patriotic tears. (It is really wonderful how copiously these men will weep in public at a moment's notice and in droves.) And then, in a little while, comes a job in the Post Office, a wife or two, several new editions of Young China on the back premises, a widening girth and fat neck, a pair of goggles and a stake in the country, and a gradual acquiescence in the established order and methods of ancient things Celestial. How many such have we not known, converted from ranting rowdyism to *bons bourgeois* habits and sober multiple paternity by the kindly hand of Time? Nevertheless, because of his noise and his numbers, and his incorrigible and inconceivable ignorance, the Chinese Babu remains for the time being a nuisance and something of a menace to the public peace.

° ON · COMING · HOME ·

CHAPTER XXI

"Home is the sailor, home from sea,
And the hunter home from the hill."
                                    STEVENSON.

E were sailing down the seven-mile reach, Jim and I, homeward bound after a day with the snipe at Chapu. The young May moon was riding serenely through shoals of fleecy clouds, and a warm south-westerly breeze driving the *Saucy Jane* gently along to the music of rippling waters. Smoking contentedly in our long cane chairs on the foredeck we were very near to that Nirvana of restfulness which man lost at the gates of Eden, and towards which his blundering steps have turned instinctively ever since. On the broad river, silence, and the shimmering message of uncounted worlds; on shore, a mysterious fairyland of silver and shadows.

I had been holding forth eloquently on the folly that wastes our powers and chances of enjoying life on the unceasing labour of getting and spending, getting and spending,—a text induced, no doubt, by the prospect of to-morrow's mechanical routine, contrasted with the Buddha-like detachment of these lotus hours. I had been comparing the life of our old friend the Cholin bonze with that of the heart-hungry, quill-driving automata of our civilisation, and Jim, who generally agrees sympathetically on such occasions, had puffed away in silence. The best of monologues is apt to pall, especially when it deals with conflicting systems, so after a while it perished on the midnight, without pain, and we sat gazing, with speculative eyes, at the inverted star-spangled bowl above our heads.

I think it was the physical effort of filling a new pipe that roused Jim from his musings to slow speech.

"I don't know that I'd like to lead that old johnny's life," he said, "at least, not yet a while. The white man's burden may gall a bit at times, but I prefer it to the yellow man's dreams, any day. And so do you, Phil. You've just been grousing because you're going home to work, but you'd grouse far worse if you had no home and no work to go back to. Human cussedness, that's all."

"The ideal of philosophic contentment is not the yellow man's exclusive dream, my dear Jim. There are superior minds in every country, as Confucius very rightly surmised."

"That's not what I'm driving at. What I mean is that half the joy of wandering comes from the thought of coming home again, just as the most subtle flavour of fireside contentment lies in the contemplation of future wanderings. Light and shadow, old chap, ebb and flow, — the flavour of life comes from its contrasts."

"Ay, keep moving, Jim — that's the thing. To see the cities of the earth and learn the minds of men; to keep your mind from rusting and your bones from getting stiff. That's the wisdom of the ancients."

"All very well up to a certain point, but restlessness is just as much a disease now as it was in the days of Ishmael. Your American tourist-wives keep moving all right, but you would hardly call them philosophers."

"*Moderata durant*," said I. "All depends on the motive. American women travel to get new frocks or new husbands, and to escape the horrors of domesticity without domestics."

"Quite so; but for the same majority of humanity, for those whose normal instincts haven't been destroyed by nerves or the hotel habit, or exceptional bad luck, there remains always, at the back of all our *wanderlust*, the homing instinct. Aren't we all of the same mould as old Ulysses, father of globe-trotters? Not all the enchantments of Circe and Calypso can destroy the vision of the old familiar places, the little headland on rock-bound Ithaca."

"Jim, you're getting poetical again. I don't blame you on a night like this, but the fact remains. I don't deny that every one of us cherishes a dim and distant ideal of settling down some day, of ending his days in stay-at-home contentment, with Penelope and her distaff in the ingle-nook. We all look forward to growing fat-headed cabbages when the wild oats' crop is garnered. Which simply amounts to admitting that every one expects to grow comfortably dull in old age, and to choose a congenial spot to be dull in."

"Don't pretend to be cynical, Phil. All the flavour of life lies, I say, in its contrasts. The man who has never worked doesn't know the blessedness of loafing, and the man who doesn't know the joys of coming home has missed half the pleasure of wandering."

"Right you are; but don't overdo the idealising. There isn't a white man east of Suez, I suppose, who hasn't got a pretty little picture at the back of his mind, a little dream that he hugs particularly tight when things are going wrong. A dream of a nice little place in the country, somewhere among the fields and lanes where he went apple-stealing as a boy, a place with cheery neighbours, and a home-farm, a little fishing, golf, and the other leisurely pastimes over which a man may potter respectably to his grave, taking his family to the parish church on Sunday mornings, and reading Dickens and Thackeray over his glass of port at night. Every one has an ideal of that sort tucked away somewhere for future use. But sensible people like you and I, Jim, know that it's only an ideal, something like the young man's fancy when it lightly turns to thoughts of love."

(This last was a shrewd thrust, deliberately dealt; for, when Jim grows poetical, the presence of Lady Betty is hovering very near us in space.)

"Well," he said, "if it is only an ideal, let's hold on to it. Anyhow, it's a fairly old one and has worn well enough in spite of your socialists and suffragettes, the restaurant mania and all your modern nonsense. Those ideas are nothing but the froth and flurry of a small and noisy set; behind them are the eternal humanities, the decent unsophisticated millions of men to whom the idea of home means something real, something that has been from the beginning, is now, and ever shall be. Did you ever hear Patti sing 'Home, Sweet Home' to a provincial audience, Phil?"

"Yes, and it brought the Vision near to every one of us. Each saw the place of his dreams, the ideal place of eternal sunshine and rest, and the old familiar faces. It brought a lump to one's throat, Jim, but it didn't bring us a bit nearer to reality. The old words, the old music, can revive transmitted memories whose roots lie centuries deep, they can touch emotional chords to an echo of forgotten music; but they can't remit the penalty that every one of us has to pay for having eaten of the fruit of the tree of knowledge."

Jim didn't answer for some minutes. The *Saucy Jane* was tacking close in shore, the moon's light-cast silver dancing in our wake, and from a fisher's hut on the bank came the plaintive high-pitched recitative of a lonely watcher by his dip-net. 'Twas a night to broaden one's ideas of relative values and the absolute unimportance of man.

Jim sighed, as one who is weary. "You're all wrong," he said, "but don't let us argue any more. Be quiet and listen to that poor benighted heathen over yonder. He's only telling you what every poet knows, the simple things that no machinery or modern fads can ever kill. You may pretend to have outgrown them, but they are there just the same."

"All right, Jim, but go slow with your poets, at least as regards the 'Home, Sweet Home' business. Remember what Keats said about it, for one. But I know what you mean, — the *basso pro-fundo* Wordsworth-Tennyson brigade, as distinguished from the untamed tenor bards. You're becoming respectable, Jim, and I'm glad of it. 'Twas high time." And I quoted softly to the stars: —

> "And Lucy at her wheel shall sing
> In russet gown and apron blue."

"Yes," said Jim, "you're right this time, for I'm going to marry Betty as soon as ever she can get her trousseau from Paris. And as we shall be going home in the autumn, this is my last trip on the *Saucy Jane* for some time, old chap. I didn't want to tell you before, Phil, because, well, I'm sorry to say good-bye to the old tub and all the good times we've had together."

I said I was glad, of course, and in a sort of a way I was; but in another, and very distinct way, I wasn't. Lady Betty could have found a husband any day without advertising, but where was I to find another Jim? Without him to talk to on long winter evenings half the joy of houseboat days would be gone, and already, in my mind's eye, the old haunts loomed cheerless ahead. Ah, well, *tout passe, tout lasse, tout casse.* The moment was a fit one for those social conventions wherewith we are wont to stifle the first signs of sentiment, and Gehazi's whisky and soda, timely brought, was appropriately consumed to the greater glory of Lady Betty.

"Good luck to you both," said I, with a silent libation, "and may all your dreams come true. May you win home to the Castle Beautiful, and live there happily ever after. And may the rest of your days, friend Jim, be as free from care as those we have passed together."

Heigho! for 'tis a sad, mad, little world! All our busy little lives, the sputtering of a brief candle, spent in building us castles in the Enchanted Isles, where everything is to be different from the grim realities we have known; in seeking and storing up toys that break and flowers that fade, against the distant day of our coming home. And then, as we learn a little wisdom, we rebuild our castles, seeking ever new toys and new flowers to satisfy our new ideals, until quickly we grow old over "the toil that each dawning quickens, and the task that is never done"; and so we come Home at last, all our plans and playthings forgotten,

> Gathered to the silent west,
> The sunset splendid and serene,
> Death.

At daybreak we anchored at the Bund. A thrush was singing lustily in the magnolias of the Public Garden, and the south wind came laden with the first fragrance of summer. Already the river was humming with traffic of men and the stir of the day's work—a morning to send all blue devils and heart-searchings to the right-about. And as Jim walked briskly ashore, whistling something which he intended to be "Queen of my Heart," I found it in mine to rejoice that he should be thus hotfoot on the quest of the Golden Girl, even though the *Saucy Jane* and I must be left behind. And there was a sneaking voice of consolation in my ears, a voice that seemed to fit in with the song of the thrush and the whisper of the south wind, which told me that some day, sooner or later, Jim would come aboard once more, and our talk would begin again where it had left off. For the call of the wild carries farther than all the voices of men.

"Dog Rex," said I to that sympathetic quadruped, as he walked solemnly by my side with the regulation muzzle on his disciplined nose, and the foreknowledge of a week's kennel and constitutionals pathetically expressed in his half masted tail, "Dog Rex, sentiment at appropriate intervals is a thing expected of all respectable Anglo-Saxons. Whether it be requisitioned to glorify my lady's eyebrow, to lament the death of Fido, or to extol the joys of home, we have got to have it in our outfit. And what's more, it has got to be of the conventional British quality, and available for immediate use, as befits a great race of successful people who buy or inherit their emotions ready-made. And so, Dog Rex, this being the end of Jim's cruises, and the last chapter, let us be sentimentally joyful, old chap. For Jim is going to be married, and there will be much rejoicing."

But we were getting out of the narrow ways of bricks and mortar, out into the country, where invisible larks overhead and warblers in the reed-beds were consigning dull care, together with all the humours and vapours of humanity, to oblivion, and as we came near home the old dog's tail gradually indicated the fact that he had weighed the pros and cons and found the balance of good righting itself once again. "God's in His heaven," it said, "and all's right with the world." And so our reflections (which otherwise might have ended this book) appropriately enough, and to the credit of all concerned, dropped all flavour of melancholy and ended, like M'Nulty's Christmas dinner, in great heartiness and good cheer.

And, in case you have never heard of that dinner (all the low-dahs on the river know of it), I will tell you now, if only to prove that, as I say, it is customary for Anglo-Saxons to put on sentiment as a garment of virtue, and also that it is a garment which sits but lightly, and somewhat shamefacedly, upon us. Finally, that, as I have reminded you once before, when a man's heart warms to his viands, he forgets a great deal of sophistry.

M'Nulty, who came of Scotch but respectable parents, had shed many of the peculiarities of his race in twenty years of boiler-making on the Pootung side. He had, however, retained a few fixed habits, one of which was a week's houseboat outing with his chum Macpherson, to wind up the year, beginning with a good old-fashioned Christmas dinner somewhere in the wilds. Just the pair of them, you understand, but with all the proper toasts, the seasonable dishes, and the songs an' a'—a very solemn business indeed. If, in the course of this pious orgy, they happened to run across other boats, they would invite all hands in for a wee drap after dinner, but the *tête-à-tête* meal itself was a sort of consecrated rite, and respected as such by both.

And one Christmas week it fell out that Macpherson had business in Soochow, so they could not start together, but they agreed to meet on Christmas morning at the mouth of the Mutu creek and hold their high festival in that romantic spot. But something went wrong — a launch broke down, I think — and at the close of a day of irritated suspense M'Nulty found himself confronted by the awful prospect of a solitary Christmas dinner.

There, in his cosy cabin, glowed the table regally set for two. There were the crackers and the little patriotic flags, the oranges, almonds, and raisins of his youth; there was the champagne on its bed of ice, and the port beaming ruddily by the stove. And outside, a shrill wintry blast came whirling through the bleak hills; just the time and place for a snug fireside feast, good fellowship, and long yarns of bygone days. But no sign of Macpherson.

M'Nulty, as I have said, comes of that Scotch breed which does not lightly forgo anything that has been planned and paid for; a hearty fellow withal, though sentimental in the Scottish manner, and with a fitting sense of the humanities. He now displayed these qualities. At eight o'clock he ordered dinner, called up the lowdah, arrayed him in Macpherson's spare dressing-gown, and solemnly invited him to take the empty chair. The pair of them then proceeded to make their way steadily through a Gargantuan menu (including a haggis from Perth). There was not much conversation for the first half-hour, M'Nulty being busily engaged in putting away Macpherson's share of the liquor in addition to his own, and the lowdah, slightly dazed by the unexpectedness of the business, but inscrutably calm and watchful, after the manner of his kind. With the plum pudding, however, M'Nulty, who by this time had begun to warm to his entertainment, pulled a couple of crackers with his guest, coiffed him with a Normandy peasant's cap and himself with a Tam o' shanter, called in the dog-coolie to enliven the proceedings, and proceeded to circulate the port.

"Gentlemen," said he, "'The Queen.' Stand up, you heathens,

and no heel-taps!"

The lowdah, looking like Dan Leno in a female part, drank his old tawny like a man, and the dog-coolie, nobly struggling with the unwonted sensation in his gullet, followed suit. Then came "Absent Friends" (in bumpers), suitably coupled with the name of Macpherson, and words of eulogy addressed to that worthy's *locum tenens*, a speech in M'Nulty's best and most discursive manner. At this stage the lowdah's eyes began to grow beadily bright, and he showed signs of increasing conviviality, which M'Nulty nipped in the bud by singing "Willie brewed a peck o' maut" in a voice that shook the boat. The next toast on the list was "The Land o' Cakes," with long-drawn reminiscences of Scottish childhood and more references to Macpherson, during which the guests helped themselves furtively to Havanas, and the host showed symptoms of unsteadiness on his pins. Then, with a second bottle of port, came "The Old Folks at Home," a magnificent, if somewhat maudlin, effort, in which M'Nulty endeavoured to bring home to his guests something of the dignity and pathos of exile. It was at this point that the lowdah unconsciously anticipated the next toast by independently and loudly draining his glass to an anonymous "Soochow girlie," for which breach of good manners he was threatened with personal violence by the indignant chair. Finally came "Auld Lang Syne" by the whole strength of the company; and it was in the midst of this solemn chant, when M'Nulty's stentorian tones were rising and falling incoherently to an accompaniment of curious nasal and guttural noises that came from his yellow brethren, and when all three, with clasped hands, were slowly circumnavigating the table, — it was then that Wilden and Thurlsby, homeward bound and attracted by the uproar, burst upon the festive scene. And M'Nulty, who had enough wine inside him to allow the truth to come out, assured them on his honour that the lowdah and the dog-coolie were jolly good fellows (he even insisted on singing it), that he did not want to meet better, and that he had never spent a jollier Christmas. Which was reported in due season to

Macpherson.

The moral of which tale is, if you take it aright, that a cheerful philosophy is worth all your sentiment. Not a bad thing to remember, Dog Rex, when the long day's work is done, our wages taken, and we are coming home.

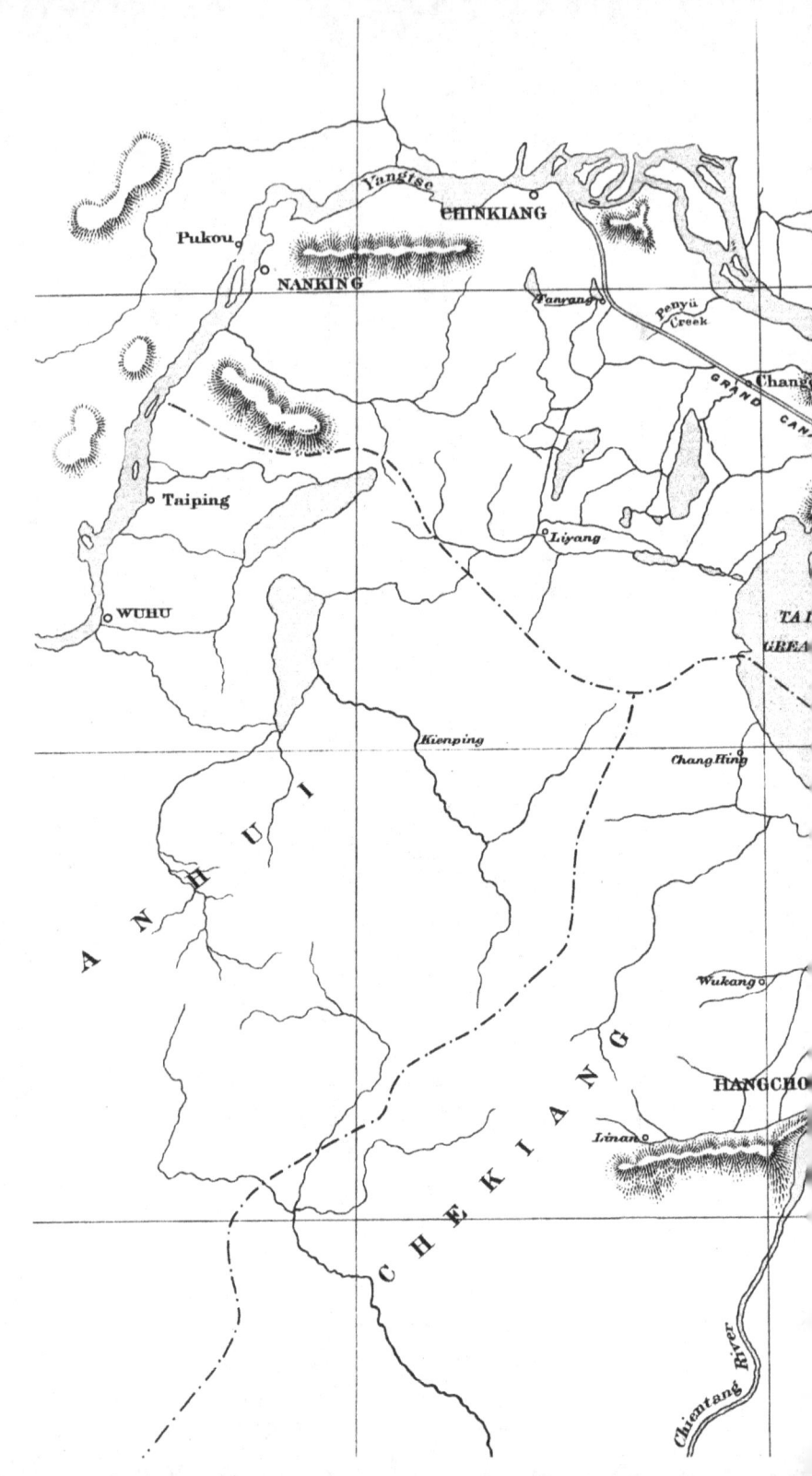

MAP OF COUNTRY
NEAR
SHANGHAI.

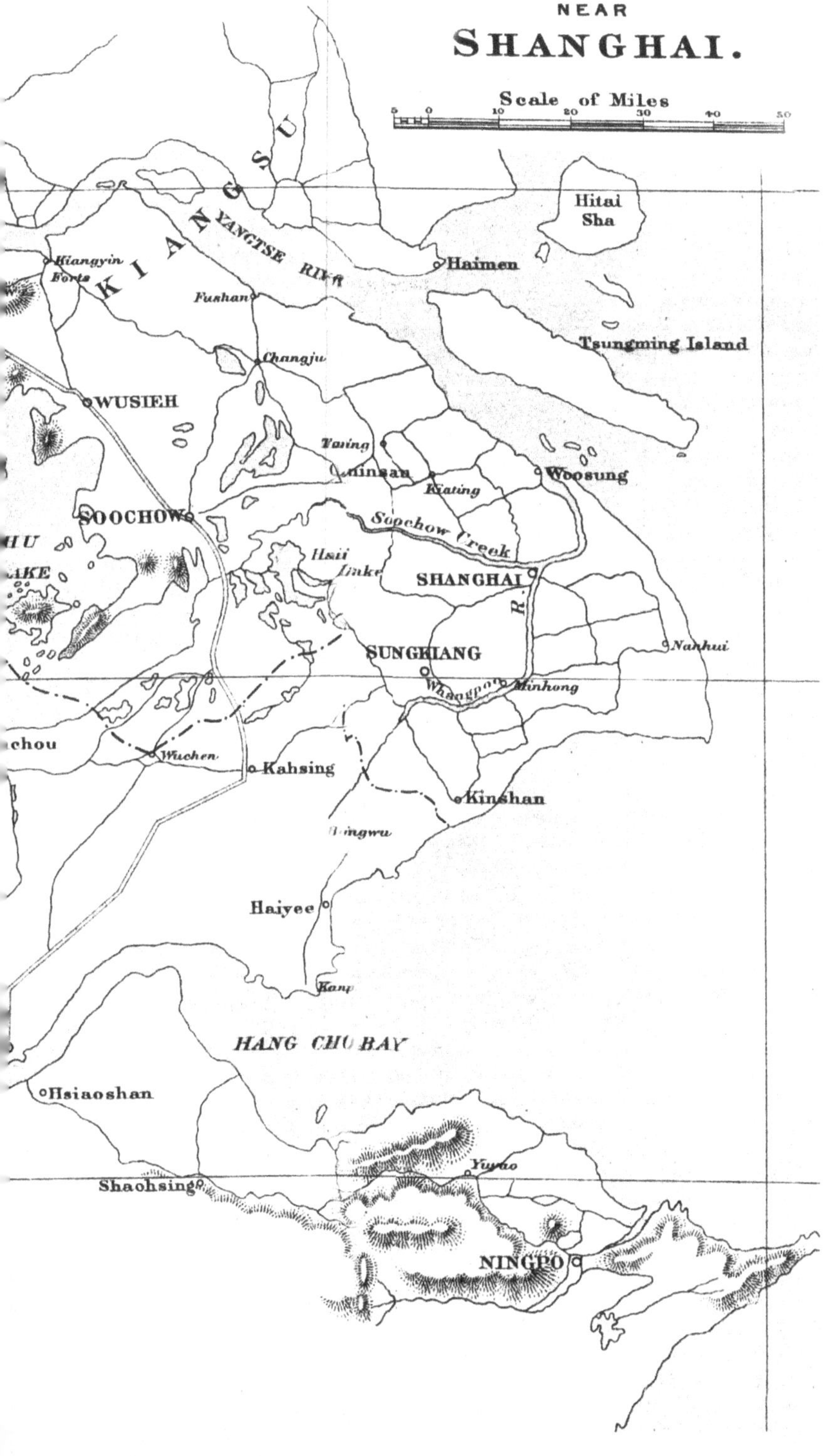

Scale of Miles

Hitai Sha

Haimen

Tsungming Island

Kiangyin Forts

Fushan

Changju

WUSIEH

YANGTSE RIVER

KIANGSU

Yasing

Minsan

Kiating

Woosung

SOOCHOW

Soochow Creek

Hsii Linke

SHANGHAI

HU LAKE

SUNGKIANG

Whangpo

Minhong

Nanhui

chou

Wuchen

Kahsing

Kinshan

Lingwu

Haiyee

Kanp

HANG CHO BAY

Hsiaoshan

Shaohsing

Yuyao

NINGPO

www.ingramcontent.com/pod-product-compliance
Lightning Source LLC
Chambersburg PA
CBHW011236120626
46549CB00009B/3281

* 9 7 8 9 8 8 1 7 6 2 1 2 2 *